SUMMER LINK

MATH *plus* READING

P9-BYJ-128

Thinking Kids®
An imprint of Carson-Dellosa Publishing LLC
Greensboro, North Carolina

Thinking Kids®
An imprint of Carson-Dellosa Publishing LLC
P.O. Box 35665
Greensboro, NC 27425 USA

ISBN 978-1-4838-0469-9

06-105197784

Table of Contents
by Section

Summer Link Math
Table of Contents

Summer Link Reading
Table of Contents

This page intentionally left blank.

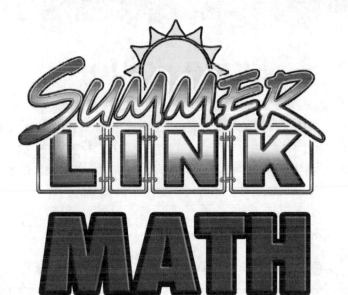

Summer Link
MATH

Place Value

Place value is the position of a digit in a number. A digit's place in a number shows its value. Numbers left of the decimal point represent **whole numbers**. Numbers right of the decimal point represent a part, or fraction, of a whole number. These parts are broken down into tenths, hundredths, thousandths, and so on.

Example:
3,443,221.621

millions	hundred thousands	ten thousands	thousands	hundreds	tens	ones	tenths	hundredths	thousandths
3	4	4	3	2	2	1	6	2	1

← ———— Whole Numbers ————→ ← Fractions →

Directions: Write the following number words as numbers.

1. Three million, forty-four thousand, six hundred twenty-one _____

2. One million, seventy-seven _____

3. Nine million, six hundred thousand, one hundred two _____

4. Twenty-nine million, one hundred three thousand and nine tenths

   _____

5. One million, one hundred thousand, one hundred seventy-one and

   thirteen hundredths _____

Directions: In each box, write the corresponding number for each place value.

1. 4,822,000.00 ☐ hundreds
2. 55,907,003.00 ☐ thousands
3. 190,641,225.07 ☐ hundred thousands
4. 247,308,211.59 ☐ tenths
5. 7,594,097.33 ☐ millions
6. 201,480,110.01 ☐ hundred thousands
7. 42,367,109,074.25 ☐ hundredths

Expanded Notation

Expanded notation is writing out the value of each digit in a number.

Example:
8,920,077 = 8,000,000 + 900,000 + 20,000 + 70 + 7
Word form: Eight million, nine hundred twenty thousand, seventy-seven

Directions: Write the following numbers using expanded notation.

1. 20,769,033 _____

_____

2. 1,183,541,029 _____

_____

3. 776,003,091 _____

_____

4. 5,920,100,808 _____

_____

5. 14,141,543,760 _____

_____

Directions: Write the following numbers.

1. 700,000 + 900 + 60 + 7 _____

2. 35,000,000 + 600,000 + 400 + 40 + 2 _____

3. 12,000,000 + 700,000 + 60,000 + 4,000 + 10 + 4 _____

4. 80,000,000,000 + 8,000,000,000 + 400,000,000 + 80,000,000 + 10,000 +

400 + 30 _____

5. 4,000,000,000 + 16,000,000 + 30 + 2 _____

Adding Integers

Example:

A number line can be used to add integers. To add positive integers, move to the right. To add negative integers, move to the left.

$4 + (-5) = (-1)$
Find 4 on the number line. Move 5 spaces to the left.

$(-3) + 4 = 1$

$(-2) + (-1) = (-3)$

Directions: Add. Use the number lines to help you.

1. $2 + (-4) =$ _____

2. $(-3) + (-1) =$ _____

3. $(-1) + 4 =$ _____

4. $(-2) + 2 =$ _____

5. $4 + (-7) =$ _____

6. $0 + (-4) =$ _____

Rounding

Follow these steps to round numbers to a given place.

Example: Round 35,634 to the nearest thousand.

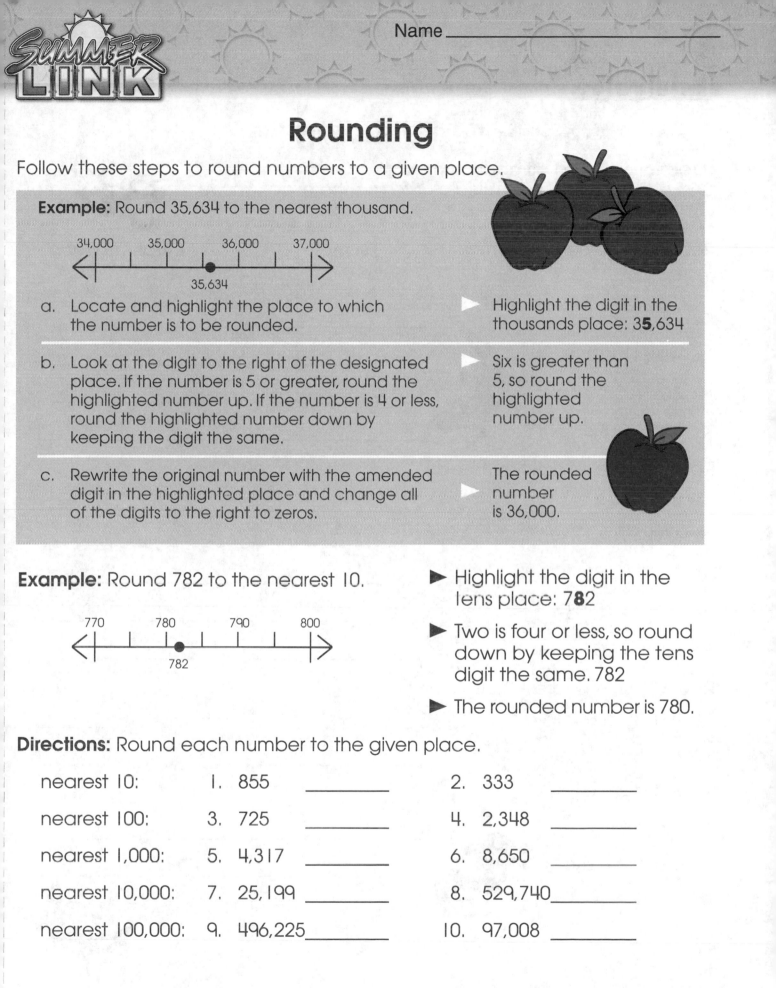

a. Locate and highlight the place to which the number is to be rounded.

► Highlight the digit in the thousands place: 3**5**,634

b. Look at the digit to the right of the designated place. If the number is 5 or greater, round the highlighted number up. If the number is 4 or less, round the highlighted number down by keeping the digit the same.

► Six is greater than 5, so round the highlighted number up.

c. Rewrite the original number with the amended digit in the highlighted place and change all of the digits to the right to zeros.

► The rounded number is 36,000.

Example: Round 782 to the nearest 10.

► Highlight the digit in the tens place: 7**8**2

► Two is four or less, so round down by keeping the tens digit the same. 782

► The rounded number is 780.

Directions: Round each number to the given place.

nearest 10:	1. 855 _____	2. 333 _____
nearest 100:	3. 725 _____	4. 2,348 _____
nearest 1,000:	5. 4,317 _____	6. 8,650 _____
nearest 10,000:	7. 25,199 _____	8. 529,740_____
nearest 100,000:	9. 496,225_____	10. 97,008 _____

Rounding

Directions: Round off each number, then estimate the answer. You can use a calculator to find the exact answer.

	Estimate	**Actual Answer**

Round to the nearest ten.

1. $86 \div 9 =$

2. $237 + 488 =$

3. $49 \times 11 =$

4. $309 + 412 =$

5. $625 - 218 =$

Round to the nearest hundred.

6. $790 - 70 =$

7. $690 \div 70 =$

8. $2,177 - 955 =$

9. $4,792 + 3,305 =$

10. $5,210 \times 90 =$

Round to the nearest thousand.

11. $4,078 + 2,093 =$

12. $5,525 - 3,065 =$

13. $6,047 \div 2,991 =$

14. $1,913 \times 4,216 =$

15. $7,227 + 8,449 =$

 Name _____

Rounding and Estimating

Rounding is expressing a number to the nearest whole number, ten, thousand, or other value. **Estimating** is using an approximate number instead of an exact one. When rounding a number, we say a country has 98,000,000 citizens instead of 98,347,425. We can round off numbers to the nearest whole number, the nearest hundred, or the nearest million—whatever is appropriate.

Here are the steps: 1) Decide where you want to round off the number. 2) If the digit to the right is less than 5, leave the digit at the rounding place unchanged. 3) If the digit to the right is 5 or more, increase the digit at the rounding place by 1.

Examples: 587 rounded to the nearest hundred is 600.
535 rounded to the nearest hundred is 500.
21,897 rounded to the nearest thousand is 22,000.
21,356 rounded to the nearest thousand is 21,000.

When we estimate numbers, we use rounded, approximate numbers instead of exact ones.

Example: A hamburger that costs $1.49 and a drink that costs $0.79 total about $2.30 ($1.50 plus $0.80).

Directions: Use rounding and estimating to find the answers to these questions. You may have to add, subtract, multiply, or divide.

1. Debbi is having a party and wants to fill 11 cups from a 67-ounce bottle of pop. About how many ounces should she pour into each cup? _____

2. Tracy studied 28 minutes every day for 4 days. About how long did she study in all? _____

3. About how much does this lunch cost? $1.19 $0.39 $0.49 _____

4. The numbers below show how long Frank spent studying last week. Estimate how many minutes he studied for the whole week.
Monday: 23 minutes Tuesday: 37 minutes Wednesday: 38 minutes
Thursday: 12 minutes _____

5. One elephant at the zoo weighs 1,417 pounds and another one weighs 1,789 pounds. About how much heavier is the second elephant? _____

6. If Tim studied a total of 122 minutes over 4 days, about how long did he study each day? _____

7. It's 549 miles to Dover and 345 miles to Albany. About how much closer is Albany? _____

Name _____

Addition

Teachers of an Earth Science class planned to take 50 students on an overnight hiking and camping experience. After planning the menu, they went to the grocery store for supplies.

Breakfast	**Lunch**	**Dinner**	**Snacks**
bacon	hot dogs/buns	pasta	crackers
eggs	apples	sauce	marshmallows
bread	chips	garlic bread	chocolate bars
cereal	juice	salad	cocoa mix
juice	granola bars	cookies	
$ 34.50	$ 52.15	$ 47.25	$ 23.40

Directions: Answer the questions. Write the total amount spent on food for the trip.

What information do you need to answer the question?_____

_____

What is the total?_____

Directions: Add.

462	918	527	386	295
+ 574	+ 359	+ 582	+ 745	+ 764

397	524	906	750	891
+ 448	+ 725	+ 337	+ 643	+ 419

1,568	3,214	5,147	7,259	9,317
+ 2,341	+ 2,896	+ 4,285	+ 2,451	+ 3,583

Addition

Bob the butcher is popular with the dogs in town. He was making a delivery this morning when he noticed he was being followed by two dogs. Bob tried to climb a ladder to escape from the dogs.

Directions: Solve the following addition problems and shade in the answers on the ladder. If all the numbers are shaded when the problems have been solved, Bob made it up the ladder. Some answers may not be on the ladder.

1.   986,145
      621,332
+   200,008
	2. 1,873,402
	    925,666
	+ 4,689
		3. 506,328
		   886,510
		+ 342,225

4.   43,015
  2,811,604
+   987,053
	5. 18,443
	  300,604
	+ 999,999
		6. 8,075
		  14,608
		+ 33,914

7.   9,162
  7,804
+ 755,122
	8. 88,714
	  213,653
	+ 5,441,298
		9. 3,244,662
		 1,986,114
		+ 521,387

10.   4,581
  22,983
+ 5,618,775
	11. 818,623
	     926
	+ 3,260,004
		12. 80,436
		   9,159
		+ 3,028,761

Ladder numbers:

1,319,046
2,803,757
5,743,665
3,118,356
56,597
4,079,553
1,807,485
2,943,230
18,344,666
1,735,063
5,752,163
896,316
3,841,672
5,646,339

Did Bob make it? _____

Name _____

Addition Word Problems

Directions: Solve the following addition word problems.

1. 100 students participated in a sports card show in the school gym. Brad brought his entire collection of 2,000 cards to show his friends. He had 700 football cards and 400 basketball cards. If the rest of his cards were baseball cards, how many baseball cards did he bring with him?

   _____

2. Refreshments were set up in one area of the gym. Hot dogs were a dollar, soda was 50 cents, chips were 35 cents, and cookies were a quarter. If you purchased two of each item, how much money would you need?

   _____

3. It took each student 30 minutes to set up for the card show and twice as long to put everything away. The show was open for 3 hours. How much time did each student spend on this event?

   _____

4. 450 people attended the card show. 55 were mothers of students, 67 were fathers, 23 were grandparents, 8 were aunts and uncles, and the rest were kids. How many kids attended?

   _____

5. Of the 100 students who set up displays, most of them sold or traded some of their cards. Bruce sold 75 cards, traded 15 cards, and collected $225. Kevin sold only 15 cards, traded 81 cards, and collected $100. Missi traded 200 cards, sold 10, and earned $35. Of those listed, how many cards were sold, how many were traded, and how much money was earned?

   sold _____   traded _____   earned $ _____

Subtraction

Subtraction is "taking away" one number from another to find the difference between the two numbers.

Directions: Subtract.

76	93	68	49	88	54
− 23	− 14	− 25	− 17	− 39	− 25

1. Brent saved $75.00 of the money he earned delivering the local newspaper in his neighborhood. He wanted to buy a new bicycle that cost $139.00. How much more would he need to save in order to buy the bike?

_____

38	74	67	92	43	85
− 29	− 25	− 49	− 35	− 26	− 37

2. When Brent finally went to buy the bicycle, he saw a light and basket for the bike. He decided to buy them both. The light was $5.95 and the basket was $10.50. He gave the clerk a twenty dollar bill his grandmother had given him for his birthday. How much change did he get back?

_____

Subtraction

When working with larger numbers, it is important to keep the numbers lined up according to place value.

Directions: Subtract.

```
  398          543          491
- 149        - 287        - 311
```

```
  786        1,825        4,172
- 597        -  495       - 2,785
```

```
  8,391       63,852       24,107       52,900
- 5,492      - 34,765     - 19,350     - 43,081
```

1. Eagle Peak is the highest mountain peak at Yellowstone National Park. It is 11,353 feet high. The next highest point at the park is Mount Washburn. It is 10,243 feet tall. How much higher is Eagle Peak?

   _____

2. The highest mountain peak in North America is Mount McKinley, which stretches 20,320 feet toward the sky. Two other mountain ranges in North America have peaks at 10,302 feet and 8,194 feet. What is the greatest difference between the peaks?

   _____

Subtraction Word Problems

Directions: Solve the following subtraction word problems.

1. Last year, 28,945 people lived in Mike's town. This year, there are 31,889. How many people have moved in? _____

2. Brad earned $227 mowing lawns. He spent $168 on tapes by his favorite rock group. How much money does he have left? _____

3. The school year has 180 days. Carrie has gone to 32 school days so far. How many more days does she have left? _____

4. Craig wants a skateboard that costs $128. He has saved $47. How much more does he need? _____

5. To get to school, Jennifer walks 1,275 steps and Carolyn walks 2,618 steps. How many more steps does Carolyn walk than Jennifer? _____

6. Amy has placed 91 of the 389 pieces in a new puzzle she purchased. How many more does she have left to finish? _____

7. From New York, it's 2,823 miles to Los Angeles and 1,327 miles to Miami. How much farther away is Los Angeles? _____

8. Sheila read that a piece of carrot cake has 236 calories, but a piece of apple pie has 427 calories. How many calories will she save by eating the cake instead of the pie? _____

9. Tim's summer camp costs $223, while Sam's costs $149. How much more does Tim's camp cost?

_____

10. Last year, the nation's budget was $45,000,000,000, but the nation spent $52,569,342,000. How much more than its budget did the nation spend?

_____

Name _____

Addition and Subtraction

Directions: Check the answers. Write **T** if the answer is true and **F** if it is false.

Example:
```
  48,973    Check:     35,856
- 35,856      F      +13,118
  13,118              48,974
```

```
  18,264    Check:              458,342    Check:
+ 17,893                      - 297,652
  36,157    _____              160,680    _____
```

```
  39,854    Check:              631,928    Check:
+ 52,713                      - 457,615
  92,577    _____              174,313    _____
```

```
  14,389    Check:              554,974    Check:
+ 93,587                      - 376,585
 107,976    _____              178,389    _____
```

```
  87,321    Check:              109,568    Check:
- 62,348                      + 97,373
  24,973    _____              206,941    _____
```

Directions: Read the story problem. Write the equation and check the answer.

A camper hikes 53,741 feet out into the wilderness. On his return trip he takes a shortcut, walking 36,752 feet back to his cabin. The shortcut saves him 16,998 feet of hiking. True or False?

Multiplying by a Three-Digit Number

Example:

Steps:

| Multiply by the ones. | Multiply by the tens. Put a zero in the ones place. | Multiply by the hundreds. Put a zero in the ones and tens place. | Add. |

```
    2, 3 1 3          2, 3 1 3            2, 3 1 3           2, 3 1 3
  x    1 3 2        x    1 3 2          x    1 3 2         x    1 3 2
    4, 6 2 6          4, 6 2 6            4, 6 2 6           4, 6 2 6
                      6 9, 3 9 0          6 9, 3 9 0         6 9, 3 9 0
                                          2 3 1, 3 0 0     +2 3 1, 3 0 0
                                                            3 0 5, 3 1 6
```

Directions: Multiply. Circle the correct answer in each clover.

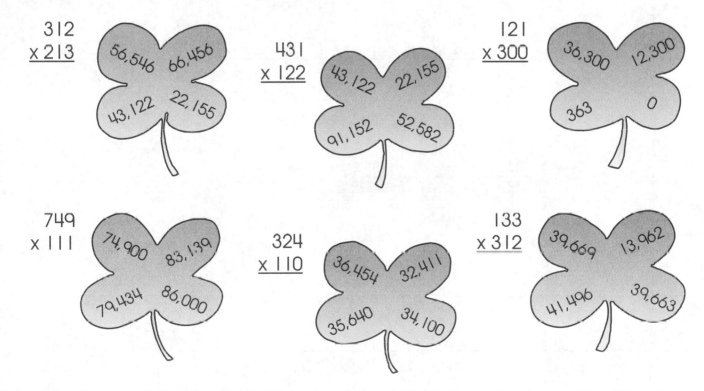

312
x 213

56,546   66,456
43,122   22,155

431
x 122

43,122   22,155
91,152   52,582

121
x 300

36,300   12,300
363   0

749
x 111

74,900   83,139
79,434   86,000

324
x 110

36,454   32,411
35,640   34,100

133
x 312

39,669   13,962
41,496   39,663

Multiplication

Be certain to keep the proper place value when multiplying by tens and hundreds.

Examples:

```
    143            250
  x 262          x 150
    286            000
    858           1250
    286           250
  37,466         37,500
```

Directions: Multiply.

```
    701            621            348            597
  x 308          x 538          x 200          x 424
```

```
    537            416            682            180
  x 189          x 727          x 472          x 340
```

```
    878            267            893            907
  x 638          x 196          x 214          x 428
```

An airplane flies 720 trips a year between the cities of Chicago and Columbus. Each trip is 375 miles. How many miles does the airplane fly each year?

_____

Multiplying Integers

Example:

Ignore the negative signs, and multiply the numbers. If two factors have the same sign, the product is positive. If two factors have different signs, the product is negative. With three or more factors, multiply two numbers at a time and keep track of the signs.

$2 \times 3 = 6$ $2 \times -3 = -6$ $-2 \times 3 = -6$ $-2 \times -3 = 6$

$2 \times 3 \times -2 = 6 \times -2 = -12$ $2 \times -3 \times -2 = -6 \times -2 = 12$

$-2 \times -3 \times -2 = 6 \times -2 = -12$

Directions: Multiply.

$3 \times -4 = $ _____ $-5 \times -5 = $ _____ $-4 \times 12 = $ _____ $7 \times 3 = $ _____

$-8 \times -9 = $ _____ $-6 \times 3 = $ _____ $2 \times 15 = $ _____ $-4 \times -10 = $ _____

$8 \times -8 = $ _____ $-1 \times -9 = $ _____ $7 \times -7 = $ _____ $-5 \times -6 = $ _____

$2 \times -12 = $ _____ $1 \times 2 \times -5 = $ _____ $3 \times -3 \times -3 = $ _____ $-4 \times -2 \times -2 = $ _____

$-3 \times -2 \times 3 = $ _____ $2 \times -2 \times 1 = $ _____ $-5 \times 0 \times 6 = $ _____

$1 \times -1 \times 1 = $ _____ $-3 \times -2 \times -2 = $ _____ $-5 \times 2 \times -2 = $ _____

Use the numbers –4, 6, –2, –18, –9 and 12 to complete this magic square. Each row, column, and diagonal should equal 216.

–36		–1
3		

Zeroes in the Quotient

Zero holds a place in the quotient.

Example:

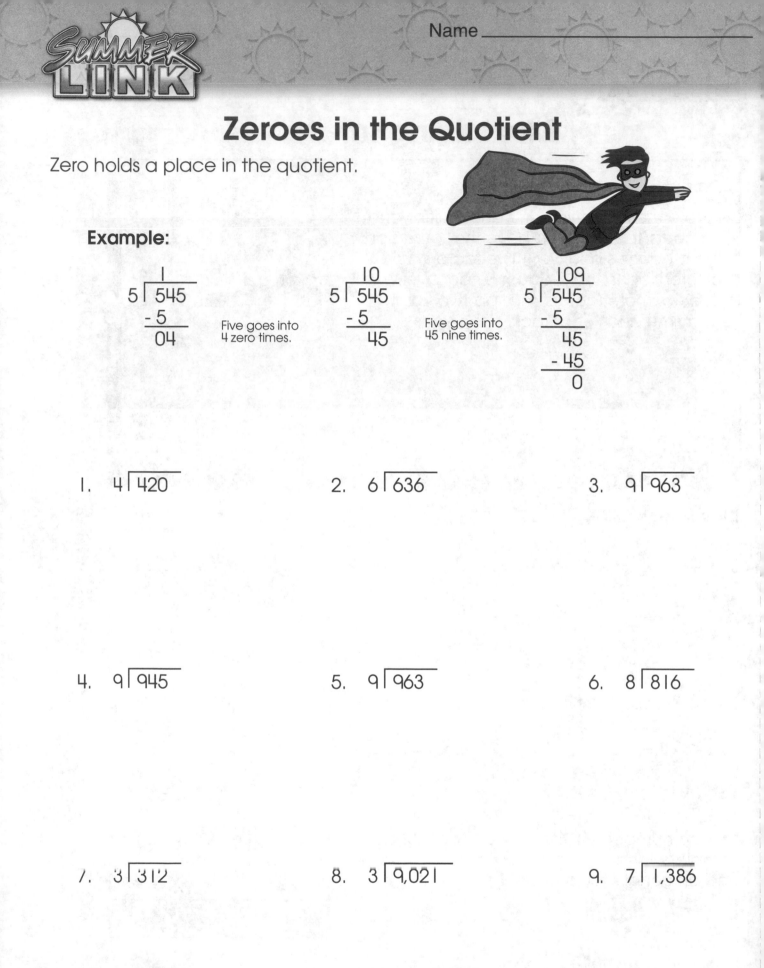

$$
\begin{array}{r}
1 \\
5\overline{)545} \\
-5 \\
\hline
04
\end{array}
$$
Five goes into 4 zero times.

$$
\begin{array}{r}
10 \\
5\overline{)545} \\
-5 \\
\hline
45
\end{array}
$$
Five goes into 45 nine times.

$$
\begin{array}{r}
109 \\
5\overline{)545} \\
-5 \\
\hline
45 \\
-45 \\
\hline
0
\end{array}
$$

1. $4\overline{)420}$

2. $6\overline{)636}$

3. $9\overline{)963}$

4. $9\overline{)945}$

5. $9\overline{)963}$

6. $8\overline{)816}$

7. $3\overline{)312}$

8. $3\overline{)9,021}$

9. $7\overline{)1,386}$

Division

The remainder in a division problem must always be less than the divisor.

Example:

```
        244 r 23
26 ) 6,367
     5 2
     1 16
     104
      127
      104
       23
```

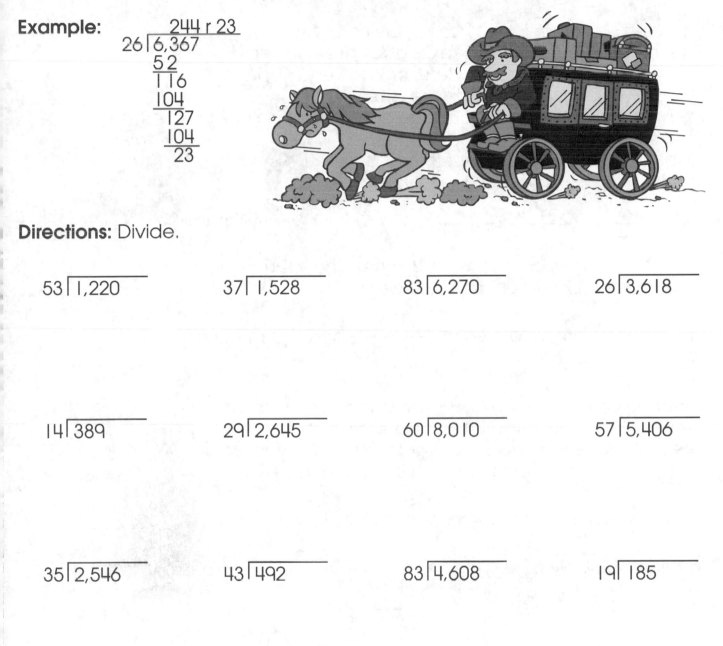

Directions: Divide.

53) 1,220   37) 1,528   83) 6,270   26) 3,618

14) 389   29) 2,645   60) 8,010   57) 5,406

35) 2,546   43) 492   83) 4,608   19) 185

The Oregon Trail is 2,197 miles long. How long would it take a covered wagon traveling 20 miles a day to complete the trip?

_____

Multiplication and Division

Directions: Multiply or divide to find the answers.

1. Brianne's summer job is mowing lawns for three of her neighbors. Each lawn takes about 1 hour to mow and needs to be done once every week. At the end of the summer, she will have earned a total of $630. She collected the same amount of money from each job. How much did each neighbor pay for her summer lawn service?

   _____

2. If the mowing season lasts for 14 weeks, how much will Brianne earn for each job each week? _____

3. If she had worked for two more weeks, how much would she have earned? _____

4. Brianne agreed to shovel snow from the driveways and sidewalks for the same three neighbors. They agreed to pay her the same rate. However, it snowed only seven times that winter. How much did she earn shoveling snow? _____

5. What was her total income for both jobs? _____

Directions: Multiply or divide.

$12\overline{)7,476}$ $\qquad$ $23\overline{)21,620}$ $\qquad$ $40\overline{)32,600}$

$32 \times 45 =$ _____ $28 \times 15 =$ _____ $73 \times 14 =$ _____ $92 \times 30 =$ _____

Money Problems

Shifty Sam sells the latest rock releases along with some oldies. You have to keep a close eye on Sam, or you may get ripped off.

Directions: Solve the problems on another sheet of paper. Write your answers in the spaces provided.

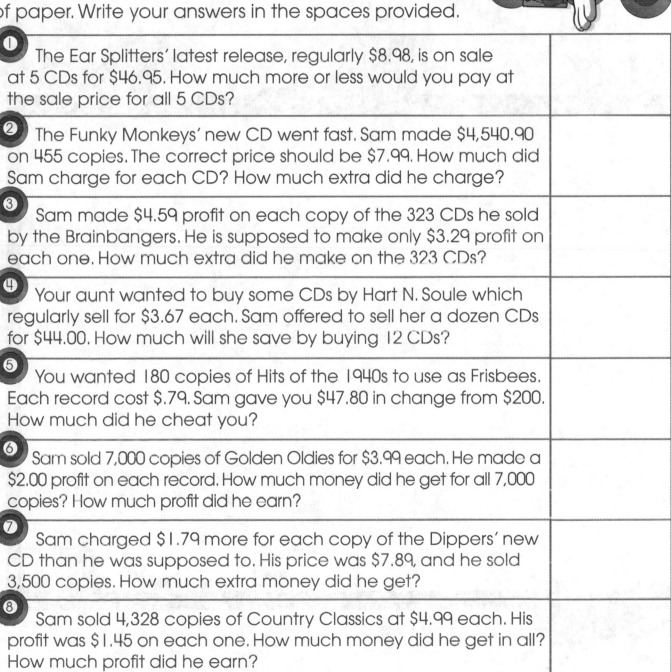

① The Ear Splitters' latest release, regularly $8.98, is on sale at 5 CDs for $46.95. How much more or less would you pay at the sale price for all 5 CDs?	
② The Funky Monkeys' new CD went fast. Sam made $4,540.90 on 455 copies. The correct price should be $7.99. How much did Sam charge for each CD? How much extra did he charge?	
③ Sam made $4.59 profit on each copy of the 323 CDs he sold by the Brainbangers. He is supposed to make only $3.29 profit on each one. How much extra did he make on the 323 CDs?	
④ Your aunt wanted to buy some CDs by Hart N. Soule which regularly sell for $3.67 each. Sam offered to sell her a dozen CDs for $44.00. How much will she save by buying 12 CDs?	
⑤ You wanted 180 copies of Hits of the 1940s to use as Frisbees. Each record cost $.79. Sam gave you $47.80 in change from $200. How much did he cheat you?	
⑥ Sam sold 7,000 copies of Golden Oldies for $3.99 each. He made a $2.00 profit on each record. How much money did he get for all 7,000 copies? How much profit did he earn?	
⑦ Sam charged $1.79 more for each copy of the Dippers' new CD than he was supposed to. His price was $7.89, and he sold 3,500 copies. How much extra money did he get?	
⑧ Sam sold 4,328 copies of Country Classics at $4.99 each. His profit was $1.45 on each one. How much money did he get in all? How much profit did he earn?	

A Number Challenge

Directions: Fill in the blanks to make each problem true. To check your work, start at the left and do each operation in order to get the given answer.

1. __ + __ - __ =   2

2. __ - __ ÷ __ =   3

3. __ + __ ÷ __ =   4

4. __ x __ - __ =   5

5. __ - __ x __ =   6

6. __ x __ ÷ __ =   3

7. __ ÷ __ + __ =   4

8. __ ÷ __ - __ =   5

9. __ ÷ __ x __ =   6

10. __ x __ + __ =   7

11. __ ÷ __ + __ =   12

12. __ ÷ __ - __ =   15

13. __ ÷ __ x __ =   20

14. __ x __ ÷ __ =   8

15. __ + __ x __ =   24

Equations

In an **equation,** the value on the left of the equal sign must equal the value on the right. Remember the order of operations: solve from left to right, multiply or divide numbers before adding or subtracting and do the operation inside parentheses first.

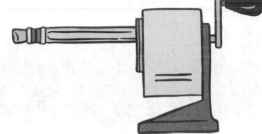

Example: $6 + 4 - 2 = 4 \times 2$

$$10 - 2 = 8$$
$$8 = 8$$

Directions: Write the correct operation signs in the blanks to make accurate equations.

1. (25 _____ 25) _____ 2 = 100 _____ 75

2. (76 _____ 24) _____ 3 = 150 _____ 2

3. 140 _____ 2 _____ 10 = 500 _____ 50 _____ 150

4. 2,100 _____ 2,000 _____ 60 = 80 _____ 2

5. 80 _____ 8 _____ 4 = 160 _____ 160 _____ 160

6. (55 _____ 100) _____ 11 = (1,000 _____ 2) _____ 4

7. 137 _____ 81 _____ 52 = 3 _____ 90

8. 3,000 _____ 10 _____ 10 = (600 _____ 300) _____ 30

9. (720 _____ 20) _____ 4 = 37 _____ 5

10. (457 _____ 43) _____ 500 = (21 _____ 40) x 0

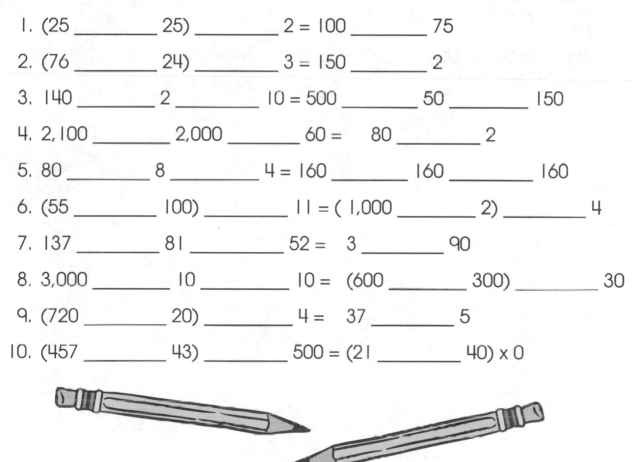

Prime Numbers

Example: 3 is a prime number.
3 ÷ 1 = 3 and 3 ÷ 3 = 1

A prime number is a positive whole number which can be divided evenly only by itself or one.

Any other divisor will result in a mixed number or fraction.

An easy way to test a number to see if it is prime is to divide by 2 and 3. If the number can be divided by 2 or 3 without a remainder, it is not a prime number. (Exceptions, 2 and 3.)

Example:

11 cannot be divided evenly by 2 or 3. It can be divided only by 1 and 11. It is a prime number.

Directions: Write the first 15 prime numbers. Test by dividing by 2 and by 3.

Prime Numbers:

_____   _____   _____   _____   _____

_____   _____   _____   _____   _____

_____   _____   _____   _____   _____

How many prime numbers are there between 0 and 100?   _____

Prime Numbers

Directions: Circle the prime numbers.

71	3	82	20	43	69
128	97	23	111	75	51
13	44	137	68	171	83
61	21	77	101	34	16
2	39	92	17	52	29
19	156	63	99	27	147
121	25	88	12	87	55
57	7	139	91	9	37
67	183	5	59	11	95

Factors

Factors are the numbers multiplied together to give a product. The **greatest common factor** (GCF) is the largest number for a set of numbers that divides evenly into each number in the set.

Example:

The factors of 12 are 3 x 4, 2 x 6, and 1 x 12.

We can write the factors like this: 3, 4, 2, 6, 12, 1.

The factors of 8 are 2, 4, 8, 1.

The common factors of 12 and 8 are 2 and 4 and 1.

The GCF of 12 and 8 is 4.

Directions: Write the factors of each pair of numbers. Then write the common factors and the GCF.

12: _____ , _____ , _____ , _____ , _____ , _____

15: _____ , _____ , _____ , _____

The common factors of 12 and 15 are _____ , _____ .

The GCF is _____ .

20: _____ , _____ , _____ , _____ , _____ , _____

10: _____ , _____ , _____ , _____

The common factors of 10 and 20 are _____ , _____ , _____ , _____ .

The GCF is _____ .

32: _____ , _____ , _____ , _____ , _____ , _____

24: _____ , _____ , _____ , _____ , _____ , _____ , _____ , _____

The common factors of 24 and 32 are _____ , _____ , _____ , _____ .

The GCF is _____ .

Directions: Write the GCF for the following pairs of numbers.

28 and 20 _____   42 and 12 _____

36 and 12 _____   20 and 5 _____

Greatest Common Factor

Directions: Write the greatest common factor for each set of numbers.

10 and 35 _____

2 and 10 _____

42 and 63 _____

16 and 40 _____

25 and 55 _____

12 and 20 _____

14 and 28 _____

8 and 20 _____

6 and 27 _____

15 and 35 _____

18 and 48 _____

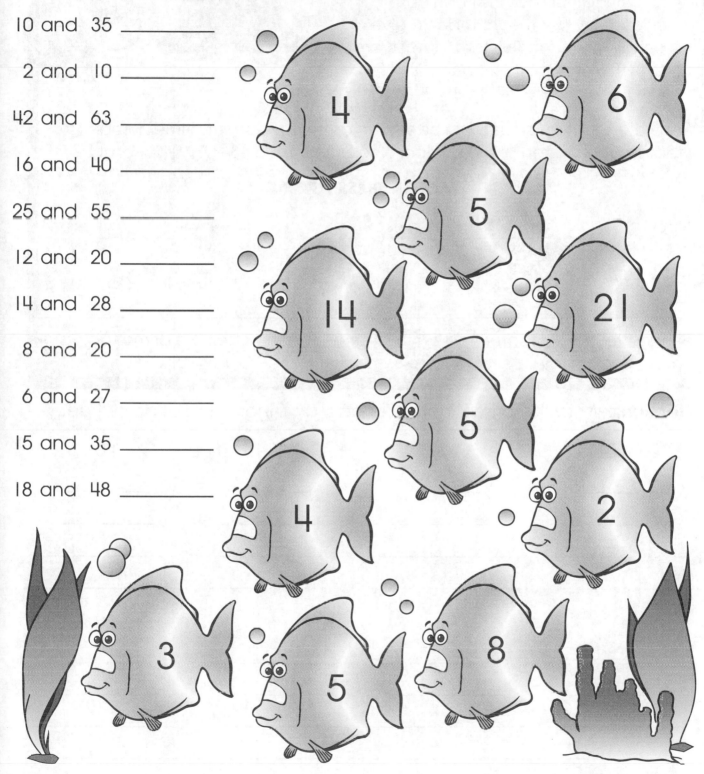

Factor Trees

A factor is a number that can be multiplied by another number to give a certain product. The factors of 24 are 1, 2, 3, 4, 6, 8, 12, and 24 because 1 x 24 = 24, 2 x 12 = 24, 3 x 8 = 24, and 4 x 6 = 24.

Any composite number can be written as the product of prime number factors. The first ten prime numbers are 2, 3, 5, 7, 11, 13, 17, 19, 23, and 29.

FACTOR TREES FOR 24

24	24	24
2 x 12	**3** x 8	4 x 6
2 x 6 x **2**	**3** x **2** x 4	**2** x **2** x **3** x **2**
2 x **3** x **2** x **2**	**3** x **2** x **2** x **2**	

No matter how a factor tree is made for a given number, the prime factors in the bottom row are always the same. $24 = 2 \times 2 \times 2 \times 3 = 2^3 \times 3$

Directions: Write the prime factors for each number, using a factor tree.

12 _____ 32 _____ 48 _____ 40 _____

_____ _____ _____ _____

_____ _____ _____ _____

_____ _____ _____ _____

9 _____ 42 _____ 96 _____ 72 _____

_____ _____ _____ _____

_____ _____ _____ _____

_____ _____ _____ _____

Common Ground

A **multiple** is the product of
any given number and a factor such as 1, 2, 3, and so on.

Example:

Multiples of **4**: 4, 8, 12, 16, 20, 24, 28, 32, 36, 40 . . .
Multiples of **10**: 10, 20, 30, 40, 50, 60, 70, 80, 90, 100 . . .
Multiples of **18**: 18, 36, 54, 72, 90, 108, 126, 144, 162, 180 . . .
Multiples of **25**: 25, 50, 75, 100, 125, 150, 175, 200, 225 . . .

Common multiples are multiples that two or more numbers share, or have in common.

Multiples of **8**: 8, 16, 24, 32, 40, 48, 56, 64, 72, 80 . . .
Multiples of **12**: 12, 24, 36, 48, 60, 72, 84 . . .

Some common multiples of 8 and 12 are 24, 48, and 72.

Find three common multiples for each set of numbers. To do this, list the first ten multiples of each number. Then, look for common multiples. The first one is done for you in the box at the bottom of the page. Show your work on another sheet of paper.

6 and 9 __18, 36, 54__   15 and 30 _____   4 and 10 _____

3 and 4 _____   5 and 25 _____   8 and 6 _____

4 and 9 _____   2 and 7 _____   18 and 3 _____

12 and 16 _____   2, 4, and 5 _____   2, 3, and 6 _____

6	12	(18)	24	30	(36)	42	48	(54)	60
9	(18)	27	(36)	45	(54)	63	72	81	90

Least Common Multiples

The **least common multiple** (LCM) is the least multiple that a group of numbers has in common. The LCM helps when adding and subtracting fractions.

One way to find the LCM is to find the common multiples and choose the least one.

Multiples of 6: 6, 12, 18, 24, 30, 36, 42, 48, 54 . . .
Multiples of 9: 9, 18, 27, 36, 45, 54, 63, 72 . . .

Common multiples of 6 and 9 include 18, 36, and 54, but the least is 18.

Find the LCM for each set of numbers. The first one is done for you in the box at the bottom of the page.

8 and 3 ___24___   7 and 21_____   5 and 8 _____   9 and 12 _____

6 and 16 _____   1 and 9 _____   4 and 7 _____   2 and 3 _____

10 and 4 _____   12 and 16 _____   6 and 8 _____   15 and 12 _____

2, 3, and 4 _____   3, 4, and 5 _____   2, 4, and 7 _____   3, 5, and 6 _____

Find two numbers that when multiplied together do not have a product of 30 but have a LCM of 30. _____

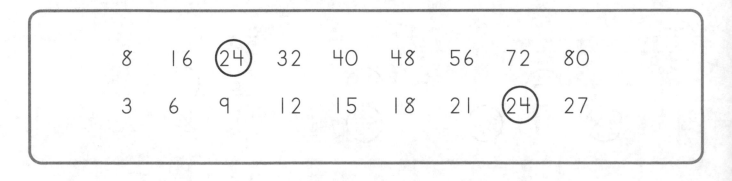

Decimals

A **decimal** is a number that includes a period called a **decimal point**. The digits to the right of the decimal point are a value less than one.

one whole	one tenth	one hundredth

The place value chart below helps explain decimals.

hundreds	tens	ones	.	tenths	hundredths	thousandths
6	3	2	.	4		
	4	7	.	0	5	
		8	.	0	0	9

A decimal point is read as "and." The first number, 632.4, is read as "six hundred thirty-two and four tenths." The second number, 47.05, is read as "forty-seven and five hundredths." The third number, 8.009, is read as "eight and nine thousandths."

Directions: Write the decimals shown below. Two have been done for you.

1. _____1.4_____   2. _____   3. _____

4. six and five tenths _____6.5_____

5. twenty-two and nine tenths _____

6. thirty-six and fourteen hundredths _____

7. forty-seven hundredths _____

8. one hundred six and four tenths _____

9. seven and three hundredths _____

10. one tenth less than 0.6 _____

11. one hundredth less than 0.34 _____

12. one tenth more than 0.2 _____

Adding and Subtracting Decimals

When adding or subtracting decimals, place the decimal points under each other. That way, you add tenths to tenths, for example, not tenths to hundredths. Add or subtract beginning on the right, as usual. Carry or borrow numbers in the same way. Adding 0 to the end of decimals does not change their value, but sometimes makes them easier to add and subtract.

Examples:	39.40	0.064	3.56	6.83
	+ 6.81	+ 0.470	– .09	– 2.14
	46.21	0.534	3.47	4.69

Directions: Solve the following problems.

1. Write each set of numbers in a column and add them.

   a. 2.56 + 0.6 + 76 = _____

   b. 93.5 + 23.06 + 1.45 = _____

   c. 3.23 + 91.34 + 0.85 = _____

2. Write each pair of numbers in a column and subtract them.

   a. 7.89 – 0.56 = _____   b. 34.56 – 6.04 = _____   c. 7.6 – 3.24 = _____

3. In a relay race, Alice ran her part in 23.6 seconds, Cindy did hers in 24.7 seconds, and Erin took 20.09 seconds. How many seconds did they take altogether? _____

4. Although Erin ran her part in 20.09 seconds today, yesterday it took her 21.55 seconds. How much faster was she today? _____

5. Add this grocery bill: potatoes—$3.49; milk—$2.09; bread—$0.99; apples—$2.30 _____

6. A yellow coat cost $47.59 and a blue coat cost $36.79. How much more did the yellow coat cost? _____

7. A box of Oat Boats cereal has 14.6 ounces. A box of Sugar Circles has 17.85 ounces. How much more cereal is in the Sugar Circles box? _____

8. The Oat Boats cereal has 4.03 ounces of sugar in it. Sugar Circles cereal has only 3.76 ounces. How much more sugar is in a box of Oats Boats? _____

Multiplying Decimals

In some problems, you may need to add zeros in order to place the decimal point correctly.

Examples:

$$
\begin{array}{r} 0.34 \\ \times\ 0.08 \\ \hline 0.0272 \end{array}
\qquad
\begin{array}{r} 0.0067 \\ \times\qquad 4 \\ \hline 0.0268 \end{array}
\qquad
\begin{array}{r} 0.046 \\ \times\ 0.07 \\ \hline 0.00322 \end{array}
$$

Directions: Solve the following problems.

1.
$$
\begin{array}{r} 0.15 \\ \times\ 0.02 \\ \hline \end{array}
$$

2.
$$
\begin{array}{r} 0.67 \\ \times\ 0.08 \\ \hline \end{array}
$$

3.
$$
\begin{array}{r} 7.3 \\ \times\ 0.06 \\ \hline \end{array}
$$

4.
$$
\begin{array}{r} 3.59 \\ \times\ 0.08 \\ \hline \end{array}
$$

5.
$$
\begin{array}{r} 0.061 \\ \times\ 0.014 \\ \hline \end{array}
$$

6.
$$
\begin{array}{r} 7.10 \\ \times\ 0.042 \\ \hline \end{array}
$$

7.
$$
\begin{array}{r} 5.05 \\ \times\ 0.08 \\ \hline \end{array}
$$

8.
$$
\begin{array}{r} 8.75 \\ \times\ 0.067 \\ \hline \end{array}
$$

9.
$$
\begin{array}{r} 0.0647 \\ \times\qquad 0.3 \\ \hline \end{array}
$$

10.
$$
\begin{array}{r} 3.62 \\ \times\ 0.003 \\ \hline \end{array}
$$

11.
$$
\begin{array}{r} 1.07 \\ \times\ 0.05 \\ \hline \end{array}
$$

12.
$$
\begin{array}{r} 3.03 \\ \times\ 0.07 \\ \hline \end{array}
$$

13.
$$
\begin{array}{r} 0.02 \\ \times\ 0.02 \\ \hline \end{array}
$$

14.
$$
\begin{array}{r} 0.501 \\ \times\ 0.03 \\ \hline \end{array}
$$

15.
$$
\begin{array}{r} 0.321 \\ \times\ 0.09 \\ \hline \end{array}
$$

16. The players and coaches gathered around for refreshments after the soccer game. Of the 30 people there, 0.50 of them had fruit drinks, 0.20 of them had fruit juice, and 0.30 of them had soft drinks. How many people had each type of drink?

fruit drink_____

fruit juice_____

soft drink_____

Dividing With Decimals

When the dividend has a decimal, place the decimal point for the answer directly above the decimal point in the dividend. The first one has been done for you.

$$
\begin{array}{r}
12.5 \\
3\overline{)37.5} \\
-3 \\
\hline
07 \\
-6 \\
\hline
15 \\
-15 \\
\hline
0
\end{array}
$$

$4\overline{)34.4}$ $2\overline{)31.6}$ $3\overline{)131.4}$

$5\overline{)187.5}$ $7\overline{)181.3}$ $6\overline{)340.8}$ $9\overline{)294.3}$

$3\overline{)135.6}$ $5\overline{)264.5}$ $2\overline{)134.6}$ $8\overline{)754.4}$

$5\overline{)35.25}$ $7\overline{)79.45}$ $9\overline{)28.71}$ $36\overline{)199.44}$

Decimals and Fractions

A **fraction** is a number that names part of something. The top number in a fraction is called the **numerator**. The bottom number is called the **denominator**. Since a decimal also names part of a whole number, every decimal can also be written as a fraction. For example, 0.1 is read as "one tenth" and can also be written $\frac{1}{10}$. The decimal 0.56 is read as "fifty-six hundredths" and can also be written $\frac{56}{100}$.

Examples:

$$0.7 = \frac{7}{10} \qquad 0.34 = \frac{34}{100} \qquad 0.761 = \frac{761}{1,000} \qquad \frac{5}{10} = 0.5 \qquad \frac{58}{100} = 0.58 \qquad \frac{729}{1,000} = 0.729$$

Even a fraction that doesn't have 10, 100, or 1,000 as the denominator can be written as a decimal. Sometimes you can multiply both the numerator and denominator by a certain number so the denominator is 10, 100, or 1,000. (You can't just multiply the denominator. That would change the amount of the fraction.)

Examples:

$$\frac{3 \times 2}{5 \times 2} = \frac{6}{10} = 0.6 \qquad\qquad \frac{4 \times 4}{25 \times 4} = \frac{16}{100} = 0.16$$

Other times, divide the numerator by the denominator.

Examples:

$$\frac{3}{4} = 4\overline{)3.00} = 0.75 \qquad\qquad \frac{5}{8} = 8\overline{)5.000} = 0.625$$

Directions: Follow the instructions below.

1. For each square, write a decimal and a fraction to show the part that is colored. The first one has been done for you.

a. 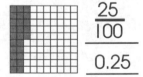 $\dfrac{25}{100}$

0.25

b. 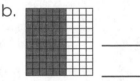 _____

_____

c. 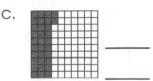 _____

_____

2. Change these decimals to fractions.

a. 0.6 =   b. 0.54 =   c. 0.751 =   d. 0.73 =   e. 0.592 =   f. 0.2 =

3. Change these fractions to decimals. If necessary, round off the decimals to the nearest hundredth.

a. $\dfrac{3}{10}$ =   b. $\dfrac{89}{100}$ =   c. $\dfrac{473}{1,000}$ =   d. $\dfrac{4}{5}$ =   e. $\dfrac{35}{50}$ =

f. $\dfrac{7}{9}$ =   g. $\dfrac{1}{3}$ =   h. $\dfrac{23}{77}$ =   i. $\dfrac{12}{63}$ =   j. $\dfrac{4}{16}$ =

Adding Fractions

When adding fractions, if the denominators are the same, simply add the numerators. When the result is an improper fraction, change it to a mixed number.

Examples: $\frac{3}{5} + \frac{1}{5} = \frac{4}{5}$ $\frac{3}{9} + \frac{7}{9} = \frac{10}{9} = 1\frac{1}{9}$

If the denominators of fractions are different, change them so they are the same. To do this, find equivalent fractions. In the first example below, $\frac{1}{4}$ and $\frac{3}{8}$ have different denominators, so change $\frac{1}{4}$ to the equivalent fraction $\frac{2}{8}$. Then add the numerators. In the second example, $\frac{5}{7}$ and $\frac{2}{3}$ also have different denominators. Find a denominator both 7 and 3 divide into. The lowest number they both divide into is 21. Multiply the numerator and denominator of $\frac{5}{7}$ by 3 to get the equivalent fraction $\frac{15}{21}$. Then multiply the numerator and denominator of $\frac{2}{3}$ by 7 to get the equivalent fraction $\frac{14}{21}$.

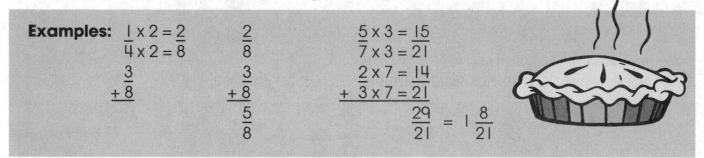

Examples:
$$\begin{array}{l} \frac{1 \times 2 = 2}{4 \times 2 = 8} \\ \frac{3}{8} \\ +\frac{3}{8} \end{array} \qquad \begin{array}{l} \frac{2}{8} \\ \frac{3}{8} \\ +\frac{3}{8} \\ \hline \frac{5}{8} \end{array} \qquad \begin{array}{l} \frac{5 \times 3 = 15}{7 \times 3 = 21} \\ \frac{2 \times 7 = 14}{+\ 3 \times 7 = 21} \\ \hline \frac{29}{21} = 1\frac{8}{21} \end{array}$$

Directions: Solve the following problems. Find equivalent fractions when necessary.

1. $\frac{3}{5}$ $+\frac{1}{5}$ 2. $\frac{7}{8}$ $+\frac{2}{16}$ 3. $\frac{1}{9}$ $+\frac{2}{3}$ 4. $\frac{2}{6}$ $+\frac{2}{3}$ 5. $\frac{2}{15}$ $+\frac{1}{5}$

6. Cora is making a cake. She needs $\frac{1}{2}$ cup butter for the cake and $\frac{1}{4}$ cup butter for the frosting. How much butter does she need altogether? _____

7. Henry is painting a wall. Yesterday he painted $\frac{1}{3}$ of it. Today he painted $\frac{1}{4}$ of it. How much has he painted altogether? _____

8. Nancy ate $\frac{1}{6}$ of a pie. Her father ate $\frac{1}{4}$ of it. How much did they eat altogether? _____

Subtracting Fractions

Subtracting fractions is very similar to adding them in that the denominators must be the same. If the denominators are different, use equivalent fractions.

Examples:

$$\frac{3}{4}$$
$$-\frac{1}{4}$$
$$\frac{2}{4} = \frac{1}{2}$$

$2 \times 8 = \frac{16}{40}$
$5 \times 8 = \frac{}{40}$
$1 \times 5 = \frac{5}{40}$
$-\frac{}{8} \times 5 = \frac{}{40}$
$$\frac{11}{40}$$

Adding and subtracting mixed numbers are also similar. Often, though, change the mixed numbers to improper fractions. If the denominators are different, use equivalent fractions.

Examples:

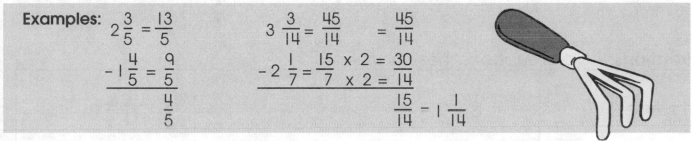

$2\frac{3}{5} = \frac{13}{5}$
$-1\frac{4}{5} = \frac{9}{5}$
$$\frac{4}{5}$$

$3\frac{3}{14} = \frac{45}{14} \qquad = \frac{45}{14}$
$-2\frac{1}{7} = \frac{15 \times 2}{7 \times 2} = \frac{30}{14}$
$$\frac{15}{14} - 1\frac{1}{14}$$

Directions: Solve the following problems. Use equivalent fractions and improper fractions where necessary.

1. $\frac{6}{7}$
    $-\frac{5}{7}$

2. $1\frac{2}{9}$
    $-\frac{4}{9}$

3. $2\frac{3}{6}$
    $-\frac{4}{5}$

4. $\frac{3}{4}$
    $-\frac{1}{2}$

5. $2\frac{1}{3}$
    $-\frac{3}{4}$

6. Carol promised to weed the flower garden for $1\frac{1}{2}$ hours this morning. So far she has pulled two weeds for $\frac{3}{4}$ of an hour. How much longer does she have to work? _____

7. Dll started out with $1\frac{1}{4}$ gallons of paint. He used $\frac{3}{8}$ gallon of the paint on his boat. How much paint is left? _____

8. A certain movie lasts $2\frac{1}{2}$ hours. Susan has already watched it for $1\frac{2}{3}$ hours. How much longer is the movie? _____

9. Bert didn't finish $\frac{1}{8}$ of the math problems on a test. He made mistakes on $\frac{1}{6}$ of the problems. The rest he answered correctly. What fraction of the problems did he answer correctly? _____

Summer Link Super Edition Grade 6

Adding and Subtracting Like Fractions

A **fraction** is a number that names part of a whole. Examples of fractions are $\frac{1}{2}$ and $\frac{1}{3}$. **Like fractions** have the same **denominator**, or bottom number. Examples of like fractions are $\frac{1}{4}$ and $\frac{3}{4}$.

To add or subtract fractions, the denominators must be the same. Add or subtract only the **numerators**, the numbers above the line in fractions.

Example:

numerators
denominators $\quad \frac{5}{8} - \frac{1}{8} = \frac{4}{8}$

$$\frac{5}{8} \qquad \frac{1}{8} \qquad \frac{4}{8}$$

Directions: Add or subtract these fractions.

$\frac{6}{12} - \frac{3}{12} =$	$\frac{4}{9} + \frac{1}{9} =$	$\frac{1}{3} + \frac{1}{3} =$	$\frac{5}{11} + \frac{4}{11} =$
$\frac{3}{5} - \frac{1}{5} =$	$\frac{5}{6} - \frac{2}{6} =$	$\frac{3}{4} - \frac{2}{4} =$	$\frac{5}{10} + \frac{3}{10} =$
$\frac{3}{8} + \frac{2}{8} =$	$\frac{1}{7} + \frac{4}{7} =$	$\frac{2}{20} + \frac{15}{20} =$	$\frac{11}{15} - \frac{9}{15} =$

Directions: Color the part of each pizza that equals the given fraction.

$$\frac{2}{4} \qquad + \qquad \frac{1}{4} \qquad =$$

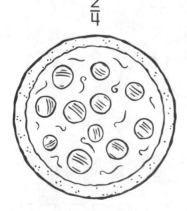 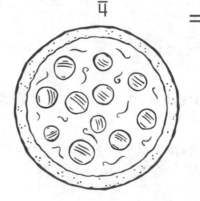 

Adding and Subtracting Unlike Fractions

Unlike fractions have different denominators. Examples of unlike fractions are $\frac{1}{4}$ and $\frac{2}{5}$. To add or subtract fractions, the denominators must be the same.

Example:

Step 1: Make the denominators the same by finding the least common denominator. The LCD of a pair of fractions is the same as the least common multiple (LCM) of their denominators.

$$\frac{1}{3} + \frac{1}{4} =$$

Multiples of 3 are 3, 6, 9, **12**, 15.
Multiples of 4 are 4, 8, **12**, 16.
LCM (and LCD) = 12

Step 2: Multiply by a number that will give the LCD. The numerator and denominator must be multiplied by the same number.

A. $\frac{1}{3} \times \frac{4}{4} = \frac{4}{12}$ **B.** $\frac{1}{4} \times \frac{3}{3} = \frac{3}{12}$

Step 3: Add the fractions. $\frac{1}{3} + \frac{1}{4} = \frac{4}{12} + \frac{3}{12} = \frac{7}{12}$

Directions: Follow the above steps to add or subtract unlike fractions. Write the LCM.

$\frac{2}{4} + \frac{3}{8} =$ LCM = _____	$\frac{3}{6} + \frac{1}{3} =$ LCM = _____	$\frac{4}{5} - \frac{1}{4} =$ LCM = _____
$\frac{2}{3} + \frac{2}{9} =$ LCM = _____	$\frac{4}{7} - \frac{2}{14} =$ LCM = _____	$\frac{7}{12} - \frac{2}{4} =$ LCM = _____

The basketball team ordered two pizzas. They left $\frac{1}{3}$ of one and $\frac{1}{4}$ of the other. How much pizza was left?

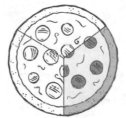 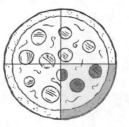

_____

Multiplying Fractions

To multiply two fractions, multiply the numerators and then multiply the denominators. If necessary, change the answer to its lowest term.

Examples: $\frac{3}{4} \times \frac{2}{3} = \frac{6}{12} = \frac{1}{2}$ $\frac{1}{8} \times \frac{4}{5} = \frac{4}{40} = \frac{1}{10}$

To multiply a whole number by a fraction, first write the whole number as a fraction (with 1 as the denominator). Then multiply as above. You may need to change an improper fraction to a mixed number.

Examples: $\frac{2}{3} \times \frac{4}{1} = \frac{8}{3} = 2\frac{2}{3}$ $\frac{3}{7} \times \frac{6}{1} = \frac{18}{7} = 2\frac{4}{7}$

Directions: Solve the following problems, writing answers in their lowest terms.

1. $\frac{1}{5} \times \frac{2}{3} =$ 2. $\frac{1}{3} \times \frac{4}{7} =$ 3. $\frac{2}{8} \times 3 =$ 4. $\frac{2}{6} \times \frac{1}{2} =$

5. Tim lost $\frac{1}{8}$ of his marbles. If he had 56 marbles, how many did he lose? _____

6. Jeff is making $\frac{2}{3}$ of a recipe for spaghetti sauce. How much will he need of each ingredient below?

   $1\frac{1}{4}$ cups water = _____   2 cups tomato paste = _____

   $\frac{3}{4}$ teaspoon oregano = _____ $4\frac{1}{2}$ teaspoons salt = _____

7. Carrie bought 2 dozen donuts and asked for $\frac{3}{4}$ of them to be chocolate. How many were chocolate? _____

8. Christy let her hair grow 14 inches long and then had $\frac{1}{4}$ of it cut off. How much was cut off? _____

9. Kurt has finished $\frac{7}{8}$ of 40 math problems. How many has he done? _____

10. If Sherryl's cat eats $\frac{2}{3}$ can of cat food every day, how many cans should Sherryl buy for a week? _____

Dividing Fractions

Reciprocals are two fractions that, when multiplied together, make 1. To divide a fraction by a fraction, turn one of the fractions upside down and multiply. The upside-down fraction is a reciprocal of its original fraction. If you multiply a fraction by its reciprocal, you always get 1.

Examples of reciprocals: $\frac{2}{3} \times \frac{3}{2} = \frac{6}{6} = 1$ $\qquad \frac{9}{11} \times \frac{11}{9} = \frac{99}{99} = 1$

Examples of dividing by fractions: $\frac{1}{2} \div \frac{2}{3} = \frac{1}{2} \times \frac{3}{2} = \frac{3}{4}$ $\qquad \frac{2}{5} \div \frac{2}{7} = \frac{2}{5} \times \frac{7}{2} = \frac{14}{10} = \frac{7}{5} = 1\frac{2}{5}$

To divide a whole number by a fraction, first write the whole number as a fraction (with a denominator of 1). (Write a mixed number as an improper fraction.) Then finish the problem as explained above.

Examples: $4 \div \frac{2}{6} = \frac{4}{1} \times \frac{6}{2} = \frac{24}{2} = 12$ $\qquad 3\frac{1}{2} \div \frac{2}{5} = \frac{7}{2} \times \frac{5}{2} = \frac{35}{4} = 8\frac{3}{4}$

Directions: Solve the following problems, writing answers in their lowest terms. Change any improper fractions to mixed numbers.

1. $\frac{1}{3} \div \frac{2}{5} =$

2. $\frac{6}{7} \div \frac{1}{3} =$

3. $3 \div \frac{3}{4} =$

4. $\frac{1}{4} \div \frac{2}{3} =$

5. Judy has 8 candy bars. She wants to give $\frac{1}{3}$ of a candy bar to everyone in her class. Does she have enough for all 24 students? _____

6. A big jar of glue holds $3\frac{1}{2}$ cups. How many little containers that hold $\frac{1}{4}$ cup each can you fill? _____

7. A container holds 27 ounces of ice cream. How many $4\frac{1}{2}$-ounce servings is that? _____

8. It takes $2\frac{1}{2}$ teaspoons of powdered mix to make 1 cup of hot chocolate. How many cups can you make with 45 teaspoons of mix? _____

9. Each cup of hot chocolate also takes $\frac{2}{3}$ cup of milk. How many cups of hot chocolate can you make with 12 cups of milk? _____

Name _____

Reducing Fractions

A fraction is in lowest terms when the GCF of both the numerator and denominator is 1. These fractions are in lowest possible terms: $\frac{2}{3}$, $\frac{5}{8}$, and $\frac{99}{100}$.

Example: Write $\frac{4}{8}$ in lowest terms.

Step 1: Write the factors of 4 and 8.

Factors of 4 are **4**, 2, 1.

Factors of 8 are 1, 8, 2, **4.**

Step 2: Find the GCF: 4.

Step 3: Divide both the numerator and denominator by 4.

$$\frac{4 \div 4}{8 \div 4} = \frac{1}{2}$$

Directions: Write each fraction in lowest terms.

$\frac{6}{8} = $ _____ lowest terms $\frac{9}{12} = $ _____ lowest terms

factors of 6: 6, 1, 2, 3   factors of 9: ____ , ____ , ____   ___ GCF

factors of 8: 8, 1, 2, 4   factors of 12: ___ , ____ , ____ , ____ , ____ , ___   ___ GCF

$\frac{2}{6} =$	$\frac{10}{15} =$	$\frac{8}{32} =$	$\frac{4}{10} =$
$\frac{12}{18} =$	$\frac{6}{8} =$	$\frac{4}{6} =$	$\frac{3}{9} =$

Directions: Color the pizzas to show that $\frac{4}{6}$ in lowest terms is $\frac{2}{3}$.

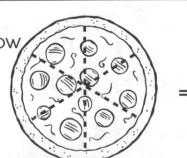 =

Improper Fractions

An **improper fraction** has a numerator that is greater than its denominator. An example of an improper fraction is $\frac{7}{6}$. An improper fraction should be reduced to its lowest terms.

Example: $\frac{5}{4}$ is an improper fraction because its numerator is greater than its denominator.

> **Step 1:** Divide the numerator by the denominator: $5 \div 4 = 1, r1$
>
> **Step 2:** Write the remainder as a fraction: $\frac{1}{4}$

$\frac{5}{4} = 1\frac{1}{4}$ $1\frac{1}{4}$ is a mixed number—a whole number and a fraction.

Directions: Follow the steps above to change the improper fractions to mixed numbers.

$\frac{9}{8} =$	$\frac{11}{5} =$	$\frac{5}{3} =$	$\frac{7}{6} =$	$\frac{8}{7} =$	$\frac{4}{3} =$
$\frac{21}{5} =$	$\frac{9}{4} =$	$\frac{3}{2} =$	$\frac{9}{6} =$	$\frac{25}{4} =$	$\frac{8}{3} =$

Sara had 29 duplicate stamps in her stamp collection. She decided to give them to four of her friends. If she gave each of them the same number of stamps, how many duplicates will she have left? _____

Name the improper fraction in this problem. _____

What step must you do next to solve the problem?

_____

Write your answer as a mixed number. _____

How many stamps could she give each of her friends? _____

Mixed Numbers

A **mixed number** is a whole number and a fraction together. An example of a mixed number is $2\frac{3}{4}$. A mixed number can be changed to an improper fraction.

Example: $2\frac{3}{4}$

Step 1: Multiply the denominator by the whole number: $4 \times 2 = 8$

Step 2: Add the numerator: $\qquad 8 + 3 = 11$

Step 3: Write the sum over the denominator: $\qquad \frac{11}{4}$

Directions: Follow the steps above to change the mixed numbers to improper fractions.

$3\frac{2}{3} =$	$6\frac{1}{5} =$	$4\frac{7}{8} =$	$2\frac{1}{2} =$
$1\frac{4}{5} =$	$5\frac{3}{4} =$	$7\frac{1}{8} =$	$9\frac{1}{9} =$
$8\frac{1}{2} =$	$7\frac{1}{6} =$	$5\frac{3}{5} =$	$9\frac{3}{8} =$
$12\frac{1}{5} -$	$25\frac{1}{2} =$	$10\frac{2}{3} -$	$14\frac{3}{8} =$

Adding Mixed Numbers

To add mixed numbers, first find the least common denominator.

Always reduce the answer to lowest terms.

Example:

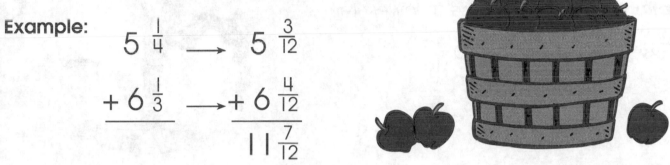

$$5\tfrac{1}{4} \longrightarrow 5\tfrac{3}{12}$$
$$+6\tfrac{1}{3} \longrightarrow +6\tfrac{4}{12}$$
$$\overline{11\tfrac{7}{12}}$$

Directions: Add. Reduce the answers to lowest terms.

$$8\tfrac{1}{2}$$
$$+7\tfrac{1}{4}$$

$$5\tfrac{1}{4}$$
$$+2\tfrac{3}{8}$$

$$9\tfrac{3}{10}$$
$$+7\tfrac{1}{5}$$

$$8\tfrac{1}{5}$$
$$+6\tfrac{7}{10}$$

$$4\tfrac{4}{5}$$
$$+3\tfrac{3}{10}$$

$$3\tfrac{1}{2}$$
$$+7\tfrac{1}{4}$$

$$4\tfrac{1}{2}$$
$$+1\tfrac{1}{3}$$

$$6\tfrac{1}{12}$$
$$+3\tfrac{3}{4}$$

$$5\tfrac{1}{3}$$
$$+2\tfrac{3}{9}$$

$$6\tfrac{1}{3}$$
$$+2\tfrac{2}{5}$$

$$2\tfrac{2}{7}$$
$$+4\tfrac{1}{14}$$

$$3\tfrac{1}{2}$$
$$+3\tfrac{1}{4}$$

The boys picked $3\tfrac{1}{2}$ baskets of apples. The girls picked $5\tfrac{1}{2}$ baskets. How many baskets of apples did the boys and girls pick in all? _____

Summer Link Super Edition Grade 6

Subtracting Mixed Numbers

To subtract mixed numbers, first find the least common denominator. Reduce the answer to its lowest terms.

Directions: Subtract. Reduce to lowest terms.

Example:

$$6 \frac{5}{8} \rightarrow 6 \frac{10}{16}$$
$$- 3 \frac{4}{16} \rightarrow - 3 \frac{4}{16}$$
$$3 \frac{6}{16} = 3 \frac{3}{8}$$

$2 \frac{3}{7}$ $7 \frac{2}{3}$ $6 \frac{3}{4}$ $9 \frac{5}{12}$
$- 1 \frac{1}{14}$ $- 5 \frac{1}{8}$ $- 2 \frac{3}{12}$ $- 5 \frac{9}{24}$

$5 \frac{1}{2}$ $7 \frac{3}{8}$ $8 \frac{3}{8}$ $11 \frac{5}{6}$
$- 3 \frac{1}{3}$ $- 5 \frac{1}{6}$ $- 6 \frac{5}{12}$ $- 7 \frac{1}{12}$

$9 \frac{3}{5}$ $4 \frac{4}{5}$ $9 \frac{2}{3}$ $14 \frac{3}{8}$
$- 7 \frac{1}{15}$ $- 2 \frac{1}{4}$ $- 4 \frac{1}{6}$ $- 9 \frac{3}{16}$

The Rodriguez Farm has $9 \frac{1}{2}$ acres of corn. The Johnson Farm has $7 \frac{1}{3}$ acres of corn. How many more acres of corn does the Rodriguez Farm have? _____

Ordering Fractions

When putting fractions in order from smallest to largest or largest to smallest, it helps to find a common denominator first.

Example:

$\frac{1}{3}$, $\frac{1}{2}$ changed to $\frac{2}{6}$, $\frac{3}{6}$

Directions: Put the following fractions in order from least to largest value.

				Least			Largest
$\frac{1}{2}$	$\frac{2}{7}$	$\frac{4}{5}$	$\frac{1}{3}$	_____	_____	_____	_____
$\frac{3}{12}$	$\frac{3}{6}$	$\frac{1}{3}$	$\frac{3}{4}$	_____	_____	_____	_____
$\frac{2}{5}$	$\frac{4}{15}$	$\frac{3}{5}$	$\frac{5}{15}$	_____	_____	_____	_____
$3\frac{4}{5}$	$3\frac{2}{5}$	$\frac{9}{5}$	$3\frac{1}{5}$	_____	_____	_____	_____
$9\frac{1}{3}$	$9\frac{2}{3}$	$9\frac{9}{12}$	$8\frac{2}{3}$	_____	_____	_____	_____
$5\frac{8}{12}$	$5\frac{5}{12}$	$5\frac{4}{24}$	$5\frac{3}{6}$	_____	_____	_____	_____
$4\frac{3}{5}$	$5\frac{7}{15}$	$6\frac{2}{5}$	$5\frac{1}{5}$	_____	_____	_____	_____

Four dogs were selected as finalists at a dog show. They were judged in four separate categories. One received a perfect score in each area. The dog with a score closest to four is the winner. Their scores are listed below. Which dog won the contest?

_____

Dog A $3\frac{4}{5}$ Dog B $3\frac{2}{3}$ Dog C $3\frac{5}{15}$ Dog D $3\frac{9}{12}$

Multiplying Fractions

To multiply fractions, follow these steps:

$\frac{1}{2} \times \frac{3}{4} =$ **Step 1**: Multiply the numerators. $1 \times 3 = \frac{3}{8}$
                                        Step 2: Multiply the denominators. $2 \times 4 = \frac{3}{8}$

When multiplying a fraction by a whole number, first change the whole number to a fraction.

Example:

$\frac{1}{2} \times 8 = \frac{1}{2} \times \frac{8}{1} = \frac{8}{2} = 4$ reduced to lowest terms

Directions: Multiply. Reduce your answers to lowest terms.

$\frac{3}{4} \times \frac{1}{6} =$	$\frac{1}{2} \times \frac{5}{8} =$	$\frac{2}{3} \times \frac{1}{6} =$	$\frac{2}{3} \times \frac{1}{2} =$
$\frac{5}{6} \times 4 =$	$\frac{3}{8} \times \frac{1}{16} =$	$\frac{1}{5} \times 5 =$	$\frac{7}{8} \times \frac{3}{4} =$
$\frac{7}{11} \times \frac{1}{3} =$	$\frac{2}{9} \times \frac{9}{4} =$	$\frac{1}{3} \times \frac{1}{3} \times \frac{1}{3} =$	$\frac{1}{8} \times \frac{1}{4} \times \frac{1}{2} =$

Jennifer has 10 pets. Two-fifths of the pets are cats, one-half are fish, and one-tenth are dogs. How many of each pet does she have?

_____

_____

Dividing Fractions

To divide fractions, follow these steps:

$$\frac{3}{4} \div \frac{1}{4} =$$

Step 1: "Invert" the divisor. That means to turn it upside down.

$$\frac{3}{4} \div \frac{4}{1}$$

Step 2: Multiply the two fractions:

$$\frac{3}{4} \times \frac{4}{1} = \frac{12}{4}$$

Step 3: Reduce the fraction to lowest terms by dividing the denominator into the numerator.

$$12 \div 4 = 3$$

$$\frac{3}{4} \div \frac{1}{4} = 3$$

Directions: Follow the above steps to divide fractions.

$\frac{1}{4} \div \frac{1}{5} =$	$\frac{1}{3} \div \frac{1}{12} =$	$\frac{3}{4} \div \frac{1}{3} =$
$\frac{5}{12} \div \frac{1}{3} =$	$\frac{3}{4} \div \frac{1}{6} =$	$\frac{2}{9} \div \frac{2}{3} =$
$\frac{3}{7} \div \frac{1}{4} =$	$\frac{2}{3} \div \frac{4}{6} =$	$\frac{1}{8} \div \frac{2}{3} =$
$\frac{4}{5} \div \frac{1}{3} =$	$\frac{4}{8} \div \frac{1}{2} =$	$\frac{5}{12} \div \frac{6}{8} =$

Least Common Demoninators

Equivalent fractions make it possible to write any fractions so that they have the same denominator. The least common denominator (LCD) is the least multiple that two or more denominators have in common.

Example: Write $\frac{3}{6}$ and $\frac{1}{4}$ with the same denominator.

Steps:

1. Find the least common multiple (LCM) of the denominators. The LCM of 6 and 4 is 12.

2. Rewrite each fraction as an equivalent fraction using the LCD as the denominator.

$$\frac{3}{6} \times \frac{2}{2} = \frac{6}{12} \qquad \frac{1}{4} \times \frac{3}{3} = \frac{3}{12}$$

The fractions $\frac{6}{12}$ and $\frac{3}{12}$ are the fractions $\frac{3}{6}$ and $\frac{1}{4}$ rewritten with the same denominator.

Rewrite each pair of fractions using the least common denominator (LCD).

$\frac{1}{2}$ and $\frac{2}{3}$ _____ $\frac{1}{2}$ and $\frac{3}{4}$ _____ $\frac{3}{8}$ and $\frac{3}{4}$ _____

$\frac{3}{4}$ and $\frac{1}{6}$ _____ $\frac{2}{3}$ and $\frac{2}{4}$ _____ $\frac{3}{10}$ and $\frac{1}{4}$ _____

$\frac{7}{12}$ and $\frac{5}{8}$ _____ $\frac{7}{8}$ and $\frac{5}{6}$ _____ $\frac{11}{22}$ and $\frac{1}{3}$ _____

One fraction in each box does not belong. Draw an **X** through the fraction that is not equivalent to the others.

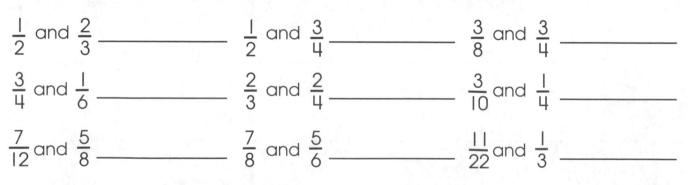

$\frac{2}{4}$	$\frac{1}{2}$
$\frac{3}{8}$	$\frac{3}{6}$

$\frac{2}{5}$	$\frac{3}{10}$
$\frac{8}{20}$	$\frac{6}{15}$

$\frac{2}{3}$	$\frac{10}{30}$
$\frac{4}{12}$	$\frac{3}{9}$

$\frac{6}{8}$	$\frac{3}{11}$
$\frac{12}{16}$	$\frac{8}{12}$

Cross My Heart

Here is a quick way to decide which fraction is greater. Cross multiply the numerator of one fraction by the denominator of the other and write the products like this:

$$42 \quad\quad 40$$
$$\frac{7}{8} \times \frac{5}{6}$$

The fraction with the greater number above it is the greater fraction. If the numbers are the same, the fractions are equivalent.

Cross multiply to compare. Write the letter from the greater fraction in each set to solve the riddle.

What is black and white, and red all over?

1. $\frac{2}{6}$ P $\frac{3}{8}$ T

2. $\frac{7}{12}$ H $\frac{9}{16}$ E

3. $\frac{3}{20}$ C $\frac{2}{15}$ D

4. $\frac{6}{8}$ M $\frac{7}{9}$ N

5. $\frac{5}{10}$ E $\frac{5}{12}$ O

6. $\frac{6}{12}$ R $\frac{6}{11}$ U

7. $\frac{3}{16}$ D $\frac{5}{24}$ S

8. $\frac{8}{9}$ P $\frac{6}{7}$ O

9. $\frac{10}{14}$ A $\frac{9}{13}$ N

10. $\frac{15}{32}$ L $\frac{2}{4}$ B

11. $\frac{16}{25}$ B $\frac{3}{4}$ I

12. $\frac{5}{20}$ G $\frac{4}{18}$ D

___ ___ ___ ___ ___ ___ ___ ___
8   5   4   12 6   11 4   7

___ ___   ___ ___ ___
9   1   1   2   5

___ ___ ___ ___ ___
10 5   9   3   2

Different Denominators

Fractions, improper fractions, and mixed numbers must have a common denominator before they can be added or subtracted.

Steps to add fractions with different denominators:
1. Find a common denominator.
2. Rewrite each number using the common denominator.
3. Add. Simplify, if necessary.

$$\frac{3}{8} + \frac{1}{4} = \frac{3}{8} + \frac{2}{8} = \frac{5}{8} \qquad \frac{5}{6} + \frac{3}{4} = \frac{10}{12} + \frac{9}{12} = \frac{19}{12} = 1\frac{7}{12}$$

$$2\frac{1}{2} + \frac{3}{10} = 2\frac{5}{10} + \frac{3}{10} = 2\frac{8}{10} = 2\frac{4}{5} \qquad 1\frac{2}{3} + 1\frac{2}{5} = 1\frac{10}{15} + 1\frac{6}{15} = 2\frac{16}{15} = 3\frac{1}{15}$$

Directions: Add. Simplify, if necessary.

$$\frac{1}{2} + \frac{1}{4} = \qquad\qquad \frac{2}{6} + \frac{1}{4} = \qquad\qquad \frac{3}{5} + \frac{2}{10} =$$

$$\frac{5}{8} + \frac{3}{4} = \qquad\qquad \frac{5}{12} + \frac{1}{2} = \qquad\qquad 1\frac{2}{5} + \frac{1}{3} =$$

$$\frac{4}{3} + \frac{3}{4} = \qquad\qquad \frac{9}{16} + \frac{7}{8} = \qquad\qquad \frac{3}{8} + \frac{2}{6} =$$

$$\frac{2}{3} + \frac{2}{6} = \qquad\qquad \frac{9}{10} + \frac{4}{15} = \qquad\qquad 1\frac{1}{4} + \frac{3}{2} =$$

$$2\frac{3}{5} + 4\frac{1}{2} = \qquad\qquad \frac{8}{9} + \frac{1}{3} = \qquad\qquad \frac{3}{8} + \frac{3}{12} =$$

$$\frac{8}{10} + \frac{1}{8} - \qquad\qquad \frac{12}{21} + \frac{2}{7} = \qquad\qquad \frac{1}{20} + \frac{1}{12} =$$

Finding Percents

Find percent by dividing the number you have by the number possible.

Example:

15 out of 20 possible: $\underline{0.75} = 75\%$

$$20 \overline{)15.00}$$
$$-140$$
$$\overline{100}$$
$$\underline{100}$$

Annie has been keeping track of the scores she earned on each spelling test during the grading period.

Directions: Find out each percentage grade she earned. The first one has been done for you.

Week	Number Correct		Total Number of Words	Score in Percent
1	14	(out of)	20	70%
2	16		20	_____
3	18		20	_____
4	12		15	_____
5	16		16	_____
6	17		18	_____
Review Test	51		60	_____

If Susan scored 5% higher than Annie on the review test, how many words did she get right? _____

Carrie scored 10% lower than Susan on the review test. How many words did she spell correctly? _____

Of the 24 students in Annie's class, 25% had the same score as Annie. Only 10% had a higher score. What percent had a lower score? _____

Is that answer possible? _____

Why? _____

Percent of a Number

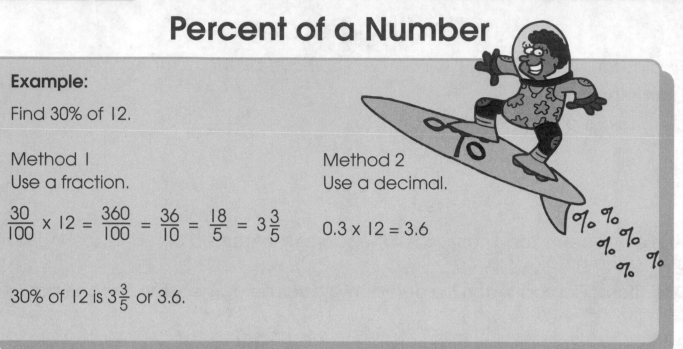

Example:

Find 30% of 12.

Method 1
Use a fraction.

$$\frac{30}{100} \times 12 = \frac{360}{100} = \frac{36}{10} = \frac{18}{5} = 3\frac{3}{5}$$

Method 2
Use a decimal.

$$0.3 \times 12 = 3.6$$

30% of 12 is $3\frac{3}{5}$ or 3.6.

Find 25% of:	Find 4% of:	Find 60% of:
16 _____	10 _____	15 _____
20 _____	96 _____	60 _____
64 _____	150 _____	100 _____
140 _____	200 _____	125 _____
10 _____	20 _____	7 _____
35 _____	35 _____	32 _____
120 _____	90 _____	110 _____
630 _____	140 _____	297 _____

Ratios

A **ratio** compares two numbers.

Example:

Put 10 pennies and 10 nickels in a bag. Without looking, pull out a small handful of coins. Draw the coins in a box below. Write each ratio. Return the coins to the bag and repeat 4 more times. The first example is shown.

pennies to nickels	3:5	coins to pennies	8:3
nickels to pennies	5:3	nickels to coins	5:8
pennies to coins	3:8	coins to nickels	8:5

pennies to nickels	____	coins to pennies	____
nickels to pennies	____	nickels to coins	____
pennies to coins	____	coins to nickels	____

pennies to nickels	____	coins to pennies	____
nickels to pennies	____	nickels to coins	____
pennies to coins	____	coins to nickels	____

pennies to nickels	____	coins to pennies	____
nickels to pennies	____	nickels to coins	____
pennies to coins	____	coins to nickels	____

pennies to nickels	____	coins to pennies	____
nickels to pennies	____	nickels to coins	____
pennies to coins	____	coins to nickels	____

pennies to nickels	____	coins to pennies	____
nickels to pennies	____	nickels to coins	____
pennies to coins	____	coins to nickels	____

Proportions

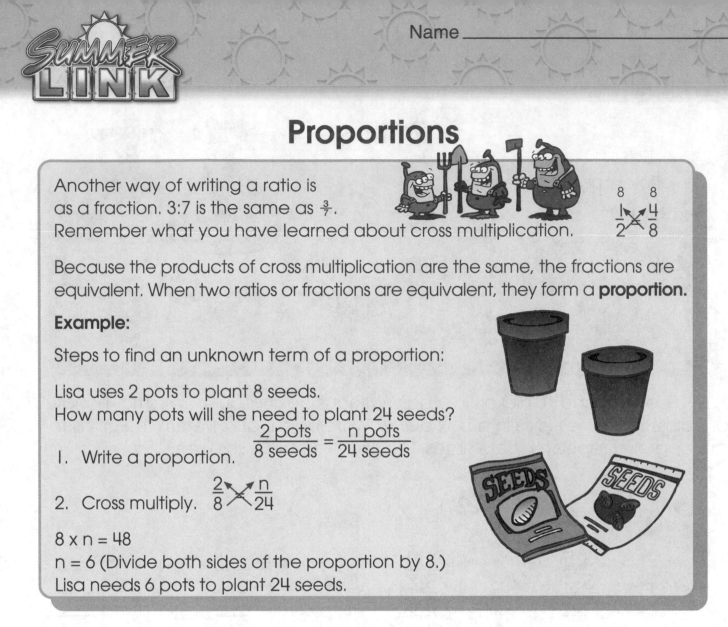

Another way of writing a ratio is as a fraction. 3:7 is the same as $\frac{3}{7}$.
Remember what you have learned about cross multiplication.

$$\frac{1}{2} \nearrow\!\!\!\!\searrow \frac{4}{8} \quad \begin{array}{c} 8 \quad 8 \end{array}$$

Because the products of cross multiplication are the same, the fractions are equivalent. When two ratios or fractions are equivalent, they form a **proportion.**

Example:

Steps to find an unknown term of a proportion:

Lisa uses 2 pots to plant 8 seeds.
How many pots will she need to plant 24 seeds?

1. Write a proportion. $\frac{2 \text{ pots}}{8 \text{ seeds}} = \frac{n \text{ pots}}{24 \text{ seeds}}$

2. Cross multiply. $\frac{2}{8} \nearrow\!\!\!\!\searrow \frac{n}{24}$

$8 \times n = 48$
$n = 6$ (Divide both sides of the proportion by 8.)
Lisa needs 6 pots to plant 24 seeds.

If the ratios form a proportion, write *yes* on the line. If not, write *no.*

$\frac{4}{5} = \frac{24}{30}$ _____ $\frac{1}{2} = \frac{36}{72}$ _____ $\frac{3}{7} = \frac{20}{35}$ _____ $\frac{1}{23} = \frac{8}{184}$ _____

$\frac{6}{13} = \frac{75}{156}$ _____ $\frac{9}{5} = \frac{171}{95}$ _____ $\frac{4}{21} = \frac{40}{210}$ _____ $\frac{11}{12} = \frac{154}{168}$ _____

Find the unknown term in each of these proportions.

$\frac{4}{5} = \frac{n}{15}$ _____ $\frac{n}{104} = \frac{5}{13}$ _____ $\frac{5}{6} = \frac{45}{n}$ _____

Probability

Probability is the ratio of favorable outcomes to possible outcomes of an experiment.

Vehicle	Number Sold
4 door	26
2 door	18
Sport	7
Van	12
Wagon	7
Compact	4
Total	75

Example:

This table records vehicle sales for 1 month. What is the probability of a person buying a van?

number of vans sold = 12   total number of cars = 75

The probability that a person will choose a van is 12 in 75 or $\frac{12}{75}$.

Directions: Look at the chart of flowers sold in a month. What is the probability that a person will buy each?

Roses _____

Tulips _____

Violets _____

Orchids _____

Flowers	Number Sold
Roses	48
Tulips	10
Violets	11
Orchids	7
Total	76

How would probability help a flower store owner keep the correct quantity of each flower in the store?

_____

_____

_____

Likely and Unlikely

The probability of an event happening can be written as a fraction between 0 and 1.

Example:

Certain if the probability is 1. The probability of spinning red, blue, or green is $\frac{6}{6}$ or 1.

More likely if its probability is greater than another. It is more likely to spin green ($\frac{3}{6}$) than red ($\frac{2}{6}$).

Less likely if its probability is less than another. It is less likely to spin blue ($\frac{1}{6}$) than red ($\frac{2}{6}$).

Equally likely if the probabilities are the same. It is equally likely to spin red or blue ($\frac{3}{6}$) or green ($\frac{3}{6}$).

Impossible if the probability is 0. It is impossible to spin white ($\frac{0}{6}$ = 0).

Look at the spinner. Write the probability for each event below. Write *certain* or *impossible*, where appropriate.

spinning a 6 _____   spinning a 4 _____

spinning a 2 _____   spinning a 4 or 5 _____

spinning an even number _____   spinning a prime number _____

spinning a number < 10 _____   spinning a zero _____

Look at the spinner to find which is **more likely, less likely,** or **equally likely**.

Spinning a 4 is _____ than spinning a 5.

Spinning a 4 is _____ than spinning a 1.

Spinning an even number is _____ than spinning an odd number.

Bar Graphs

Another way to organize information is a **bar graph**. The bar graph in the example compares the number of students in 4 elementary schools. Each bar stands for 1 school. You can easily see that School A has the most students and School C has the least. The numbers along the left show how many students attend each school.

Example:

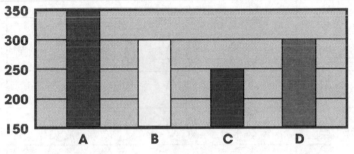

Directions: Complete the following exercises.

1. This bar graph will show how many calories are in 1 serving of 4 kinds of cereal. Draw the bars the correct height and label each with the name of the cereal. After completing the bar graph, answer the questions. Data: Korn Kernals— 150 calories; Oat Floats— 160 calories; Rite Rice— 110 calories; Sugar Shapes— 200 calories.

   a. Which cereal is the best to eat if you're trying to lose weight?_____
   b. Which cereal has nearly the same number of calories as Oat Floats? _____

2. On another sheet of paper, draw your own graph, showing the number of TV commercials in 1 week for each of the 4 cereals in the graph above. After completing the graph, answer the questions. Data: Oat Boats—27 commercials; Rite Rice— 15; Sugar Shapes—35; Korn Kernals—28.

   a. Which cereal is most heavily advertised?_____
   b. What similarities do you notice between the graph of calories and the graph of TV commercials?_____

   _____

Picture Graphs

Newspapers and textbooks often use **pictures** in graphs instead of bars. Each picture stands for a certain number of objects. Half a picture means half the number. The picture graph in the example indicates the number of games each team won. The Astros won 7 games, so they have $3\frac{1}{2}$ balls.

Example:

	Games Won			
Astros	⚾	⚾	⚾	🌓
Orioles	⚾	⚾		
Bluebirds	⚾	⚾	⚾	⚾
Sluggers	⚾			

(1 ball = 2 games)

Directions: Complete the following exercises.

Finish this picture graph, showing the number of students who have dogs in 4 sixth-grade classes. Draw simple dogs in the graph, letting each drawing stand for 2 dogs.

Data: Class 1—12 dogs; Class 2—16 dogs; Class 3—22 dogs; Class 4—12 dogs. After completing the graph, answer the questions.

	Dogs Owned by Students
Class 1	
Class 2	
Class 3	
Class 4	

(One dog drawing = 2 students' dogs)

1. Why do you think newspapers use picture graphs?_____

_____

2. Would picture graphs be appropriate to show exact number of dogs living in America? Why or why not?_____

_____

Name _____

Line Graphs

Still another way to display information is a **line graph**. The same data can often be shown in both a bar graph and a line graph. Nevertheless, line graphs are especially useful in showing changes over a period of time.

The line graph in the example shows changes in the number of students enrolled in a school over a 5-year period. Enrollment was highest in 2000 and has decreased gradually each year since then. Notice how labeling the years and enrollment numbers make the graph easy to understand.

Example:

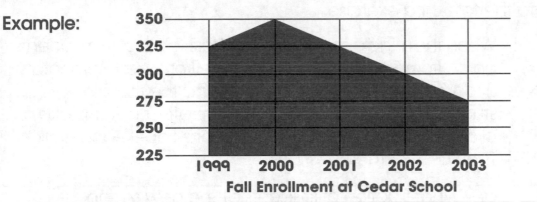

Fall Enrollment at Cedar School

Directions: Complete the following exercises.

1. On another sheet of paper, draw a line graph that displays the growth of a corn plant over a 6-week period. Mark the correct points, using the data below, and connect them with a line. After completing the graph, answer the questions. Data: week 1— 3.5 in.; week 2—4.5 in.; week 3—5 in.; week 4—5.5 in.; week 5—5.75 in.; week 6—6 in.

   a. Between which weeks was the growth fastest?_____

   b. Between which weeks was the growth slowest?_____

2. On another sheet of paper draw a line graph to show how the high temperature varied during one week. Then answer the questions. Data: Sunday—high of 53 degrees; Monday—51; Tuesday—56; Wednesday—60; Thursday—58; Friday—67; Saturday—73. Don't forget to label the numbers.

   a. In general, did the days get warmer or cooler?_____

   b. Do you think this data would have been as clear in a bar graph?_____
   Explain your answer.

   _____

   _____

Circle Graphs

Circle graphs are useful in showing how something is divided into parts. The circle graph in the example shows how Carly spent her $10 allowance. Each section is a fraction of her whole allowance. For example, the movie tickets section is $\frac{1}{2}$ of the circle, showing that she spent $\frac{1}{2}$ of her allowance, $5, on movie tickets.

Directions: Complete the following exercises.

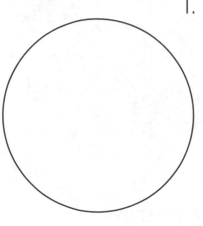

1. When the middle school opened last fall, $\frac{1}{2}$ of the students came from East Elementary, $\frac{1}{4}$ came from West Elementary, $\frac{1}{8}$ came from North Elementary, and the remaining students moved into the town from other cities. Make a circle graph showing these proportions. Label each section. Then answer the questions.

   a. What fraction of students at the new school moved into the area from other cities?_____

   b. If the new middle school has 450 students enrolled, how many used to go to East Elementary?_____

2. This circle graph will show the hair color of 24 students in one class. Divide the circle into 4 sections to show this data: black hair—8 students; brown hair—10 students; blonde hair—4 students; red hair—2 students. (Hint: 8 students are $\frac{8}{24}$ or $\frac{1}{3}$ of the class.) Be sure to label each section by hair color. Then answer the questions.

   a. Looking at your graph, what fraction of the class is the combined group of blonde- and red-haired students? _____

   b. Which two fractions of hair color combine to total half the class?_____

Length in Customary Units

The **customary system** of measurement is the most widely used in the United States. It measures length in inches, feet, yards, and miles.

Examples:

    12 inches (in.) = 1 foot (ft.)
    3 ft. (36 in.) = 1 yard (yd.)
    5,280 ft. (1,760 yds.) = 1 mile (mi.)

To change to a larger unit, divide. To change to a smaller unit, multiply.

Examples:

To change inches to feet, divide by 12.	24 in. = 2 ft.	27 in. = 2 ft. 3 in.
To change feet to inches, multiply by 12.	3 ft. = 36 in.	4 ft. = 48 in.
To change inches to yards, divide by 36.	108 in. = 3 yd.	80 in. = 2 yd. 8 in.
To change feet to yards, divide by 3.	12 ft. = 4 yd.	11 ft. = 3 yd. 2 ft.

Sometimes in subtraction you have to borrow units.

Examples:

3 ft. 4 in.	= 2 ft. 16 in.	3 yd.	= 2 yd. 3 ft.
− 1 ft. 11 in.	− 1 ft. 11 in.	− 1 yd. 2 ft.	− 1 yd. 2 ft.
	1 ft. 5 in.		1 yd. 1 ft.

Directions: Solve the following problems.

1. 108 in. = _____ ft.

2. 68 in. = _____ ft. _____ in.

3. 8 ft. = _____ yd. _____ ft.

4. 3,520 yd. = _____ mi.

5. What form of measurement (inches, feet, yards, or miles) would you use for each item below?

    a. pencil _____

    b. vacation trip _____

    c. playground _____

    d. wall _____

6. One side of a square box is 2 ft. 4 in. What is the perimeter of the box? _____

7. Jason is 59 in. tall. Kent is 5 ft. 1 in. tall. Who is taller and by how much? _____

8. Karen bought a doll 2 ft. 8 in. tall for her little sister. She found a box that is 29 in. long. Will the doll fit in that box? _____

9. Dan's dog likes to go out in the backyard, which is 85 ft. wide. The dog's chain is 17 ft. 6 in. long. If Dan attaches one end of the chain to a pole in the middle of the yard, will his dog be able to leave the yard? _____

Name _____

Length in Metric Units

The **metric system** measures length in meters, centimeters, millimeters, and kilometers.

Examples:

A **meter (m)** is about 40 inches or 3.3 feet.
A **centimeter (cm)** is $\frac{1}{100}$ of a meter or 0.4 inches.
A **millimeter (mm)** is $\frac{1}{1000}$ of a meter or 0.04 inches.
A **kilometer (km)** is 1,000 meters or 0.6 miles.

As before, divide to find a larger unit and multiply to find a smaller unit.

Examples:

To change cm to mm, multiply by 10.
To change cm to meters, divide by 100.
To change mm to meters, divide by 1,000.
To change km to meters, multiply by 1,000.

Directions: Solve the following problems.

1. 600 cm = ___ m   2. 12 cm = _____ mm   3. 47 m = _____ cm   4. 3 km = _____ m

5. In the sentences below, write the missing unit: m, cm, mm, or km.

   a. A fingernail is about 1 _____ thick.

   b. An average car is about 5 _____ long.

   c. Someone could walk 1 _____ in 10 minutes.

   d. A finger is about 7 _____ long.

   e. A street could be 3 _____ long.

   f. The Earth is about 40,000 _____ around at the equator.

   g. A pencil is about 17 _____ long.

   h. A noodle is about 4 _____ wide.

   i. A teacher's desk is about 1 _____ wide.

6. A nickel is about 1 mm thick. How many nickels would
   be in a stack 1 cm high?   _____

7. Is something 25 cm long closer to 10 inches or 10 feet?   _____

8. Is something 18 mm wide closer to 0.7 inch or 7 inches?   _____

9. Would you get more exercise running 4 km or 500 m?   _____

10. Which is taller, something 40 m or 350 cm?   _____

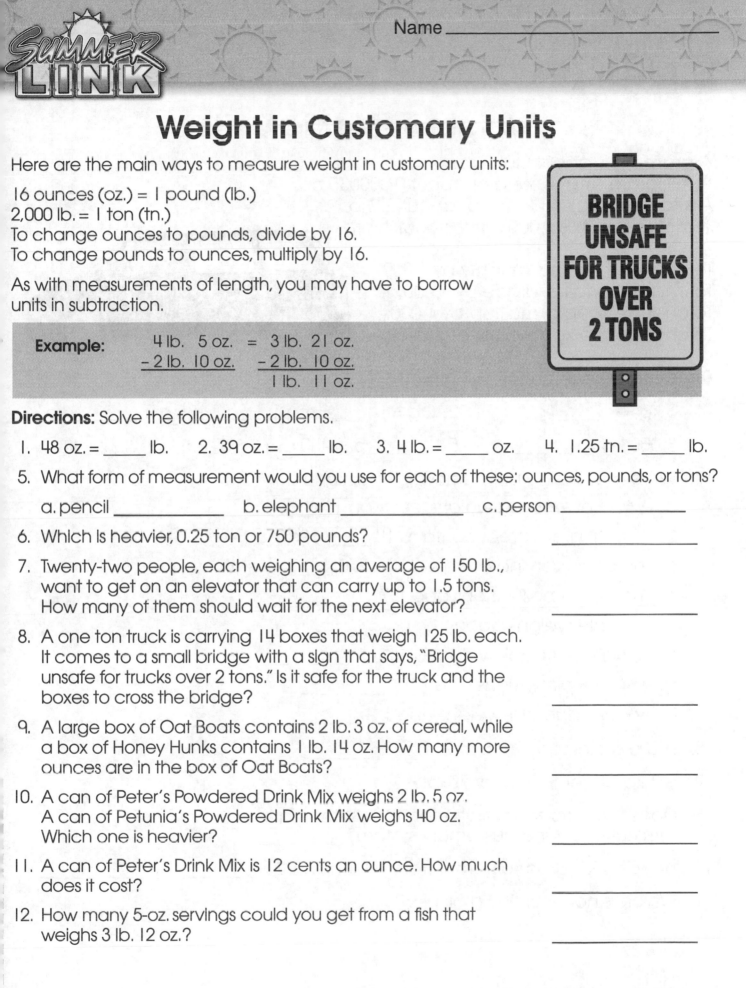

Weight in Customary Units

Here are the main ways to measure weight in customary units:

16 ounces (oz.) = 1 pound (lb.)
2,000 lb. = 1 ton (tn.)
To change ounces to pounds, divide by 16.
To change pounds to ounces, multiply by 16.

As with measurements of length, you may have to borrow units in subtraction.

BRIDGE UNSAFE FOR TRUCKS OVER 2 TONS

Example:	4 lb. 5 oz.	=	3 lb. 21 oz.
	– 2 lb. 10 oz.		– 2 lb. 10 oz.
			1 lb. 11 oz.

Directions: Solve the following problems.

1. 48 oz. = _____ lb.   2. 39 oz. = _____ lb.   3. 4 lb. = _____ oz.   4. 1.25 tn. = _____ lb.

5. What form of measurement would you use for each of these: ounces, pounds, or tons?

   a. pencil _____   b. elephant _____   c. person _____

6. Which is heavier, 0.25 ton or 750 pounds? _____

7. Twenty-two people, each weighing an average of 150 lb., want to get on an elevator that can carry up to 1.5 tons. How many of them should wait for the next elevator? _____

8. A one ton truck is carrying 14 boxes that weigh 125 lb. each. It comes to a small bridge with a sign that says, "Bridge unsafe for trucks over 2 tons." Is it safe for the truck and the boxes to cross the bridge? _____

9. A large box of Oat Boats contains 2 lb. 3 oz. of cereal, while a box of Honey Hunks contains 1 lb. 14 oz. How many more ounces are in the box of Oat Boats? _____

10. A can of Peter's Powdered Drink Mix weighs 2 lb. 5 oz. A can of Petunia's Powdered Drink Mix weighs 40 oz. Which one is heavier? _____

11. A can of Peter's Drink Mix is 12 cents an ounce. How much does it cost? _____

12. How many 5-oz. servings could you get from a fish that weighs 3 lb. 12 oz.? _____

Weight in Metric Units

A **gram (g)** is about 0.035 oz.
A **milligram (mg)** is $\frac{1}{1000}$ g or about 0.000035 oz.
A **kilogram (kg)** is 1,000 g or about 2.2 lb.
A **metric ton (t)** is 1,000 kg or about 1.1 tn.

To change g to mg, multiply by 1,000.
To change g to kg, divide by 1,000.
To change kg to g, multiply by 1,000.
To change t to kg, multiply by 1,000.

Directions: Solve the following problems.

1. 3 kg = _____ g
2. 2 g = _____ mg
3. 145 g = _____ kg
4. 3,000 kg = _____ t
5. _____ g = 450 mg
6. 3.5 t = _____ kg

7. Write the missing units below: g, mg, kg, or t.

    a. A sunflower seed weighs less than 1 _____.

    b. A serving of cereal contains 14 ____ of sugar.

    c. The same serving of cereal has 250 ____ of salt.

    d. A bowling ball weighs about 7 _____.

    e. A whale weighs about 90 _____.

    f. A math textbook weighs about 1 _____.

    g. A safety pin weighs about 1 _____.

    h. An average car weighs about 1 _____.

8. Is 200 g closer to 7 oz. or 70 oz.? _____

9. Is 3 kg closer to 7 lb. or 70 lb.? _____

10. Does a metric ton weigh more or less than a ton
    measured by the customary system? _____

11. How is a kilogram different from a kilometer? _____

12. Which is heavier, 300 g or 1 kg? _____

Capacity in Customary Units

Here are the main ways to measure capacity (how much something will hold) in customary units:

8 fluid ounces (fl. oz.) = 1 cup (c.)
2 c. = 1 pint (pt.)
2 pt. = 1 quart (qt.)
4 qt. = 1 gallon (gal.)

To change ounces to cups, divide by 8.
To change cups to ounces, multiply by 8.
To change cups to pints or quarts, divide by 2.
To change pints to cups or quarts to pints, multiply by 2.

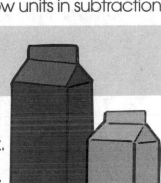

As with measurements of length and weight, you may have to borrow units in subtraction.

Example:

$$3 \text{ gal. } 2 \text{ qt. } = \quad 2 \text{ gal. } 6 \text{ qt.}$$
$$\underline{- 1 \text{ gal. } 3 \text{ qt.} \quad \underline{- 1 \text{ gal. } 3 \text{ qt.}}}$$
$$1 \text{ gal. } 3 \text{ qt.}$$

Directions: Solve the following problems.

1. 32 fl. oz. = _____ pt. 2. 4 gal. = _____ pt. 3. _____ c. = 24 fl. oz.

4. 5 pt. = _____ qt. 5. 16 pt. = _____ gal. 6. 3 pt. = _____ fl. oz.

7. A large can of soup contains 19 fl. oz. A serving is about 8 oz. How many cans should you buy if you want to serve 7 people? _____

8. A container of strawberry ice cream holds 36 fl. oz. A container of chocolate ice cream holds 2 pt. Which one has more ice cream? How much more? _____

9. A day-care worker wants to give 15 children each 6 fl. oz. of milk. How many quarts of milk does she need? _____

10. This morning, the day-care supervisor bought 3 gal. of milk. The kids drank 2 gal. 3 c. How much milk is left for tomorrow? _____

11. Harriet bought 3 gal. 2 qt. of paint for her living room. She used 2 gal. 3 qt. How much paint is left over? _____

12. Jason's favorite punch takes a pint of raspberry sherbet. If he wants to make $1\frac{1}{2}$ times the recipe, how many fl. oz. of sherbet does he need? _____

Capacity in Metric Units

A **liter** (L) is a little over 1 quart.
A **milliliter** (mL) is $\frac{1}{1000}$ of a liter or about 0.03 oz.
A **kiloliter** (kL) is 1,000 liters or about 250 gallons.

Directions: Solve the following problems.

1. 5,000 mL = _____ L

2. 2,000 L = _____ kL

3. 3 L = _____ mL

4. Write the missing unit: L, mL, or kL.

   a. A swimming pool holds about 100 _____ of water.

   b. An eyedropper is marked for 1 and 2 _____.

   c. A pitcher could hold 1 or 2 _____ of juice.

   d. A teaspoon holds about 5 _____ of medicine.

   e. A birdbath might hold 5 _____ of water.

   f. A tablespoon holds about 15 _____ of salt.

   g. A bowl holds about 250 _____ of soup.

   h. We drank about 4 _____ of punch at the party.

5. Which is more, 3 L or a gallon?   _____

6. Which is more, 400 mL or 40 oz.?   _____

7. Which is more, 1 kL or 500 L?   _____

8. Is 4 L closer to a quart or a gallon?   _____

9. Is 480 mL closer to 2 cups or 2 pints?   _____

10. Is a mL closer to 4 drops or 4 teaspoonsful?   _____

11. How many glasses of juice containing 250 mL
    each could you pour from a 1-L jug'?   _____

12. How much water would you need to water an
    average-sized lawn, 1 kL or 1 L?   _____

Temperature in Customary and Metric Units

The customary system measures temperature in Fahrenheit (F°)

The metric system uses Celsius (C°) degrees.

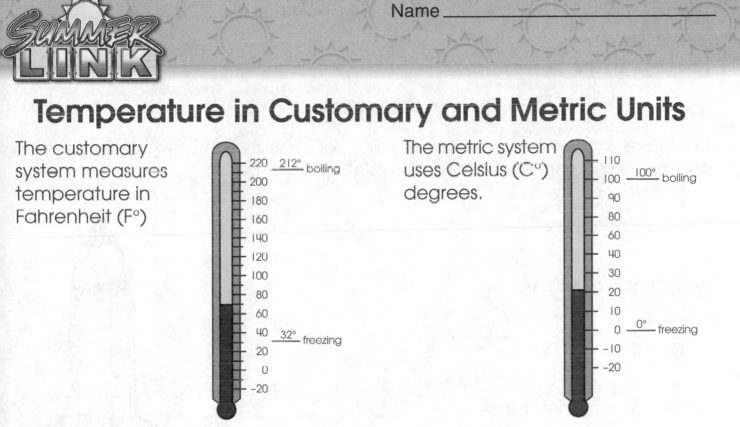

Directions: Study the thermometers and answer these questions.

1. Write in the temperature from both systems:

	Fahrenheit	Celsius
a. freezing	_____	_____
b. boiling	_____	_____
c. comfortable room temperature	_____	_____
d. normal body temperature	_____	_____

2. Underline the most appropriate temperature for both systems.

a. a reasonably hot day	34°	54°	84°	10°	20°	35°
b. a cup of hot chocolate	95°	120°	190°	60°	90°	120°
c. comfortable water to swim in	55°	75°	95°	10°	25°	40°

3. If the temperature is 35°C, is it summer or winter? _____

4. Would ice cream stay frozen at 35°F? _____

5. Which is colder, –10°C or –10°F? _____

6. Which is warmer, 60°C or 60°F? _____

Review

Directions: Write the best unit to measure each item: inch, foot, yard, mile, ounce, pound, ton, fluid ounce, cup, pint, quart, or gallon.

distance from New York to Chicago _____

weight of a goldfish _____

height of a building _____

water in a large fish tank _____

glass of milk _____

weight of a whale _____

length of a pencil _____

distance from first base to second base _____

distance traveled by a space shuttle _____

length of a soccer field _____

amount of paint needed to cover a house _____

material needed to make a dress _____

Name _____

Geometric Figures

Example	Description	Symbol	Read
Point •A	A point is an end of a line segment (an exact location in space).	A	point A
Line E D	A line is a collection of points in a straight path that extends in two directions without end.	$\overleftrightarrow{DE}$	line DE
Line Segment R S	A line segment is part of a line with two endpoints.	$\overline{RS}$	segment RS
Ray B C	A ray is part of a line having only one endpoint.	$\overrightarrow{BC}$	ray BC
Angle C D E	An angle is two rays having a common endpoint.	$\angle CDE$	angle CDE
Plane T S U	A plane is an endless flat surface.	plane STU	plane STU

Use the figure to write the symbol for each.

1. 1 ray _____

2. a plane _____

3. 3 points _____ , _____ , _____

4. 2 lines _____ , _____

5. 3 angles _____ , _____ , _____

6. 3 line segments _____ , _____ , _____

Figuring Angles

To find the answers to the two riddles below, find the answer that matches each figure and write the figure's corresponding letter above it.

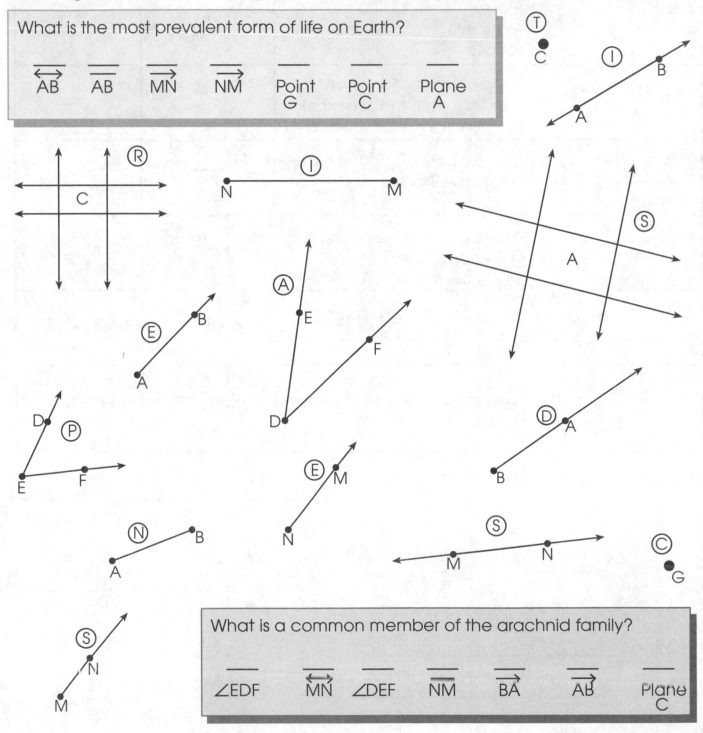

What is the most prevalent form of life on Earth?

| $\overleftrightarrow{AB}$ | $\overline{AB}$ | $\overrightarrow{MN}$ | $\overrightarrow{NM}$ | Point G | Point C | Plane A |

What is a common member of the arachnid family?

| $\angle EDF$ | $\overleftrightarrow{MN}$ | $\angle DEF$ | $\overrightarrow{NM}$ | $\overrightarrow{BA}$ | $\overrightarrow{AB}$ | Plane C |

Triangle Groups

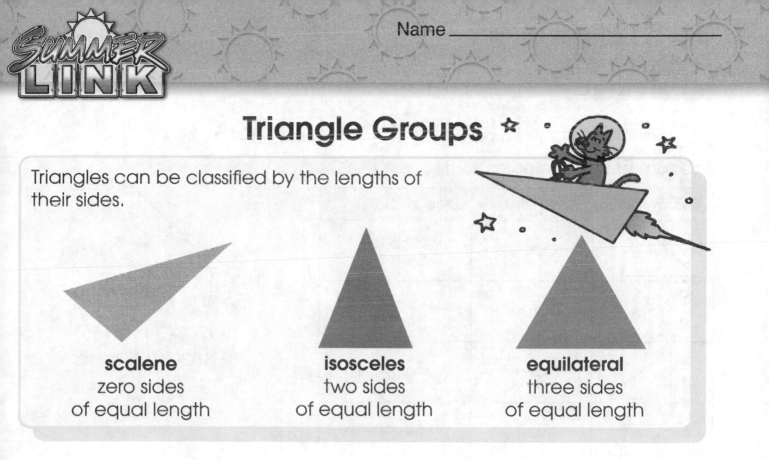

Triangles can be classified by the lengths of their sides.

scalene
zero sides
of equal length

isosceles
two sides
of equal length

equilateral
three sides
of equal length

Directions: Draw each triangle.

scalene triangle

equilateral triangle

isosceles triangle

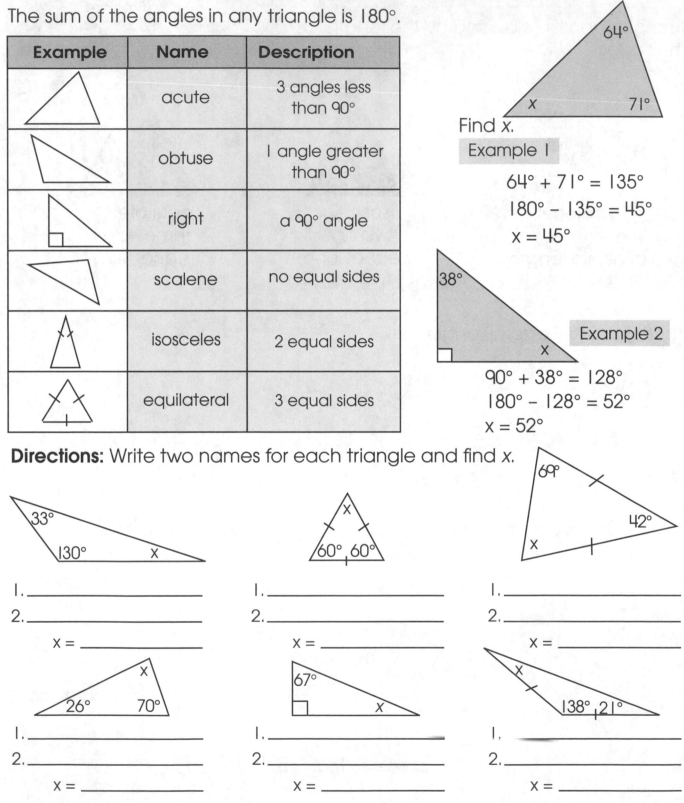

Classifying Triangles

The sum of the angles in any triangle is 180°.

Example	Name	Description
	acute	3 angles less than 90°
	obtuse	1 angle greater than 90°
	right	a 90° angle
	scalene	no equal sides
	isosceles	2 equal sides
	equilateral	3 equal sides

Find x.

Example 1

$$64° + 71° = 135°$$
$$180° - 135° = 45°$$
$$x = 45°$$

Example 2

$$90° + 38° = 128°$$
$$180° - 128° = 52°$$
$$x = 52°$$

Directions: Write two names for each triangle and find x.

1. _____
2. _____
   x = _____

1. _____
2. _____
   x = _____

1. _____
2. _____
   x = _____

1. _____
2. _____
   x = _____

1. _____
2. _____
   x = _____

1. _____
2. _____
   x = _____

Perimeter

Perimeter is the distance around an area.

Directions: Find the perimeter of each figure.

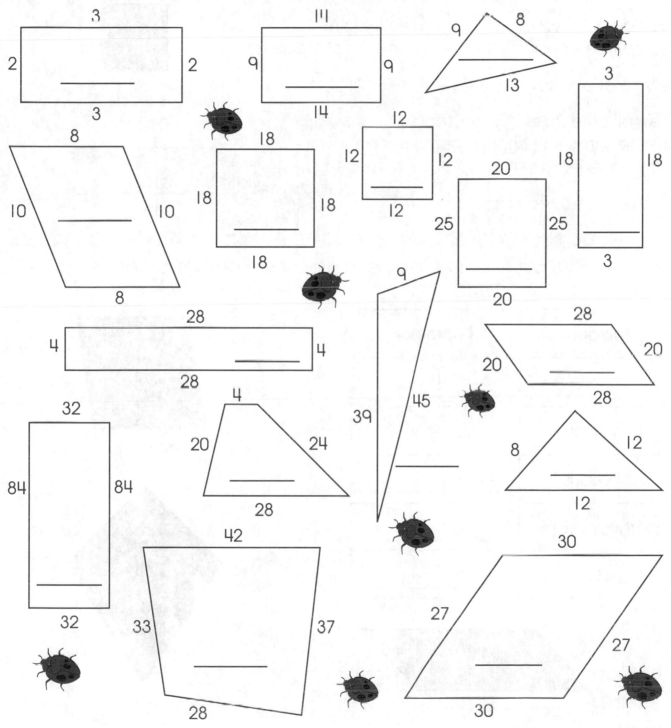

Perimeter Formula

The perimeter of some polygons can be given as a formula.

Examples:

The sides of a square are the same length.
The perimeter equals 4 times the length of a side (s).

Perimeter of a square: s + s + s + s = 4 x s = 4s

The opposite sides of a rectangle
are the same length. The perimeter equals
2 times the length (l) plus 2 times the width (w).

Perimeter of a rectangle: 2l + 2w

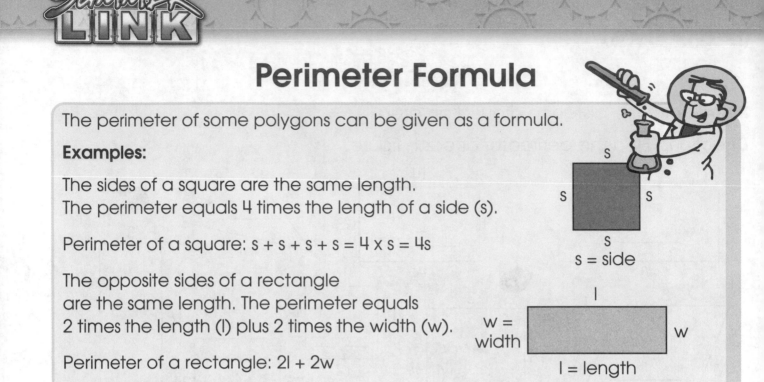

Directions: Find a formula for the perimeter of a rhombus, a parallelogram, and a kite.

Polygon	Perimeter
square	4s
rectangle	2l + 2w
rhombus	_____
parallelogram	_____
kite	_____

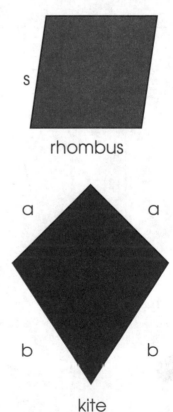

rhombus

kite

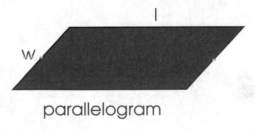

parallelogram

The Circle Game

The perimeter of a circle is called the **circumference.** There is a formula for finding the circumference of a circle. The formula uses this special number **3.14**. We call this number **pi** (π). To find the circumference of a circle, use this formula:

Circumference = π x diameter
Circumference = πd

or

Circumference = π x 2 x radius
Circumference = 2πr

Examples:

C = πd   C = 2πr
C = 3.14 x 4   C = 2 x 3.14 x 2
C = 12.56   C = 12.56

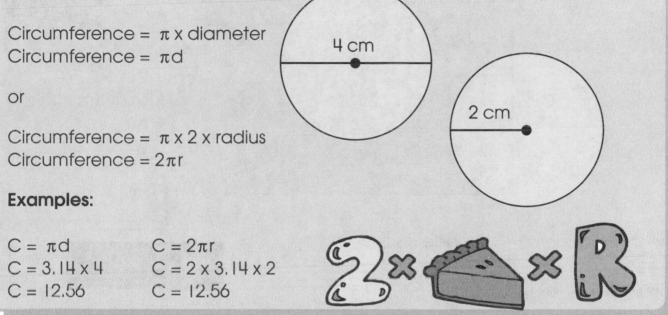

Directions: Find the circumference for each circle.

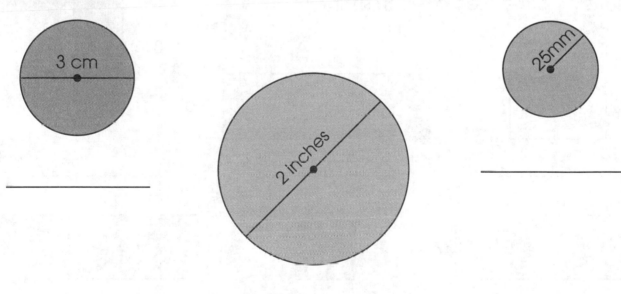

3 cm

2 inches

25mm

_____   _____

_____

Formula One

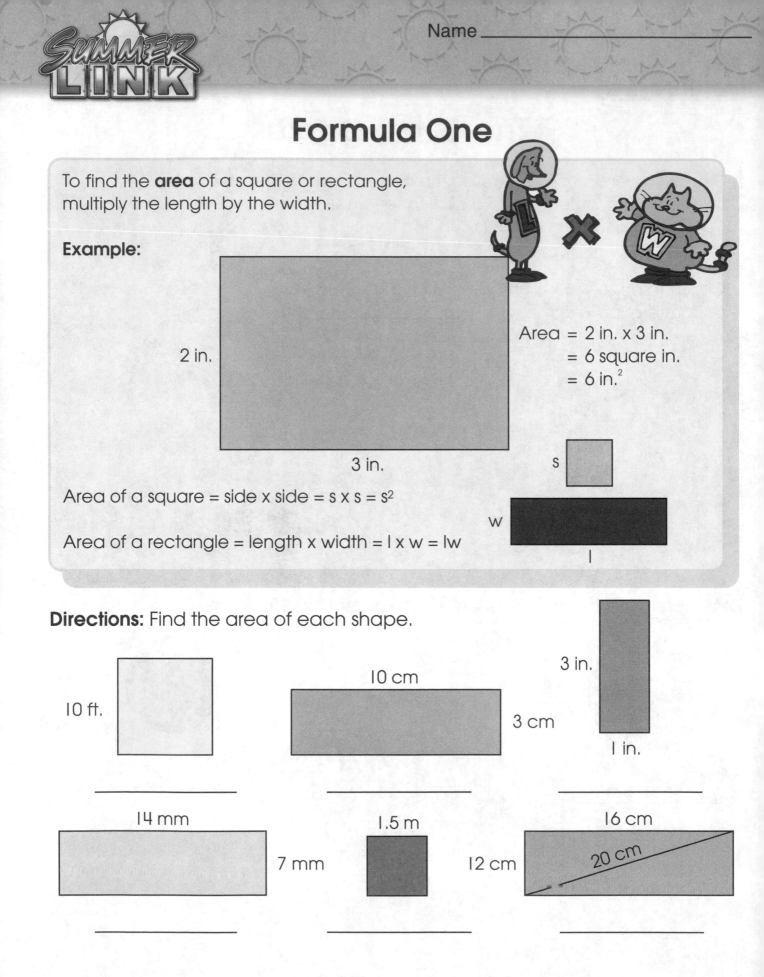

To find the **area** of a square or rectangle, multiply the length by the width.

Example:

2 in.

3 in.

Area = 2 in. x 3 in.
= 6 square in.
= 6 in.^{2}

s

w

l

Area of a square = side x side = s x s = s^2

Area of a rectangle = length x width = l x w = lw

Directions: Find the area of each shape.

10 ft.

10 cm

3 cm

3 in.

1 in.

_____

_____

_____

14 mm

7 mm

1.5 m

16 cm

20 cm

12 cm

_____

_____

_____

Area: Squares and Rectangles

The **area** is the number of square units that covers a certain space. To find the area, multiply the length by the width. The answer is in square units, shown by adding a superscript 2 (^{2}) to the number.

Examples:

 3 in.

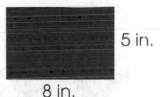 5 in.

8 in.

For the rectangle, use this formula: **A = l x w**
$$A = 8 \times 5$$
$$A = 40 \text{ in.}^2$$

For the square formula, **s** stands for side: **A = s x s** (or s^2)
$$A = 3 \times 3 \text{ (or } 3^2)$$
$$A = 9 \text{ in.}^2$$

Directions: Find the area of each shape below.

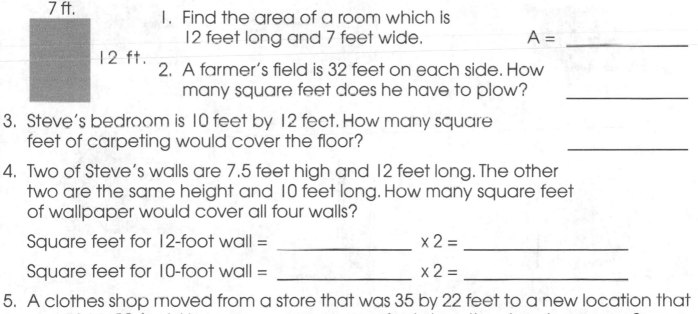

7 ft.

1. Find the area of a room which is 12 feet long and 7 feet wide.   A = _____

12 ft.

2. A farmer's field is 32 feet on each side. How many square feet does he have to plow?   _____

3. Steve's bedroom is 10 feet by 12 feet. How many square feet of carpeting would cover the floor?   _____

4. Two of Steve's walls are 7.5 feet high and 12 feet long. The other two are the same height and 10 feet long. How many square feet of wallpaper would cover all four walls?

Square feet for 12-foot wall = _____ x 2 = _____

Square feet for 10-foot wall = _____ x 2 = _____

5. A clothes shop moved from a store that was 35 by 22 feet to a new location that was 53 by 32 feet. How many more square feet does the store have now?

Square feet for first location = _____

Square feet for new location = _____   Difference = _____

6. A school wanted to purchase a climber for the playground. The one they selected would need 98 square feet of space. The only space available on the playground was 12 feet long and 8 feet wide. Will there be enough space for the climber? _____

Volume of Prisms

Volume is measured in cubic units.

Volume of a nonrectangular prism
    = base area • height

$V = b \cdot h$

$V = (\frac{1}{2} \cdot 4 \cdot 6) \cdot 12$

$V = 144 \text{ in}^3$

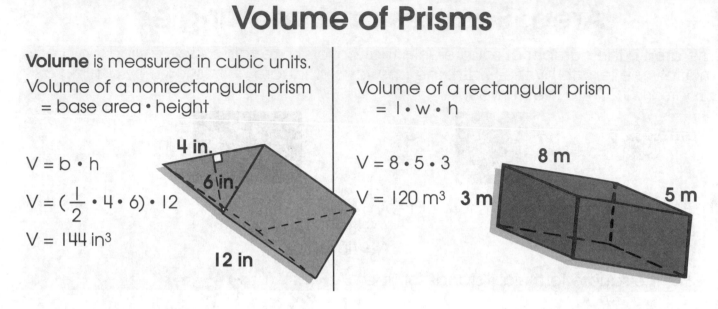

4 in.

6 in.

12 in

Volume of a rectangular prism
    = l • w • h

$V = 8 \cdot 5 \cdot 3$

$V = 120 \text{ m}^3$

8 m

3 m

5 m

Directions: Find the volume of each prism.

1.
5 cm
15 cm
14 cm

4.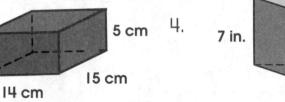
7 in.   7 in.
7 in.

7.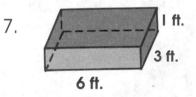
1 ft.
3 ft.
6 ft.

2.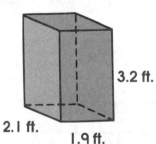
3.2 ft.
2.1 ft.
1.9 ft.

5.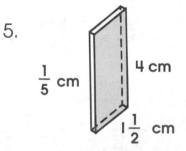
$\frac{1}{5}$ cm
4 cm
$1\frac{1}{2}$ cm

8.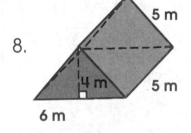
5 m
4 m
5 m
6 m

3.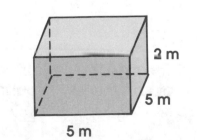
2 m
5 m
5 m

6.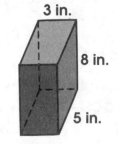
3 in.
8 in.
5 in.

Name _____

Geometric Patterns

Geometric patterns can be described in several ways. **Similar shapes** have the same shape but in differing sizes. **Congruent shapes** have the same geometric pattern but may be facing in different directions. **Symmetrical shapes** are identical when divided in half.

Directions: Use the terms **similar**, **congruent**, or **symmetrical** to describe the following patterns.

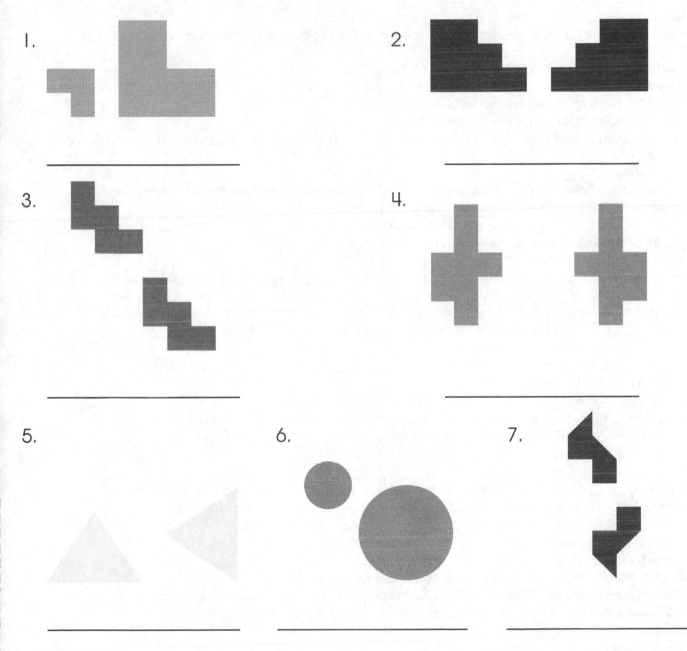

1. _____

2. _____

3. _____

4. _____

5. _____   6. _____   7. _____

Glossary

angle: two rays having a common endpoint.

area: the amount of surface in a given boundary, found by multiplying length by width.

bar graph: a way to organize information in which bars represent numbers.

circle graph: a graph that shows how something is divided into parts.

circumference: the perimeter of a circle.

common multiples: multiples that two or more numbers share or have in common.

customary system: the type of measurement most widely used in the United States.

decimal: a number that includes a period called a decimal point.

denominator: the bottom number in a fraction.

diameter: a line segment running through the center of a circle.

equation: a number sentence in which the value on the left of the equal sign must equal the value on the right.

estimating: using an approximate number instead of an exact one.

expanded notation: writing out the value of each digit in a number.

factors: numbers multiplied together to give a product.

fraction: a number that names part of something.

greatest common factor: the largest number for a set of numbers that divides evenly into each number in the set.

improper fraction: has a numerator that is greater than its denominator.

least common multiples: the least common multiple that a group of numbers has in common.

like fractions: have the same denominator, or bottom number.

line: a collection of points in a straight path that extends in two directions without end.

line graph: a way of presenting information over a period of time.

line segment: a part of a line with two endpoints.

metric system: a system of measurement based on counting by tens, such as liter, milliliter, gram, kilogram, centimeter, meter, kilometer.

mixed number: a whole number and a fraction together.

multiple: the product of any given number and a factor such as 1, 2, 3, and so on.

numerator: the top number in a fraction.

percent: a portion of 100 expressed with a % sign.

perimeter: the distance around an area.

pi: equals 3.14, used to find the circumference of a circle.

picture graph: a type of graph where a picture stands for a certain number of objects.

place value: the position of a digit in a number.

plane: an endless flat surface.

point: the end of a line segment.

prime number: a positive whole number which can be divided evenly only by itself or one.

probability: the ratio of favorable outcomes to possible outcomes of an experiment.

proportion: formed when two ratios or fractions are equivalent.

ratio: compares two numbers.

ray: part of a line having only one endpoint.

reciprocals: two fractions that, when multiplied together, make 1.

rounding: means to express a given number to the nearest ten, hundred, thousand, and so on.

unlike fractions: have different denominators that must be reduced to find a like denominator.

volume: the amount of space a three-dimensional object takes up.

whole numbers: numbers to the left of a decimal point.

Page 8

Place Value

Place value is the position of a digit in a number. A digit's place in a number shows its value. Numbers left of the decimal point represent **whole numbers**. Numbers right of the decimal point represent a part, or fraction, of a whole number. These parts are broken down into tenths, hundredths, thousandths, and so on.

Example:

3	4	4	3	2	2	1	6	2	1
← Whole Numbers					Fractions →				

Directions: Write the following number words as numbers.

1. Three million, forty-four thousand, six hundred twenty-one. 3,044,621
2. One million, seventy-seven. 1,000,077
3. Nine million, six hundred thousand, one hundred two. 9,600,102
4. Twenty-nine million, one hundred three thousand and nine tenths. 29,103,000.9
5. One million, one hundred thousand, one hundred seventy-one and thirteen hundredths. 1,100,171.13

Directions: In each box, write the corresponding number for each place value.

1. 4,822,000.00 — 0 hundreds
2. 55,907,003.00 — 7 thousands
3. 190,641,225.07 — 6 hundred thousands
4. 247,308,211.59 — 5 tenths
5. 7,594,097.33 — 7 millions
6. 201,480,110.01 — 4 hundred thousands
7. 42,367,109,074.25 — 5 hundredths

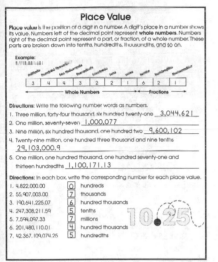
10.25

Page 9

Expanded Notation

Expanded notation is writing out the value of each digit in a number.

Example:
8,920,077 = 8,000,000 + 900,000 + 20,000 + 70 + 7
Word form: Eight million, nine hundred twenty thousand, seventy-seven

Directions: Write the following numbers using expanded notation.

1. 20,769,033 20,000,000 + 700,000 + 60,000 + 9,000 + 30 + 3
2. 1,183,541,029 1,000,000,000 + 100,000,000 + 80,000,000 + 3,000,000 + 500,000 + 40,000 + 1,000 + 20 + 9
3. 776,003,091 700,000,000 + 70,000,000 + 6,000,000 + 3,000 + 90 + 1
4. 5,920,100,808 5,000,000,000 + 900,000,000 + 20,000,000 + 100,000 + 800 + 8
5. 14,141,543,760 10,000,000,000 + 4,000,000,000 + 100,000,000 + 40,000,000 + 1,000,000 + 500,000 + 40,000 + 3,000 + 700 + 60

Directions: Write the following numbers.

1. 700,000 + 900 + 60 + 7 700,967
2. 35,000,000 + 600,000 + 400 + 40 + 2 35,600,442
3. 12,000,000 + 700,000 + 60,000 + 4,000 + 10 + 4 12,764,014
4. 80,000,000 + 8,000,000 + 400,000,000 + 80,000,000 + 10,000 + 400 + 30 88,480,010,430
5. 4,000,000,000 + 16,000,000 + 30 + 2 4,016,000,032

Page 10

Adding Integers

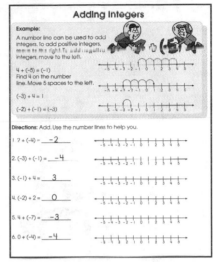

Example:
A number line can be used to add integers. To add positive integers, move to the right. To add negative integers, move to the left.

4 + (-5) = (-1)
Find 4 on the number line. Move 5 spaces to the left.

(-3) + 4 = 1

(-2) + (-1) = (-3)

Directions: Add. Use the number lines to help you.

1. 2 + (-4) = -2
2. (-3) + (-1) = -4
3. (-1) + 4 = 3
4. (-2) + 2 = 0
5. 4 + (-7) = -3
6. 0 + (-4) = -4

Page 11

Rounding

Follow these steps to round numbers to a given place.

Example: Round 35,634 to the nearest thousand.

a. Locate and highlight the place to which the number is to be rounded. ► Highlight the digit in the thousands place: 35,634
b. Look at the digit to the right of the designated place. If the number is 5 or greater, round the highlighted number up. If the number is 4 or less, round the highlighted number down by keeping the digit the same. ► Six is greater than 5, so round the highlighted number up.
c. Rewrite the original number with the amended digit in the highlighted place and change all of the digits to the right to zeros. ► The rounded number is 36,000.

Example: Round 782 to the nearest 10.

► Highlight the digit in the tens place: 782
► Two is four or less, so round down by keeping the tens digit the same. 782
► The rounded number is 780.

Directions: Round each number to the given place.

nearest 10: 1. 855 — 860 ; 2. 333 — 330
nearest 100: 3. 725 — 700 ; 4. 2,348 — 2,300
nearest 1,000: 5. 4,317 — 4,000 ; 6. 8,650 — 9,000
nearest 10,000: 7. 25,199 — 30,000 ; 8. 529,740 — 530,000
nearest 100,000: 9. 496,225 — 500,000 ; 10. 97,008 — 100,000

Page 12

Rounding

Directions: Round off each number, then estimate the answer. You can use a calculator to find the exact answer.

Round to the nearest ten.	Estimate	Actual Answer
1. 86 ÷ 9 =	9	9.56
2. 237 + 488 =	730	725
3. 49 × 11 =	500	539
4. 309 + 412 =	720	721
5. 625 − 218 =	410	407
Round to the nearest hundred.		
6. 790 − 70 =	700	720
7. 690 ÷ 70 =	7	9.86
8. 2,177 − 955 =	1,200	1,222
9. 4,792 + 3,305 =	8,100	8,097
10. 5,210 × 90 =	520,00	468,900
Round to the nearest thousand.		
11. 4,078 + 2,093 =	6,000	6,171
12. 5,625 − 3,065 =	3,000	2,460
13. 6,047 ÷ 2,991 =	2	2.02
14. 1,913 × 4,216 =	8,000,000	8,065,208
15. 7,227 + 8,449 =	15,000	15,676

Page 13

Rounding and Estimating

Rounding is expressing a number to the nearest whole number, ten, thousand, or other value. **Estimating** is using an approximate number instead of an exact one. When rounding a number, we say a country has 98,000,000 citizens instead of 98,347,425. We can round off numbers to the nearest whole number, the nearest hundred, or the nearest million—whatever is appropriate.

Here are the steps: 1) Decide where you want to round off the number. 2) If the digit to the right is less than 5, leave the digit at the rounding place unchanged. 3) If the digit to the right is 5 or more, increase the digit at the rounding place by 1.

Examples: 587 rounded to the nearest hundred is 600.
535 rounded to the nearest hundred is 500.
21,847 rounded to the nearest thousand is 22,000.
21,356 rounded to the nearest thousand is 21,000.

When we estimate numbers, we use rounded, approximate numbers instead of exact ones.

Example: A hamburger that costs $1.49 and a drink that costs $0.79 total about $2.30 ($1.50 plus $0.80).

Directions: Use rounding and estimating to find the answers to these questions. You may have to add, subtract, multiply, or divide.

1. Debbi is having a party and wants to fill 11 cups from a 67-ounce bottle of pop. About how many ounces should she pour into each cup? — 6 ounces
2. Tracy studied 28 minutes every day for 4 days. About how long did she study in all? — 120 minutes
3. About how much does this lunch cost? — $2.00
4. The numbers below show how long Frank spent studying last week. Estimate how many minutes he studied for the whole week. Monday: 23 minutes Tuesday: 37 minutes Wednesday: 38 minutes Thursday: 12 minutes — 110 minutes
5. One elephant at the zoo weighs 1,417 pounds and another one weighs 1,789 pounds. About how much heavier is the second elephant? — 400 lbs.
6. If Tim studied a total of 122 minutes over 4 days, about how long did he study each day? — 30 minutes
7. It's 544 miles to Dover and 345 miles to Albany. About how much closer is Albany? — 200 miles

Page 14

Addition

Teachers of an Earth Science class planned to take 50 students on an overnight hiking and camping experience. After planning the menu, they went to the grocery store for supplies.

Breakfast	Lunch	Dinner	Snacks
bacon	hot dogs/buns	pasta	crackers
eggs	apples	sauce	marshmallows
bread	chips	garlic bread	chocolate bars
cereal	juice	salad	cocoa mix
juice	granola bars	cookies	
$34.50	$52.15	$47.25	$23.40

Directions: Answer the questions. Write the total amount spent on food for the trip.

What information do you need to answer the question? the total for each meal and snacks added together

What is the total? $157.30

Directions: Add.

462 +574	418 +359	527 +582	386 +745	295 +764
1,036	1,277	1,109	1,131	1,059

397 +448	524 +725	906 +337	760 +643	891 +419
845	1,249	1,243	1,403	1,310

1,568 +2,341	3,214 +2,896	5,147 +4,285	7,259 +2,451	9,317 +3,583
3,909	6,110	9,432	9,710	12,900

Page 15

Addition

Bob the butcher is popular with the dogs in town. He was making a delivery this morning when he noticed he was being followed by two dogs. Bob tried to climb a ladder to escape from the dogs.

Directions: Solve the following addition problems and shade in the answers on the ladder. If all the numbers are shaded when the problems have been solved, Bob made it up the ladder. Some answers may not be on the ladder.

1. 986,145 621,332 +200,008	2. 1,873,402 926,666 +4,689	3. 506,328 886,510 +342,225
1,807,485	2,803,757	1,735,063

4. 43,015 2,811,604 +987,053	5. 18,443 300,604 +999,999	6. 8,075 14,608 +33,914
3,841,672	1,319,046	56,597

7. 9,162 7,804 +755,122	8. 88,714 213,653 +5,441,298	9. 3,244,662 1,986,114 +521,387
772,088	5,743,665	5,752,163

10. 4,581 22,983 +5,618,775	11. 818,623 926 +3,260,004	12. 80,436 9,159 +3,028,761
5,646,339	4,079,553	3,118,356

Did Bob make it? no

Page 16

Addition Word Problems

Directions: Solve the following addition word problems.

1. 100 students participated in a sports card show in the school gym. Brad brought his entire collection of 2,000 cards to show his friends. He had 700 football cards and 400 basketball cards. If the rest of his cards were baseball cards, how many baseball cards did he bring with him? — 900 baseball cards
2. Refreshments were set up in one area of the gym. Hot dogs were a dollar, soda was 50 cents, chips were 35 cents, and cookies were a quarter. If you purchased two of each item, how much money would you need? — $4.20
3. It took each student 30 minutes to set up for the card show and twice as long to put everything away. The show was open for 3 hours. How much time did each student spend on this event? — 4½ hours
4. 450 people attended the card show. 55 were mothers of students, 67 were fathers, 23 were grandparents, 8 were aunts and uncles, and the rest were kids. How many kids attended? — 297 kids
5. Of the 100 students who set up displays, most of them sold or traded some of their cards. Bruce sold 75 cards, traded 15 cards, and collected $225. Kevin sold only 15 cards, traded 81 cards, and collected $100. Missi traded 200 cards, sold 10, and earned $35. Of those listed, how many cards were sold, how many were traded, and how much money was earned? sold 100 traded 296 earned $ 360

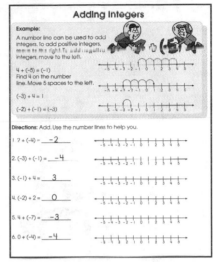

Summer Link Super Edition Grade 6

Page 17

Subtraction

Subtraction is "taking away" one number from another to find the difference between the two numbers.

Directions: Subtract.

| 76 −23 = **53** | 93 −14 = **79** | 68 −25 = **43** | 49 −17 = **32** | 88 −39 = **49** | 54 −25 = **29** |

1. Brent saved $75.00 of the money he earned delivering the local newspaper in his neighborhood. He wanted to buy a new bicycle that cost $139.00. How much more would he need to save in order to buy the bike?

$64.00

| 38 −29 = **9** | 74 −25 = **49** | 67 −49 = **18** | 92 −35 = **57** | 43 −26 = **17** | 85 −37 = **48** |

2. When Brent finally went to buy the bicycle, he saw a light and basket for the bike. He decided to buy them both. The light was $5.95 and the basket was $10.50. He gave the clerk a twenty dollar bill his grandmother had given him for his birthday. How much change did he get back?

$3.55

Page 18

Subtraction

When working with larger numbers, it is important to keep the numbers lined up according to place value.

Directions: Subtract.

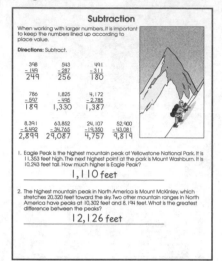

348 −149 = **249**	543 −287 = **256**	491 −311 = **180**
786 −597 = **189**	1,825 −495 = **1,330**	4,172 −2,785 = **1,387**
8,391 −5,492 = **2,899**	63,852 −19,350 = **29,087**	24,107 −19,350 = **4,757**	52,900 −43,081 = **9,819**

1. Eagle Peak is the highest mountain peak at Yellowstone National Park. It is 11,353 feet high. The next highest point at the park is Mount Washburn. It is 10,243 feet tall. How much higher is Eagle Peak?

1,110 feet

2. The highest mountain peak in North America is Mount McKinley, which stretches 20,320 feet toward the sky. Two other mountain ranges in North America have peaks at 10,302 feet and 8,194 feet. What is the greatest difference between the peaks?

12,126 feet

Page 19

Subtraction Word Problems

Directions: Solve the following subtraction word problems.

1. Last year, 28,945 people lived in Mike's town. This year, there are 31,889. How many people have moved in? **2,944 people**

2. Brad earned $227 mowing lawns. He spent $168 on tapes by his favorite rock group. How much money does he have left? **$59**

3. The school year has 180 days. Carrie has gone to 32 school days so far. How many more days does she have left? **148 days**

4. Craig wants a skateboard that costs $128. He has saved $47. How much more does he need? **$81**

5. To get to school, Jennifer walks 1,275 steps and Carolyn walks 2,618 steps. How many more steps does Carolyn walk than Jennifer? **1,343 steps**

6. Amy has placed 91 of the 389 pieces in a new puzzle she purchased. How many more does she have left to finish? **298 pieces**

7. From New York, it's 2,823 miles to Los Angeles and 1,327 miles to Miami. How much farther away is Los Angeles? **1,496 miles**

8. Sheila read that a piece of carrot cake has 236 calories, but a piece of apple pie has 427 calories. How many calories will she save by eating the cake instead of the pie? **191 calories**

9. Tim's summer camp costs $223, while Sam's costs $149. How much more does Tim's camp cost? **$74**

10. Last year, the nation's budget was $45,000,000,000, but the nation spent $52,569,342,000. How much more than its budget did the nation spend? **$ 7,569,342,000**

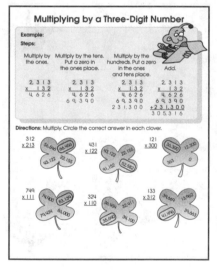

Page 20

Addition and Subtraction

Directions: Check the answers. Write **T** if the answer is true and **F** if it is false.

Example: 48,973 −35,856 = 13,118 Check: 35,856 +13,118 = 48,974 **F**

18,264 +17,893 = 36,157 Check: 36,157 −17,893 = 18,264 **T**	458,342 −297,652 = 160,680 Check: 160,680 +297,652 = 458,332 **F**
39,854 +52,713 = 92,577 Check: 92,577 −52,713 = 39,864 **F**	631,928 −457,615 = 174,313 Check: 174,313 +457,615 = 631,928 **T**
14,389 +93,587 = 107,976 Check: 107,976 −93,587 = 14,389 **T**	554,974 −376,585 = 178,389 Check: 178,389 +376,585 = 554,974 **T**
87,321 −62,348 = 24,973 Check: 24,973 +62,348 = 87,321 **T**	109,568 +97,373 = 206,941 Check: 206,941 −97,373 = 109,568 **T**

Directions: Read the story problem. Write the equation and check the answer.

A camper hikes 53,741 feet out into the wilderness. On his return trip he takes a shortcut, walking 36,752 feet back to his cabin. The shortcut saves him 16,998 feet of hiking. True or False?

| 53,741 −36,752 = 16,989 | 16,989 +36,752 = 53,741 |

Page 21

Multiplying by a Three-Digit Number

Example:

Steps:

Multiply by the ones. / Multiply by the tens. Put a zero in the ones place. / Multiply by the hundreds. Put a zero in the ones and tens place. / Add.

| 2,313 ×132 = 4,626 | 2,313 ×132 = 4,626 69,390 | 2,313 ×132 = 4,626 69,390 231,300 | 2,313 ×132 = 4,626 69,390 +231,300 = 305,316 |

Directions: Multiply. Circle the correct answer in each clover.

| 312 ×213 = **56,460 / 66,456 / 63,456 / 72,156** | 431 ×122 = **43,282 / 52,582 / 61,152** | 121 ×300 = **36,300 / 363 / 12,300** |
| 749 ×111 = **74,000 / 83,139 / 75,434 / 86,000** | 324 ×110 = **36,484 / 35,640 / 32,411 / 34,100** | 133 ×312 = **39,509 / 91,490 / 43,062 / 39,603** |

Page 22

Multiplication

Be certain to keep the proper place value when multiplying by tens and hundreds.

Examples:

| 143 ×262 = 286 858 286 = 37,466 | 250 ×150 = 000 1250 250 = 37,500 |

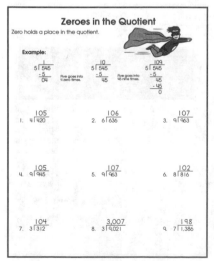

Directions: Multiply.

701 ×308 = **215,908**	621 ×538 = **334,098**	348 ×200 = **69,600**	597 ×424 = **253,128**
537 ×189 = **101,493**	416 ×727 = **302,432**	682 ×472 = **321,904**	180 ×340 = **61,200**
878 ×638 = **560,164**	267 ×196 = **52,332**	893 ×214 = **191,102**	907 ×428 = **388,196**

An airplane flies 720 trips a year between the cities of Chicago and Columbus. Each trip is 375 miles. How many miles does the airplane fly each year?

270,000

Page 23

Multiplying Integers

Example:

Ignore the negative signs, and multiply the numbers. If two factors have the same sign, the product is positive. If two factors have different signs, the product is negative. With three or more factors, multiply two numbers at a time and keep track of the signs.

2 x 3 = 6   2 x −3 = −6   −2 x 3 = −6   −2 x −3 = 6

2 x 3 x 2 = 6 x 2 = 12   2 x −3 x −2 = −6 x −2 = 12

−2 x −3 x −2 = 6 x −2 = −12

Directions: Multiply.

3 x −4 = **−12**   −5 x −5 = **25**   −4 x 12 = **−48**   7 x 3 = **21**

−8 x −9 = **72**   −6 x 3 = **−18**   2 x 15 = **30**   −4 x −10 = **40**

8 x −8 = **−64**   −1 x −9 = **9**   7 x −7 = **−49**   −5 x −6 = **30**

2 x −12 = **−24**   1 x 2 x −5 = **−10**   3 x −3 x 3 = **27**   −4 x −2 x −2 = **−16**

−3 x −2 x 3 = **18**   2 x −2 x 1 = **−4**   −5 x 0 x 6 = **0**

1 x −1 x 1 = **−1**   −3 x −2 x −2 = **−12**   −5 x 2 x −2 = **20**

Use the numbers −4, 6, −2, −18, −9 and 12 to complete this magic square. Each row, column, and diagonal should equal 216.

−2	9	12
−36	6	−1
3	−4	−18

Page 24

Zeroes in the Quotient

Zero holds a place in the quotient.

Example:

| 5⟌545 −5 = 04 Five goes into 4 zero times. | 10 5⟌545 −5 = 45 Five goes into 45 nine times. | 109 5⟌545 −5 = 45 −45 = 0 |

Directions: Divide.

1. **105** 4⟌420   2. **106** 6⟌636   3. **107** 9⟌963

4. **105** 9⟌945   5. **107** 9⟌963   6. **102** 8⟌816

7. **104** 3⟌312   8. **3,007** 3⟌9,021   9. **198** 7⟌1,386

Page 25

Division

The remainder in a division problem must always be less than the divisor.

Example:

| 244 r 23 26⟌6,367 −52 = 116 −104 = 127 −104 = 23 |

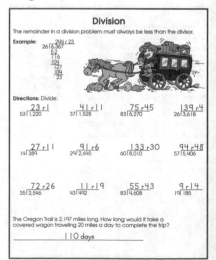

Directions: Divide.

23 r 1 53⟌1,220	**41 r 11** 37⟌1,528	**75 r 45** 83⟌6,270	**139 r 4** 26⟌3,618
27 r 1 14⟌389	**91 r 6** 29⟌2,645	**133 r 30** 60⟌8,010	**94 r 48** 57⟌5,406
72 r 26 35⟌2,546	**11 r 19** 43⟌492	**55 r 43** 83⟌4,608	**9 r 14** 19⟌185

The Oregon Trail is 2,197 miles long. How long would it take a covered wagon traveling 20 miles a day to complete the trip?

110 days

Page 26

Multiplication and Division

Directions: Multiply or divide to find the answers.

1. Brianne's summer job is mowing lawns for three of her neighbors. Each lawn takes about 1 hour to mow and needs to be done once every week. At the end of the summer, she will have earned a total of $630. She collected the same amount of money from each job. How much did each neighbor pay for her summer lawn service? **$210**

2. If the mowing season lasts for 14 weeks, how much will Brianne earn for each job each week? **$15**

3. If she had worked for two more weeks, how much would she have earned? **$90**

4. Brianne agreed to shovel snow from the driveways and sidewalks for the same three neighbors. They agreed to pay her the same rate. However, it snowed only seven times that winter. How much did she earn shoveling snow? **$315**

5. What was her total income for both jobs? **$945**

Directions: Multiply or divide.

623 — 12)7,476   940 — 23)21,620   815 — 40)32,600

32 × 45 = **1,440**   28 × 15 = **420**   73 × 14 = **1,022**   92 × 30 = **2,760**

Page 27

Money Problems

Shifty Sam sells the latest rock releases along with some oldies. You have to keep a close eye on Sam, or you may get ripped off.

Directions: Solve the problems on another sheet of paper. Write your answers in the spaces provided.

Problem	Answer
The Ear Splitters' latest release, regularly $8.98, is on sale at 5 CDs for $46.95. How much more or less would you pay at the sale price for all 5 CDs?	$2.05 more
The Funky Monkeys' new CD went fast. Sam made $4,540.90 on 455 copies. The correct price should be $7.99. How much did Sam charge for each CD? How much extra did he charge?	$9.98 each $1.99 extra
Sam made $4.59 profit on each copy of the 323 CDs he sold by the Brainbangers. He is supposed to make only $3.29 profit on each one. How much extra did he make on the 323 CDs?	$419.90 extra
Your aunt wanted to buy some CDs by Hart N. Soule which regularly sell for $3.67 each. Sam offered to sell her a dozen CDs for $44.00. How much will she save by buying 12 CDs?	She will save $.04
You wanted 180 copies of the 1940s to use as Frisbees. Each record cost $.79. Sam gave you $147.80 in change from $200. How much did he cheat you?	$10.00
Sam sold 7,000 copies of Golden Oldies for $3.99 each. He made a $2.00 profit on each record. How much money did he get for all 7,000 copies? How much profit did he earn?	$27,930.00 for all $14,000.00 profit
Sam charged $1.79 more for each copy of the Dippers' new CD than he was supposed to. His price was $7.84, and he sold 3,500 copies. How much extra money did he get?	$6,265.00 extra
Sam sold 4,328 copies of Country Classics at $4.99 each. His profit was $1.45 on each one. How much money did he get in all? How much profit did he earn?	$21,596.72 total $6,275.60 profit

Page 28

A Number Challenge

Directions: Fill in the blanks to make each problem true. To check your work, start at the left and do each operation in order to get the given answer.

1. __ + __ − __ = 2
2. __ − __ + __ = 3
3. __ + __ − __ = 4
4. __ × __ − __ = 5
5. __ ___ ___ ___ = ___
6. __ × __ ÷ __ = ___
7. __ ÷ __ + __ = 4
8. __ ÷ __ − __ = 5
9. __ ÷ __ × __ = 6
10. __ × __ + __ = 7
11. __ + __ − __ = 12
12. __ ÷ __ − __ = 15
13. __ ___ ___ ___ = 20
14. __ ___ ___ ___ = 8
15. __ + __ × __ = 24

Answers will vary.

Page 29

Equations

In an **equation**, the value on the left of the equal sign must equal the value on the right. Remember the order of operations: solve from left to right, multiply or divide numbers before adding or subtracting and do the operation inside parentheses first.

Example:
$$6 + 4 − 2 = 4 × 2$$
$$10 − 2 = 8$$
$$8 = 8$$

Directions: Write the correct operation signs in the blanks to make accurate equations.

1. (25 **+** 25) **÷** 2 = 100 **−** 75
2. (76 **+** 24) **×** 3 = 150 **×** 2
3. 140 **+** 10 **×** 10 = 500 **−** 50 **+** 150
4. 2,100 **−** 2,000 **+** 60 − 80 **×** 2
5. 80 **×** 8 **÷** 4 = 160 **+** 160 **−** 160
6. (55 **×** 100) **÷** 11 = (1,000 **−** 500) **÷** __
7. 137 **+** 81 **+** 52 = 3 **×** 90
8. 3,000 **÷** 10 **÷** 10 = (800 **−** 300) **−** 30
9. (720 **+** 20) **÷** 4 = 37 **×** 5
10. (457 **+** 43) **−** 500 = (21 **+** 40) × 0

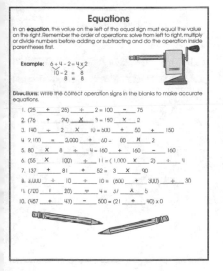

Page 30

Prime Numbers

Example: 3 is a prime number.
$$3 ÷ 1 = 3 \text{ and } 3 ÷ 3 = 1$$

Any other divisor will result in a mixed number or fraction.

An easy way to test a number to see if it is prime is to divide by 2 and 3. If the number can be divided by 2 or 3 without a remainder, it is not a prime number. (Exceptions, 2 and 3.)

Example:

11 cannot be divided evenly by 2 or 3. It can be divided only by 1 and 11. It is a prime number.

Directions: Write the first 15 prime numbers. Test by dividing by 2 and by 3.

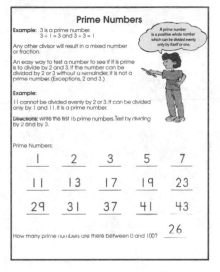

> A prime number is a positive whole number which can be divided evenly only by itself and one.

Prime Numbers:

1	2	3	5	7
11	13	17	19	23
29	31	37	41	43

How many prime numbers are there between 0 and 100? **26**

Page 31

Prime Numbers

Directions: Circle the prime numbers.

(71)	(3)	82	20	(43)	69
128	(97)	(23)	111	75	51
(13)	44	(137)	68	171	(83)
(61)	21	77	(101)	34	16
(2)	39	92	(17)	52	(29)
(19)	156	63	99	27	147
121	25	88	12	87	55
57	(7)	(139)	91	9	(37)
(67)	183	(5)	(59)	(11)	95

Page 32

Factors

Factors are the numbers multiplied together to give a product. The **greatest common factor** (GCF) is the largest number for a set of numbers that divides evenly into each number in the set.

Example:

The factors of 12 are 3 × 4, 2 × 6, and 1 × 12.
We can write the factors like this: 3, 4, 2, 6, 12, 1.
The factors of 8 are 2, 4, 8, 1.
The common factors of 12 and 8 are 2 and 4 and 1.
The GCF of 12 and 8 is 4.

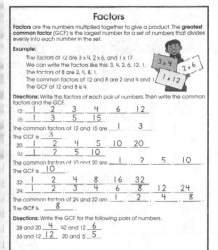

Directions: Write the factors of each pair of numbers. Then write the common factors and the GCF.

12: 1 2 3 4 6 12
15: 1 3 5 15
The common factors of 12 and 15 are 1 3
The GCF is **3**.

20: 1 2 4 5 10 20
10: 1 2 5 10
The common factors of 10 and 20 are 1 2 5 10
The GCF is **10**.

32: 1 2 4 8 16 32
24: 1 2 3 4 6 8 12 24
The common factors of 24 and 32 are 1 2 4 8
The GCF is **8**.

Directions: Write the GCF for the following pairs of numbers.

28 and 20 **4**   42 and 12 **6**
36 and 12 **12**   20 and 5 **5**

Page 33

Greatest Common Factor

Directions: Write the greatest common factor for each set of numbers.

10 and 35 **5**
2 and 10 **2**
42 and 63 **21**
16 and 40 **8**
25 and 55 **5**
12 and 20 **4**
14 and 28 **14**
8 and 20 **4**
6 and 27 **3**
15 and 35 **5**
18 and 48 **6**

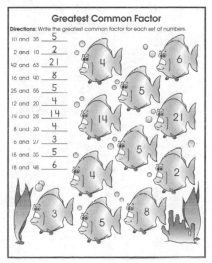

Page 34

Factor Trees

A **factor** is a number that can be multiplied by another number to give a certain product. The factors of 24 are 1, 2, 3, 4, 6, 8, 12, and 24 because 1 × 24 = 24, 2 × 12 = 24, 3 × 8 = 24, and 4 × 6 = 24.

Any composite number can be written as the product of prime number factors. The first ten prime numbers are 2, 3, 5, 7, 11, 13, 17, 19, 23, and 29.

FACTOR TREES FOR 24

24	24	24
2 × 12	3 × 8	4 × 6
2 × 6 × 2	3 × 2 × 4	2 × 2 × 3 × 2
2 × 3 × 2 × 2	3 × 2 × 2 × 2	

No matter how a factor tree is made for a given number, the prime factors in the bottom row are always the same. $24 = 2 × 2 × 2 × 3 = 2^3 × 3$

Directions: Write the prime factors for each number, using a factor tree.

12	32	48	40
4×3	4×8	8×6	10×4
2×2×3	2×2×4×2	2×4×3×2	2×5×2×2
	2×2×2×2×2	2×2×2×2×3	
$12=2^2×3$	$32=2^5$	$48=2^4×3$	$40=2^3×5$

9	42	96	72
3×3	7×6	12×8	8×9
	7×2×3	4×3×4×2	2×4×3×3
		2×2×3×7×2×2	2×2×2×3×3
$9=3^2$	$42=7×2×3$	$96=2^5×3$	$72=2^3×3^2$

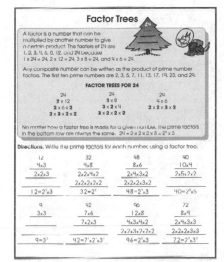

Page 35

Common Ground

A **multiple** is the product of any given number and a factor such as 1, 2, 3, and so on.

Example:

Multiples of **4**: 4, 8, 12, 16, 20, 24, 28, 32, 36, 40 . . .
Multiples of **10**: 10, 20, 30, 40, 50, 60, 70, 80, 90, 100 . . .
Multiples of **18**: 18, 36, 54, 72, 90, 108, 126, 144, 162, 180 . . .
Multiples of **25**: 25, 50, 75, 100, 125, 150, 175, 200, 225 . . .

Common multiples are multiples that two or more numbers share, or have in common.

Multiples of **8**: 8, 16, 24, 32, 40, 48, 56, 64, 72, 80 . . .
Multiples of **12**: 12, 24, 36, 48, 60, 72, 84 . . .

Some common multiples of 8 and 12 are 24, 48, and 72.

Find three common multiples for each set of numbers. To do this, list the first ten multiples of each number. Then, look for common multiples. The first one is done for you in the box at the bottom of the page. Show your work on another sheet of paper.

6 and 9 18, 36, 54 — 15 and 30 30, 60, 90 — 4 and 10 20, 40, 60
3 and 4 12, 24, 36 — 5 and 25 25, 50, 75 — 8 and 6 24, 48, 72
4 and 9 36, 72, 108 — 2 and 7 14, 28, 42 — 18 and 3 18, 36, 54
12 and 16 48, 96, 144 — 2, 4, and 5 20, 40, 60 — 2, 3, and 6 6, 12, 18

6 12 (18) 24 30 (36) 42 48 (54) 60
9 (18) 27 (36) 45 (54) 63 72 81 90

Page 36

Least Common Multiples

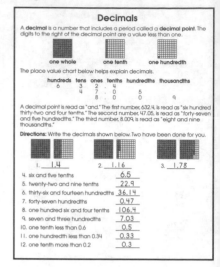

The **least common multiple** (LCM) is the least multiple that a group of numbers has in common. The LCM helps when adding and subtracting fractions.

One way to find the LCM is to find the common multiples and choose the least one.

Multiples of 6: 6, 12, 18, 24, 30, 36, 42, 48, 54 . . .
Multiples of 9: 9, 18, 27, 36, 45, 54, 63, 72 . . .

Common multiples of 6 and 9 include 18, 36, and 54, but the least is 18.

Find the LCM for each set of numbers. The first one is done for you in the box at the bottom of the page.

8 and 3 24 — 7 and 21 21 — 5 and 8 40 — 9 and 12 36
6 and 16 48 — 1 and 9 9 — 4 and 7 28 — 2 and 3 6
10 and 4 20 — 12 and 16 48 — 6 and 8 24 — 15 and 12 60
2, 3, and 4 12 — 3, 4, and 5 60 — 2, 4, and 7 28 — 3, 5, and 6 30

Find two numbers that when multiplied together do not have a product of 30 but have a LCM of 30. Sample answer: 6, 10

8 16 (24) 32 40 48 56 72 80
3 6 9 12 15 18 21 (24) 27

Page 37

Decimals

A **decimal** is a number that includes a period called a **decimal point**. The digits to the right of the decimal point are a value less than one.

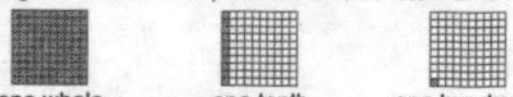

one whole — one tenth — one hundredth

The place value chart below helps explain decimals.

hundreds	tens	ones		tenths	hundredths	thousandths
6	3	2	.	4		
	4	7	.	0	5	
		8	.	0	0	9

A decimal point is read as "and." The first number, 632.4, is read as "six hundred thirty-two and four tenths." The second number, 47.05, is read as "forty-seven and five hundredths." The third number, 8.009, is read as "eight and nine thousandths."

Directions: Write the decimals shown below. Two have been done for you.

1. 1.4
2. 1.16
3. 1.78
4. six and five tenths 6.5
5. twenty-two and nine tenths 22.9
6. thirty-six and fourteen hundredths 36.14
7. forty-seven hundredths 0.47
8. one hundred six and four tenths 106.4
9. seven and three hundredths 7.03
10. one tenth less than 0.6 0.5
11. one hundredth less than 0.34 0.33
12. one tenth more than 0.2 0.3

Page 38

Adding and Subtracting Decimals

When adding or subtracting decimals, place the decimal points under each other. That way, you add tenths to tenths, for example, not tenths to hundredths. Add or subtract beginning on the right, as usual. Carry or borrow numbers in the same way. Adding 0 to the end of decimals does not change their value, but sometimes makes them easier to add and subtract.

Examples: 39.40 + 6.81 = 46.21; 0.064 + 0.470 = 0.534; 3.56 − .09 = 3.47; 6.83 − 2.14 = 4.69

Directions: Solve the following problems.

1. Write each set of numbers in a column and add them.
   a. 2.56 + 0.6 + 76 = 79.16
   b. 93.5 + 23.06 + 1.45 = 118.01
   c. 3.23 + 91.34 + 0.85 = 95.42
2. Write each pair of numbers in a column and subtract them.
   a. 7.89 − 0.56 = 7.33 b. 34.56 − 6.04 = 28.52 c. 7.6 − 3.24 = 4.36
3. In a relay race, Alice ran her part in 23.6 seconds, Cindy did hers in 24.7 seconds, and Erin took 20.09 seconds. How many seconds did they take altogether? 68.39 seconds
4. Although Erin ran her part in 20.09 seconds today, yesterday it took her 21.55 seconds. How much faster was she today? 1.46 seconds
5. Add this grocery bill: potatoes—$3.49; milk—$2.09; bread—$0.99; apples—$2.30 $8.87
6. A yellow coat cost $47.59 and a blue coat cost $36.79. How much more did the yellow coat cost? $10.80
7. A box of Oat Boats cereal has 14.6 ounces. A box of Sugar Circles has 17.85 ounces. How much more cereal is in the Sugar Circles box? 3.25 ounces
8. The Oat Boats cereal has 4.03 ounces of sugar in it. Sugar Circles cereal has only 3.76 ounces. How much more sugar is in a box of Oats Boats? 0.27 ounces

Page 39

Multiplying Decimals

In some problems, you may need to add zeros in order to place the decimal point correctly.

Examples: 0.34 × 0.08 = 0.0272; 0.0067 × 4 = 0.0268; 0.046 × 0.07 = 0.00322

Directions: Solve the following problems.

1. 0.15 × 0.02 = 0.003
2. 0.67 × 0.08 = 0.0536
3. 7.3 × 0.06 = 0.438
4. 3.59 × 0.08 = 0.2872
5. 0.061 × 0.014 = 0.000854
6. 7.10 × 0.042 = 0.2982
7. 5.05 × 0.08 = 0.404
8. 8.75 × 0.067 = 0.58625
9. 0.0647 × 0.3 = 0.01941
10. 3.62 × 0.003 = 0.01086
11. 1.07 × 0.05 = 0.0535
12. 3.03 × 0.07 = 0.2121
13. 0.02 × 0.02 = 0.0004
14. 0.501 × 0.03 = 0.01503
15. 0.321 × 0.09 = 0.02889
16. The players and coaches gathered around for refreshments after the soccer game. Of the 30 people there, 0.50 of them had fruit drinks, 0.20 of them had fruit juice, and 0.30 of them had soft drinks. How many people had each type of drink?

fruit drink 15
fruit juice 6
soft drink 9

Page 40

Dividing With Decimals

When the dividend has a decimal, place the decimal point for the answer directly above the decimal point in the dividend. The first one has been done for you.

37.5 ÷ 3 = 12.5	34.4 ÷ 4 = 8.6	31.6 ÷ 2 = 15.8	131.4 ÷ 3 = 43.8
187.5 ÷ 5 = 37.5	181.3 ÷ 7 = 25.9	340.8 ÷ 6 = 56.8	294.3 ÷ 9 = 32.7
135.6 ÷ 3 = 45.2	264.5 ÷ 5 = 52.9	134.6 ÷ 2 = 67.3	754.4 ÷ 8 = 94.3
35.25 ÷ 5 = 7.05	79.45 ÷ 7 = 11.35	28.71 ÷ 9 = 3.19	199.44 ÷ 36 = 5.54

(Worked example: 3 ⟌37.5; −3; 07; −6; 15; −15; 0)

Page 41

Decimals and Fractions

A **fraction** is a number that names part of something. The top number in a fraction is called the **numerator**. The bottom number is called the **denominator**. Since a decimal also names part of a whole number, every decimal can also be written as a fraction. For example, 0.1 is read as "one tenth" and can also be written $\frac{1}{10}$. The decimal 0.56 is read as "fifty-six hundredths" and can also be written $\frac{56}{100}$.

Examples: $0.7 = \frac{7}{10}$ $0.34 = \frac{34}{100}$ $0.761 = \frac{761}{1,000}$ $\frac{5}{10} = 0.5$ $\frac{58}{100} = 0.58$ $\frac{729}{1,000} = 0.729$

Even a fraction that doesn't have 10, 100, or 1,000 as the denominator can be written as a decimal. Sometimes you can multiply both the numerator and denominator by a certain number so the denominator is 10, 100, or 1,000. (You can't just multiply the denominator. That would change the amount of the fraction.)

Examples: $\frac{3 \times 2}{5 \times 2} = \frac{6}{10} = 0.6$ $\frac{4 \times 4}{25 \times 4} = \frac{16}{100} = 0.16$

Other times, divide the numerator by the denominator.

Examples: $\frac{3}{4} = 4\overline{)3.00} = 0.75$ $\frac{5}{8} = 8\overline{)5.000} = 0.625$

Directions: Follow the instructions below.

1. For each square, write a decimal and a fraction to show the part that is colored. The first one has been done for you.
   a. 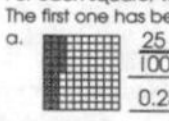 $\frac{25}{100}$ 0.25 b. 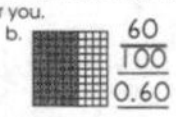 $\frac{60}{100}$ 0.60 c. 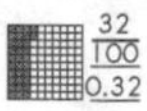 $\frac{32}{100}$ 0.32
2. Change these decimals to fractions.
   a. $0.6 = \frac{6}{10}$ b. $0.54 = \frac{54}{100}$ c. $0.751 = \frac{751}{1,000}$ d. $0.73 = \frac{73}{100}$ e. $0.592 = \frac{592}{1,000}$ f. $0.2 = \frac{2}{10}$
3. Change these fractions to decimals. If necessary, round off the decimals to the nearest hundredth.
   a. $\frac{3}{10} = 0.3$ b. $\frac{89}{100} = 0.89$ c. $\frac{473}{1,000} = 0.473$ d. $\frac{4}{5} = 0.8$ e. $\frac{35}{50} = 0.7$
   f. $\frac{7}{9} = 0.78$ g. $\frac{1}{3} = 0.33$ h. $\frac{23}{77} = 0.30$ i. $\frac{12}{63} = 0.19$ j. $\frac{4}{16} = 0.25$

Page 42

Adding Fractions

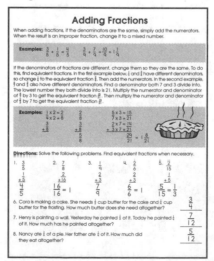

When adding fractions, if the denominators are the same, simply add the numerators. When the result is an improper fraction, change it to a mixed number.

Examples: $\frac{3}{5} + \frac{1}{5} = \frac{4}{5}$ $\frac{3}{9} + \frac{7}{9} = \frac{10}{9} = 1\frac{1}{9}$

If the denominators of fractions are different, change them so they are the same. To do this, find equivalent fractions. In the first example below, $\frac{1}{4}$ and $\frac{3}{8}$ have different denominators, so change $\frac{1}{4}$ to the equivalent fraction $\frac{2}{8}$. Then add the numerators. In the second example, $\frac{5}{7}$ and $\frac{2}{3}$ also have different denominators. Find a denominator both 7 and 3 divide into. The lowest number they both divide into is 21. Multiply the numerator and denominator of $\frac{5}{7}$ by 3 to get the equivalent fraction $\frac{15}{21}$. Then multiply the numerator and denominator of $\frac{2}{3}$ by 7 to get the equivalent fraction $\frac{14}{21}$.

Examples: $\frac{1 \times 2}{4 \times 2} = \frac{2}{8}$; $\frac{2}{8} + \frac{3}{8} = \frac{5}{8}$ $\frac{5 \times 3}{7 \times 3} = \frac{15}{21}$; $+\frac{2 \times 7}{3 \times 7} = \frac{14}{21}$; $\frac{29}{21} = 1\frac{8}{21}$

Directions: Solve the following problems. Find equivalent fractions when necessary.

1. $\frac{3}{5} + \frac{1}{5} = \frac{4}{5}$
2. $\frac{7}{8} + \frac{2}{16} = \frac{16}{16} = 1$
3. $\frac{1}{9} + \frac{2}{3} = \frac{7}{9}$
4. $\frac{2}{6} + \frac{2}{3} = \frac{6}{6} = 1$
5. $\frac{2}{15} + \frac{1}{5} = \frac{5}{15} = \frac{1}{3}$
6. Cora is making a cake. She needs $\frac{1}{2}$ cup butter for the cake and $\frac{1}{4}$ cup butter for the frosting. How much butter does she need altogether? $\frac{3}{4}$
7. Henry is painting a wall. Yesterday he painted $\frac{1}{3}$ of it. Today he painted $\frac{1}{4}$ of it. How much has he painted altogether? $\frac{7}{12}$
8. Nancy ate $\frac{1}{6}$ of a pie. Her father ate $\frac{1}{4}$ of it. How much did they eat altogether? $\frac{5}{12}$

Page 43

Subtracting Fractions

Subtracting fractions is very similar to adding them in that the denominators must be the same. If the denominators are different, use equivalent fractions.

Examples: $\frac{3}{4} - \frac{1}{4} = \frac{2}{4} = \frac{1}{2}$ $\frac{2 \times 8}{5 \times 8} = \frac{16}{40}$; $-\frac{1 \times 5}{8 \times 5} = \frac{5}{40}$; $\frac{11}{40}$

Adding and subtracting mixed numbers are also similar. Often, though, change the mixed numbers to improper fractions. If the denominators are different, use equivalent fractions.

Examples: $2\frac{3}{5} = \frac{13}{5}$; $-1\frac{4}{5} = \frac{9}{5}$; $\frac{4}{5}$ $3\frac{3}{14} = \frac{45}{14} = \frac{45}{14}$; $-2\frac{1}{7} = \frac{15 \times 2}{7 \times 2} = \frac{30}{14}$; $\frac{15}{14} = 1\frac{1}{14}$

Directions: Solve the following problems. Use equivalent fractions and improper fractions where necessary.

1. $\frac{6}{7}$ − $\frac{5}{7}$ = $\frac{1}{7}$
2. $1\frac{2}{9}$ − $\frac{4}{9}$ = $\frac{7}{9}$
3. $2\frac{3}{6}$ − $\frac{4}{5}$ = $\frac{51}{30} = 1\frac{7}{10}$
4. $\frac{3}{4}$ − $\frac{1}{2}$ = $\frac{1}{4}$
5. $2\frac{1}{3}$ − $\frac{3}{4}$ = $\frac{19}{12} = 1\frac{7}{12}$
6. Carol promised to weed the flower garden for $1\frac{1}{2}$ hours this morning. So far she has pulled two weeds for $\frac{3}{4}$ of an hour. How much longer does she have to work? $\frac{3}{4}$ hour
7. Dil started out with $1\frac{1}{4}$ gallons of paint. He used $\frac{3}{8}$ gallon of the paint on his boat. How much paint is left? $\frac{7}{8}$ gallon
8. A certain movie lasts $2\frac{1}{2}$ hours. Susan has already watched it for $1\frac{2}{3}$ hours. How much longer is the movie? $\frac{5}{6}$ hour
9. Bert didn't finish $\frac{1}{8}$ of the math problems on a test. He made mistakes on $\frac{1}{6}$ of the problems. The rest he answered correctly. What fraction of the problems did he answer correctly? $\frac{17}{24}$ problems

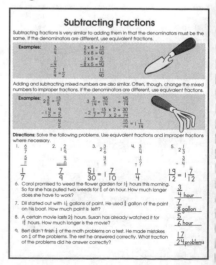

Adding and Subtracting Like Fractions

A **fraction** is a number that names part of a whole. Examples of fractions are $\frac{1}{2}$ and $\frac{3}{4}$. **Like fractions** have the same **denominator**, or bottom number. Examples of like fractions are $\frac{2}{8}$ and $\frac{3}{8}$.

To add or subtract fractions, the denominators must be the same. Add or subtract only the **numerators**, the numbers above the line in fractions.

Example:

numerators
denominators $\frac{5}{8} - \frac{1}{8} = \frac{4}{8}$

Directions: Add or subtract these fractions.

$\frac{6}{12} - \frac{3}{12} = \frac{3}{12}$	$\frac{3}{4} + \frac{1}{4} = \frac{4}{4}$	$\frac{1}{3} + \frac{1}{3} = \frac{2}{3}$	$\frac{5}{11} + \frac{4}{11} = \frac{9}{11}$
$\frac{3}{5} - \frac{1}{5} = \frac{2}{5}$	$\frac{5}{6} - \frac{2}{6} = \frac{3}{6}$	$\frac{3}{4} - \frac{2}{4} = \frac{1}{4}$	$\frac{5}{10} + \frac{3}{10} = \frac{8}{10}$
$\frac{3}{8} + \frac{2}{8} = \frac{5}{8}$	$\frac{1}{7} + \frac{4}{7} = \frac{5}{7}$	$\frac{3}{20} + \frac{14}{20} = \frac{17}{20}$	$\frac{13}{15} - \frac{11}{15} = \frac{2}{15}$

Directions: Color the part of each pizza that equals the given fraction.

$\frac{2}{4}$ + $\frac{1}{4}$ = $\frac{3}{4}$

Adding and Subtracting Unlike Fractions

Unlike fractions have different denominators. Examples of unlike fractions are $\frac{1}{4}$ and $\frac{2}{3}$. To add or subtract fractions, the denominators must be the same.

Example:

Step 1: Make the denominators the same by finding the least common denominator. The LCD of a pair of fractions is the same as the least common multiple (LCM) of their denominators.

$\frac{1}{3} + \frac{1}{4} = $ Multiples of 3 are 3, 6, **9, 12**, 15.
Multiples of 4 are 4, 8, **12**, 16.
LCM (and LCD) = 12

Step 2: Multiply by a number that will give the LCD. The numerator and denominator must be multiplied by the same number.

A. $\frac{1}{3} \times \frac{4}{4} = \frac{4}{12}$ B. $\frac{1}{4} \times \frac{3}{3} = \frac{3}{12}$

Step 3: Add the fractions. $\frac{1}{3} + \frac{1}{4} = \frac{4}{12} + \frac{3}{12} = \frac{7}{12}$

Directions: Follow the above steps to add or subtract unlike fractions. Write the LCM.

$2\frac{1}{4} + \frac{3}{8} = \frac{7}{8}$	$\frac{3}{6} + \frac{1}{3} = \frac{5}{6}$	$\frac{5}{4} - \frac{1}{4} = \frac{11}{20}$
LCM = 8	LCM = 6	LCM = 20
$\frac{2}{3} + \frac{2}{9} = \frac{8}{9}$	$\frac{4}{7} - \frac{2}{14} = \frac{6}{14}$	$\frac{7}{12} - \frac{2}{4} = \frac{1}{12}$
LCM = 9	LCM = 14	LCM = 12

The basketball team ordered two pizzas. They left $\frac{1}{3}$ of one and $\frac{1}{4}$ of the other. How much pizza was left? $\frac{7}{12}$

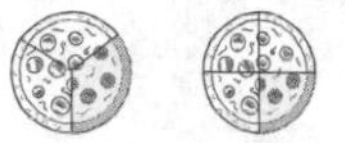

Multiplying Fractions

To multiply two fractions, multiply the numerators and then multiply the denominators. If necessary, change the answer to its lowest term.

Examples: $\frac{2}{3} \times \frac{1}{4} = \frac{2}{12} = \frac{1}{6}$ $\frac{1}{4} \times \frac{4}{10} = \frac{4}{40} = \frac{1}{10}$

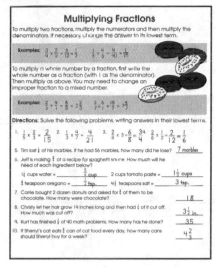

To multiply a whole number by a fraction, first write the whole number as a fraction (with 1 as the denominator). Then multiply as above. You may need to change an improper fraction to a mixed number.

Examples: $\frac{2}{3} \times \frac{4}{1} = \frac{8}{3} = 2\frac{2}{3}$ $\frac{2}{7} \times \frac{9}{1} = \frac{18}{7} = 2\frac{4}{7}$

Directions: Solve the following problems, writing answers in their lowest terms.

1. $\frac{1}{5} \times \frac{2}{3} = \frac{2}{15}$ 2. $\frac{1}{3} \times \frac{4}{7} = \frac{4}{21}$ 3. $\frac{2}{3} \times 3 = \frac{6}{8} = \frac{34}{}$ 4. $\frac{2}{3} \times \frac{1}{12} = \frac{2}{6}$

5. Tim lost $\frac{1}{8}$ of his marbles. If he had 56 marbles, how many did he lose?   7 marbles

6. Jeff is making $\frac{3}{4}$ of a recipe for spaghetti sauce. How much will he need of each ingredient below?

   1½ cups water = $\frac{5}{4}$ cup   2 cups tomato paste = $1\frac{1}{2}$ cups

   $\frac{2}{3}$ teaspoon oregano = $\frac{1}{2}$ tsp.   4½ teaspoons salt = 3 tsp.

7. Carrie bought 2 dozen donuts and asked for $\frac{3}{4}$ of them to be chocolate. How many were chocolate?   18

8. Christy let her hair grow 14 inches long and then had $\frac{1}{4}$ of it cut off. How much was cut off?   3½ in.

9. Kurt has finished $\frac{7}{8}$ of 40 math problems. How many has he done?   35

10. If Sherryl's cat eats $\frac{2}{3}$ can of cat food every day, how many cans should Sherryl buy for a week? $4\frac{2}{3}$

Dividing Fractions

Reciprocals are two fractions that, when multiplied together, make 1. To divide a fraction by a fraction, turn one of the fractions upside down and multiply. The upside-down fraction is a reciprocal of its original fraction. If you multiply a fraction by its reciprocal, you always get 1.

Examples of reciprocals: $\frac{2}{3} \times \frac{3}{2} = 1$ $\frac{9}{11} \times \frac{11}{9} = 1$

Examples of dividing by fractions: $\frac{1}{2} \div \frac{1}{3} = \frac{1}{2} \times \frac{3}{1} = \frac{3}{2}$ $\frac{2}{5} \div \frac{7}{2} = \frac{2}{5} \times \frac{2}{7} = \frac{14}{35}$

To divide a whole number by a fraction, first write the whole number as a fraction (with a denominator of 1). (Write a mixed number as an improper fraction.) Then finish the problem as explained above.

Examples: $4 \div \frac{2}{3} = \frac{4}{1} \times \frac{3}{2} = \frac{12}{2} = 12$ $3\frac{1}{2} \div \frac{2}{5} = \frac{7}{2} \times \frac{5}{2} = \frac{35}{4} = 8\frac{3}{4}$

Directions: Solve the following problems, writing answers in their lowest terms. Change any improper fractions to mixed numbers.

1. $1\frac{1}{3} \div \frac{5}{6}$ 2. $\frac{2}{3} \div \frac{18}{7} = 2\frac{3}{5}$ 3. $3 \div \frac{3}{4} = \frac{12}{3} = 4$ 4. $\frac{1}{4} \div \frac{2}{3} = \frac{3}{8}$

5. Judy has 8 candy bars. She wants to give $\frac{1}{3}$ of a candy bar to everyone in her class. Does she have enough for all 24 students?   Yes

6. A big jar of glue holds 3½ cups. How many little containers that hold ¼ cup each can you fill?   14 containers

7. A container holds 27 ounces of ice cream. How many 4½-ounce servings is that?   6 servings

8. It takes 2½ teaspoons of powdered mix to make 1 cup of hot chocolate. How many cups can you make with 45 teaspoons of milk?   18 cups

9. Each cup of hot chocolate also takes $\frac{2}{3}$ cup of milk. How many cups of hot chocolate can you make with 12 cups of milk?   18 cups

Reducing Fractions

A fraction is in lowest terms when the GCF of both the numerator and denominator is 1. These fractions are in lowest possible terms: $\frac{2}{3}$, $\frac{3}{8}$, and $\frac{1}{100}$.

Example: $\frac{4}{8}$ is lowest terms.

Step 1: Write the factors of 4 and 8.
Factors of 4 are **4**, 2, 1.
Factors of 8 are 1, 8, 2, **4**.
Step 2: Find the GCF: 4.
Step 3: Divide both the numerator and denominator by 4.

4 ÷ 4 = 1
8 ÷ 4 = 2

Directions: Write each fraction in lowest terms.

$\frac{6}{8} = \frac{3}{4}$ lowest terms $\frac{9}{12} = \frac{3}{4}$ lowest terms

factors of 6: 6, 1, 2, 3   factors of 9: 1, 3, 9   3 GCF
factors of 8: 8, 1, 2, 4   factors of 12: 1, 2, 3, 4, 6, 12   4 GCF

$\frac{2}{6} = \frac{1}{3}$	$\frac{10}{15} = \frac{2}{3}$	$\frac{8}{32} = \frac{1}{4}$	$\frac{4}{10} = \frac{2}{5}$	
$\frac{4}{6} = \frac{2}{3}$	$\frac{9}{12} = \frac{3}{4}$	$\frac{2}{6} = \frac{1}{3}$	$\frac{6}{9} = \frac{2}{3}$	

Directions: Color the pizzas to show that $\frac{2}{6}$ in lowest terms is $\frac{1}{3}$.

=

Improper Fractions

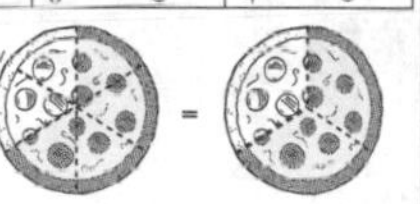

An **improper fraction** has a numerator that is greater than its denominator. An example of an improper fraction is $\frac{5}{4}$. An improper fraction should be reduced to its lowest terms.

Example: $\frac{5}{4}$ is an improper fraction because its numerator is greater than its denominator.

Step 1: Divide the numerator by the denominator: 5 ÷ 4 = 1, r1
Step 2: Write the remainder as a fraction: $\frac{1}{4}$

$\frac{5}{4} = 1\frac{1}{4}$ $1\frac{1}{4}$ is a mixed number—a whole number and a fraction.

Directions: Follow the steps above to change the improper fractions to mixed numbers.

$\frac{9}{8} = 1\frac{1}{8}$	$\frac{11}{5} = 2\frac{1}{5}$	$\frac{5}{3} = 1\frac{2}{3}$	$\frac{7}{6} = 1\frac{1}{6}$	$\frac{9}{7} = 1\frac{1}{7}$	$\frac{4}{3} = 1\frac{1}{3}$
$\frac{21}{2} = 4\frac{1}{2}$	$\frac{9}{4} = 2\frac{1}{4}$	$\frac{3}{2} = 1\frac{1}{2}$	$\frac{9}{5} = 1\frac{1}{2}$	$\frac{25}{4} = 6\frac{1}{4}$	$\frac{8}{3} = 2\frac{2}{3}$

Sara had 29 duplicate stamps in her stamp collection. She decided to give them to four of her friends. If she gave each of them the same number of stamps, how many duplicates will she have left?   1

Name the improper fraction in this problem. $\frac{29}{4}$

What step must you do next to solve the problem?
   change to a mixed number

Write your answer as a mixed number. $7\frac{1}{4}$

How many stamps could she give each of her friends?   7

Mixed Numbers

A **mixed number** is a whole number and a fraction together. An example of a mixed number is $2\frac{3}{4}$. A mixed number can be changed to an improper fraction.

Example: $2\frac{3}{4}$

Step 1: Multiply the denominator by the whole number: 4 × 2 = 8
Step 2: Add the numerator: 8 + 3 = 11
Step 3: Write the sum over the denominator: $\frac{11}{4}$

Directions: Follow the steps above to change the mixed numbers to improper fractions.

$3\frac{2}{3} = \frac{11}{3}$	$6\frac{1}{5} = \frac{31}{5}$	$4\frac{7}{8} = \frac{39}{8}$	$2\frac{1}{2} = \frac{5}{2}$
$1\frac{4}{5} = \frac{9}{5}$	$5\frac{3}{4} = \frac{23}{4}$	$7\frac{1}{8} = \frac{57}{8}$	$9\frac{1}{9} = \frac{82}{9}$
$8\frac{1}{2} = \frac{17}{2}$	$7\frac{1}{6} = \frac{43}{6}$	$5\frac{3}{5} = \frac{28}{5}$	$9\frac{3}{8} = \frac{75}{8}$
$12\frac{1}{5} = \frac{61}{5}$	$25\frac{1}{2} = \frac{51}{2}$	$10\frac{2}{3} = \frac{32}{3}$	$14\frac{3}{8} = \frac{115}{8}$

Adding Mixed Numbers

To add mixed numbers, first find the least common denominator. Always reduce the answer to lowest terms.

Example:

$5\frac{1}{4} \rightarrow 5\frac{3}{12}$
$+6\frac{1}{3} \rightarrow +6\frac{4}{12}$
$\quad\quad\quad\quad 11\frac{7}{12}$

Directions: Add. Reduce the answers to lowest terms.

$8\frac{1}{2}$ $+7\frac{1}{4}$ $15\frac{3}{4}$	$5\frac{1}{4}$ $+2\frac{3}{8}$ $7\frac{5}{8}$	$9\frac{3}{10}$ $+7\frac{1}{2}$ $16\frac{4}{5}$	$8\frac{1}{2}$ $+6\frac{7}{10}$ $14\frac{1}{5}$
$\frac{4}{5}$ $+3\frac{1}{10}$ $8\frac{3}{10}$	$3\frac{1}{2}$ $+7\frac{1}{4}$ $10\frac{3}{4}$	$4\frac{1}{5}$ $+1\frac{3}{10}$ $5\frac{1}{2}$	$6\frac{1}{4}$ $+3\frac{1}{2}$ $9\frac{3}{4}$
$5\frac{1}{3}$ $+2\frac{1}{3}$ $7\frac{2}{3}$	$6\frac{1}{2}$ $+2\frac{1}{8}$ $8\frac{5}{8}$	$2\frac{2}{3}$ $+4\frac{7}{12}$ $6\frac{5}{12}$	$3\frac{1}{4}$ $+3\frac{1}{2}$ $6\frac{3}{4}$

The boys picked 3½ baskets of apples. The girls picked 5½ baskets. How many baskets of apples did the boys and girls pick in all?   9

Subtracting Mixed Numbers

To subtract mixed numbers, first find the least common denominator. Reduce the answer to its lowest terms.

Directions: Subtract. Reduce to lowest terms.

Example:

$6\frac{5}{8} \rightarrow 6\frac{10}{16}$
$-3\frac{1}{4} \rightarrow 3\frac{4}{16}$
$\quad\quad\quad 3\frac{6}{16} = 3\frac{3}{8}$

$2\frac{3}{4}$ $-1\frac{1}{4}$ $1\frac{5}{14}$	$7\frac{2}{3}$ $-5\frac{1}{8}$ $2\frac{13}{24}$	$6\frac{3}{4}$ $-2\frac{3}{8}$ $4\frac{1}{2}$	$9\frac{5}{12}$ $-5\frac{1}{24}$ $4\frac{1}{24}$
$5\frac{1}{2}$ $-3\frac{3}{4}$ $2\frac{1}{4}$	$7\frac{5}{6}$ $-5\frac{1}{4}$ $2\frac{5}{24}$	$8\frac{3}{8}$ $-6\frac{1}{12}$ $1\frac{23}{24}$	$11\frac{5}{6}$ $-7\frac{1}{12}$ $4\frac{3}{4}$
$4\frac{8}{10}$ $-1\frac{1}{5}$ $2\frac{8}{10}$	$4\frac{1}{4}$ $-2\frac{1}{5}$ $2\frac{11}{20}$	$9\frac{3}{4}$ $-4\frac{1}{8}$ $5\frac{1}{2}$	$14\frac{3}{8}$ $-9\frac{3}{16}$ $5\frac{3}{16}$

The Rodriguez Farm has 4½ acres of corn. The Johnson Farm has 7½ acres of corn. How many more acres of corn does the Rodriguez Farm have? $2\frac{1}{6}$

Summer Link Super Edition Grade 6

Page 53

Ordering Fractions

When putting fractions in order from smallest to largest or largest to smallest, it helps to find a common denominator first.

Example:

$\frac{1}{3}, \frac{1}{2}$ changed to $\frac{2}{6}, \frac{3}{6}$

Directions: Put the following fractions in order from least to largest value.

				Least			Largest
$\frac{1}{2}$	$\frac{2}{7}$	$\frac{4}{5}$	$\frac{1}{3}$	$\frac{2}{7}$	$\frac{1}{3}$	$\frac{1}{2}$	$\frac{4}{5}$
$\frac{3}{12}$	$\frac{2}{6}$	$\frac{3}{4}$	$\frac{1}{3}$	$\frac{3}{12}$	$\frac{1}{3}$	$\frac{2}{6}$	$\frac{3}{4}$
$\frac{2}{5}$	$\frac{4}{15}$	$\frac{2}{3}$	$\frac{5}{15}$	$\frac{4}{15}$	$\frac{5}{15}$	$\frac{2}{5}$	$\frac{2}{3}$
$3\frac{4}{5}$	$3\frac{2}{6}$	$3\frac{2}{5}$	$3\frac{1}{6}$	$3\frac{1}{6}$	$3\frac{1}{5}$	$3\frac{2}{5}$	$3\frac{4}{5}$
$9\frac{1}{3}$	$9\frac{2}{3}$	$9\frac{9}{12}$	$8\frac{2}{3}$	$8\frac{2}{3}$	$9\frac{1}{3}$	$9\frac{2}{3}$	$9\frac{9}{12}$
$5\frac{8}{12}$	$5\frac{5}{6}$	$5\frac{4}{24}$	$5\frac{3}{6}$	$5\frac{4}{24}$	$5\frac{5}{12}$	$5\frac{3}{6}$	$5\frac{8}{12}$
$4\frac{3}{5}$	$5\frac{7}{15}$	$6\frac{2}{5}$	$5\frac{1}{3}$	$4\frac{3}{5}$	$5\frac{1}{3}$	$5\frac{7}{15}$	$6\frac{2}{5}$

Four dogs were selected as finalists at a dog show. They were judged in four separate categories. One received a perfect score in each area. The dog with a score closest to four is the winner. Their scores are listed below. Which dog won the contest?

Dog A

Dog A $3\frac{4}{5}$ Dog B $3\frac{2}{3}$ Dog C $3\frac{5}{15}$ Dog D $3\frac{9}{12}$

Page 54

Multiplying Fractions

To multiply fractions, follow these steps:

$\frac{1}{2} \times \frac{3}{4} =$ **Step 1:** Multiply the numerators. $1 \times 3 = 3$
   Step 2: Multiply the denominators. $2 \times 4 = 8$

When multiplying a fraction by a whole number, first change the whole number to a fraction.

Example:

$\frac{1}{2} \times 8 = \frac{1}{2} \times \frac{8}{1} = \frac{8}{2} = 4$ reduced to lowest terms

Directions: Multiply. Reduce your answers to lowest terms.

$\frac{3}{8} \times \frac{1}{3} = \frac{1}{8}$	$\frac{1}{2} \times \frac{5}{8} = \frac{5}{16}$	$\frac{2}{3} \times \frac{1}{6} = \frac{1}{9}$	$\frac{2}{3} \times \frac{1}{2} = \frac{1}{3}$
$\frac{5}{6} \times 4 = 3\frac{1}{3}$	$\frac{3}{16} \times \frac{1}{16} = \frac{3}{128}$	$\frac{1}{5} \times 5 = 1$	$\frac{7}{8} \times \frac{3}{4} = \frac{21}{32}$
$\frac{7}{11} \times \frac{1}{3} = \frac{7}{33}$	$\frac{2}{9} \times \frac{9}{4} = \frac{1}{2}$	$\frac{1}{3} \times \frac{1}{3} \times \frac{1}{3} = \frac{1}{27}$	$\frac{1}{8} \times \frac{1}{4} \times \frac{1}{2} = \frac{1}{64}$

Jennifer has 10 pets. Two-fifths of the pets are cats, one-half are fish, and one-tenth are dogs. How many of each pet does she have?

Cats = 4
Fish = 5
Dogs = 1

Page 55

Dividing Fractions

To divide fractions, follow these steps:

$\frac{3}{4} \div \frac{1}{4} =$

Step 1: "Invert" the divisor. That means to turn it upside down.

$\frac{3}{4} \div \frac{4}{1}$

Step 2: Multiply the two fractions:

$\frac{3}{4} \times \frac{4}{1} = \frac{12}{4}$

Step 3: Reduce the fraction to lowest terms by dividing the denominator into the numerator.

$12 \div 4 = 3$
$\frac{3}{4} \div \frac{1}{4} = 3$

Directions: Follow the above steps to divide fractions.

$\frac{1}{4} \div \frac{1}{5} = 1\frac{1}{4}$	$\frac{1}{3} \div \frac{1}{12} = 4$	$\frac{3}{4} \div \frac{1}{3} = 2\frac{1}{4}$
$\frac{5}{12} \div \frac{1}{3} = 1\frac{1}{4}$	$\frac{3}{4} \div \frac{1}{6} = 4\frac{1}{2}$	$\frac{2}{3} \div \frac{2}{3} = \frac{1}{3}$
$\frac{3}{4} \div \frac{1}{4} = 1\frac{5}{7}$	$\frac{2}{3} \div \frac{4}{6} = 1$	$\frac{1}{8} \div \frac{2}{3} = \frac{3}{16}$
$\frac{4}{9} \div \frac{1}{3} = 2\frac{2}{5}$	$\frac{6}{8} \div \frac{1}{2} = 1$	$\frac{5}{12} \div \frac{3}{4} = \frac{5}{9}$

Page 56

Least Common Demoninators

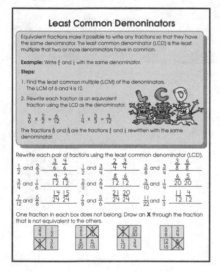

Equivalent fractions make it possible to write any fractions so that they have the same denominator. The least common denominator (LCD) is the least multiple that two or more denominators have in common.

Example: Write $\frac{2}{6}$ and $\frac{1}{4}$ with the same denominator.

Steps:

1. Find the least common multiple (LCM) of the denominators. The LCM of 6 and 4 is 12.

2. Rewrite each fraction as an equivalent fraction using the LCD as the denominator.

$\frac{2}{6} \times \frac{2}{2} = \frac{4}{12}$ $\frac{1}{4} \times \frac{3}{3} = \frac{3}{12}$

The fractions $\frac{4}{12}$ and $\frac{3}{12}$ are the fractions $\frac{2}{6}$ and $\frac{1}{4}$ rewritten with the same denominator.

Rewrite each pair of fractions using the least common denominator (LCD).

$\frac{1}{2}$ and $\frac{2}{3}$ $\frac{3}{6} \frac{4}{6}$	$\frac{1}{2}$ and $\frac{3}{4}$ $\frac{2}{4} \frac{3}{4}$	$\frac{3}{8}$ and $\frac{3}{4}$ $\frac{3}{8} \frac{6}{8}$
$\frac{3}{4}$ and $\frac{1}{12}$ $\frac{9}{12} \frac{1}{12}$	$\frac{2}{3}$ and $\frac{2}{4}$ $\frac{8}{12} \frac{6}{12}$	$\frac{1}{4}$ and $\frac{6}{20}$ $\frac{5}{20} \frac{6}{20}$
$\frac{7}{12}$ and $\frac{5}{8}$ $\frac{14}{24} \frac{15}{24}$	$\frac{7}{8}$ and $\frac{5}{24}$ $\frac{21}{24} \frac{5}{24}$	$\frac{11}{12}$ and $\frac{1}{3}$ $\frac{11}{12} \frac{4}{12}$

One fraction in each box does not belong. Draw an **X** through the fraction that is not equivalent to the others.

Page 57

Cross My Heart

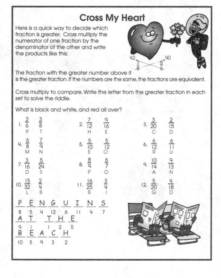

Here is a quick way to decide which fraction is greater. Cross multiply the numerator of one fraction by the denominator of the other and write the products like this:

The fraction with the greater number above it is the greater fraction. If the numbers are the same, the fractions are equivalent.

Cross multiply to compare. Write the letter from the greater fraction in each set to solve the riddle.

What is black and white, and red all over?

1. $\frac{2}{6}$ $\frac{3}{7}$ P T	2. $\frac{7}{12}$ $\frac{9}{16}$ H E	3. $\frac{3}{20}$ $\frac{2}{15}$ C D
4. $\frac{1}{3}$ $\frac{2}{4}$ M N	5. $\frac{5}{10}$ $\frac{3}{12}$ E O	6. $\frac{4}{12}$ $\frac{1}{11}$ R U
7. $\frac{3}{16}$ $\frac{5}{24}$ D S	8. $\frac{8}{9}$ $\frac{6}{7}$ P O	9. $\frac{10}{14}$ $\frac{9}{13}$ A N
10. $\frac{15}{32}$ $\frac{7}{16}$ L S	11. $\frac{16}{21}$ $\frac{5}{7}$ B I	$\frac{5}{20}$ $\frac{4}{18}$ G D

P E N G U I N S
8 5 4 3 9 12 3 7

A T   T H E
9 1 11 3 7

B E A C H
10 5 9 3 2

Page 58

Different Denominators

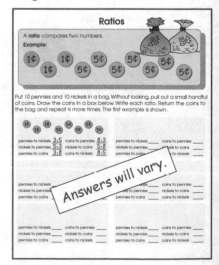

Fractions, improper fractions, and mixed numbers must have a common denominator before they can be added or subtracted.

Steps to add fractions with different denominators:
1. Find a common denominator.
2. Rewrite each number using the common denominator.
3. Add. Simplify, if necessary.

$\frac{3}{8} + \frac{1}{4} = \frac{3}{8} + \frac{2}{8} = \frac{5}{8}$ $\frac{5}{6} + \frac{3}{4} = \frac{10}{12} + \frac{9}{12} = \frac{19}{12} = 1\frac{7}{12}$

$2\frac{1}{2} + \frac{3}{10} = 2\frac{5}{10} + \frac{3}{10} = 2\frac{8}{10} = 2\frac{4}{5}$ $1\frac{3}{5} + \frac{1}{15} = 1\frac{10}{15} + \frac{6}{15} = 1\frac{16}{15} = 3\frac{1}{15}$

Directions: Add. Simplify, if necessary.

$\frac{1}{2} + \frac{1}{4} = \frac{3}{4}$	$\frac{2}{6} + \frac{1}{4} = \frac{7}{12}$	$\frac{3}{5} + \frac{2}{10} = \frac{4}{5}$
$\frac{5}{8} + \frac{3}{4} = 1\frac{3}{8}$	$\frac{5}{12} + \frac{1}{2} = 1\frac{11}{12}$	$1\frac{2}{3} + \frac{1}{13} = 1\frac{11}{15}$
$\frac{4}{9} + \frac{3}{4} = 2\frac{1}{2}$	$\frac{9}{10} + \frac{7}{12} = 1\frac{29}{60}$	$\frac{3}{8} + \frac{2}{16} = 1\frac{17}{24}$
$\frac{3}{8} + \frac{2}{3} = 1$	$\frac{9}{10} + \frac{4}{15} = 1\frac{1}{6}$	$1\frac{1}{4} + \frac{3}{12} = \frac{3}{4}$
$2\frac{3}{5} + 4\frac{1}{2} = 7\frac{1}{10}$	$\frac{2}{3} + \frac{1}{3} = 1\frac{2}{3}$	$\frac{3}{8} + \frac{3}{12} = \frac{3}{4}$
$\frac{8}{10} + \frac{1}{8} = \frac{37}{40}$	$\frac{12}{21} + \frac{2}{7} = \frac{6}{7}$	$\frac{7}{20} + \frac{1}{12} = \frac{2}{15}$

Page 59

Finding Percents

Find percent by dividing the number you have by the number possible.

Example:

15 out of 20 possible: $\frac{0.75}{20)15.00} = 75\%$
$\frac{-140}{100}$
$\frac{-100}{}$

Annie has been keeping track of the scores she earned on each spelling test during the grading period.

Directions: Find out each percentage grade she earned. The first one has been done for you.

Week	Number Correct		Total Number of Words	Score in Percent
1	14	(out of)	20	70%
2	16		20	80%
3	18		20	90%
4	12		15	80%
5	16		16	100%
6	17		18	94%
Review Test	51		60	85%

If Susan scored 5% higher than Annie on the review test, how many words did she get right?   54

Carrie scored 10% lower than Susan on the review test. How many words did she spell correctly?   48

Of the 24 students in Annie's class, 25% had the same score as Annie. Only 10% had a higher score. What percent had a lower score? 65%

Is that answer possible? no   65% of 24 is 15.6

Why? cannot have a percent of a person

Page 60

Percent of a Number

Example:
Find 30% of 12.

Method 1
Use a fraction.

$\frac{30}{100} \times 12 = \frac{360}{100} = \frac{36}{10} = \frac{18}{5} = 3\frac{3}{5}$

Method 2
Use a decimal.

$0.3 \times 12 = 3.6$

30% of 12 is $3\frac{3}{5}$ or 3.6.

Find 25% of:	Find 4% of:	Find 60% of:
16 $\underline{4}$	10 $\underline{0.4}$ or $\frac{2}{5}$	15 $\underline{9}$
20 $\underline{5}$	96 $\underline{3.84}$ or $3\frac{21}{25}$	60 $\underline{36}$
64 $\underline{16}$	160 $\underline{6}$	100 60
140 $\underline{35}$	200 $\underline{8}$	125 75
10 $\underline{2.5}$ or $2\frac{1}{2}$	20 $\underline{0.8}$ or $\frac{4}{5}$	7 $\underline{4.2}$ or $4\frac{1}{5}$
35 $\underline{8.75}$ or $8\frac{3}{4}$	35 $\underline{1.4}$ or $1\frac{2}{5}$	32 $\underline{19.2}$ or $19\frac{1}{5}$
120 $\underline{30}$	90 $\underline{3.6}$ or $3\frac{3}{5}$	110 $\underline{66}$
630 $\underline{157.5}$ or $157\frac{1}{2}$	140 $\underline{5.6}$ or $5\frac{3}{5}$	297 $\underline{178.2}$ or $178\frac{1}{5}$

Page 61

Ratios

A ratio compares two numbers.

Example:

1¢ 1¢ 5¢ 5¢ 5¢ 5¢
1¢   5¢ 5¢

Put 10 pennies and 10 nickels in a bag. Without looking, pull out a small handful of coins. Draw the coins in a box below. Write each ratio. Return the coins to the bag and repeat 4 more times. The first example is shown.

5¢ 5¢ 5¢ 5¢ 1¢ 5¢

pennies to nickels $\underline{3:5}$ coins to pennies $\underline{8:3}$
nickels to pennies $\underline{5:3}$ nickels to coins $\underline{5:8}$
pennies to coins $\underline{3:8}$ coins to nickels $\underline{8:5}$

Answers will vary.

pennies to nickels ____	coins to pennies ____
nickels to pennies ____	nickels to coins ____
pennies to coins ____	coins to nickels ____

pennies to nickels ____	coins to pennies ____
nickels to pennies ____	nickels to coins ____
pennies to coins ____	coins to nickels ____

Proportions

Another way of writing a ratio is as a fraction. 3:7 is the same as $\frac{3}{7}$.
Remember what you have learned about cross multiplication.

Because the products of cross multiplication are the same, the fractions are equivalent. When two ratios or fractions are equivalent, they form a **proportion**.

Example:

Steps to find an unknown term of a proportion.
Lisa uses 2 pots to plant 8 seeds.
How many pots will she need to plant 24 seeds?

1. Write a proportion. $\frac{2 \text{ pots}}{8 \text{ seeds}} = \frac{n \text{ pots}}{24 \text{ seeds}}$

2. Cross multiply. $\frac{2}{8} \times \frac{n}{24}$

$8 \times n = 48$
$n = 6$ (Divide both sides of the proportion by 8.)
Lisa needs 6 pots to plant 24 seeds.

If the ratios form a proportion, write yes on the line. If not, write no.

$\frac{4}{30} = \frac{24}{?}$ __yes__ $\frac{1}{2} = \frac{36}{72}$ __yes__ $\frac{3}{35} = \frac{20}{35}$ __no__ $\frac{1}{23} = \frac{8}{184}$ __yes__

$\frac{6}{13} = \frac{75}{156}$ __no__ $\frac{9}{5} = \frac{171}{95}$ __yes__ $\frac{4}{21} = \frac{40}{210}$ __yes__ $\frac{11}{12} = \frac{154}{168}$ __yes__

Find the unknown term in each of these proportions.

$\frac{4}{15} = \frac{n}{?}$ __12__ $\frac{n}{104} = \frac{5}{13}$ __40__ $\frac{6}{?} = \frac{45}{?}$ __54__

Probability

Probability is the ratio of favorable outcomes to possible outcomes of an experiment.

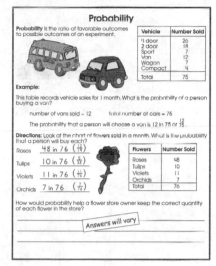

Vehicle	Number Sold
4 door	26
2 door	18
Sport	7
Van	12
Wagon	7
Compact	4
Total	75

Example:

This table records vehicle sales for 1 month. What is the probability of a person buying a van?

number of vans sold = 12   total number of cars = 75

The probability that a person will choose a van is 12 in 75 or $\frac{12}{75}$.

Directions: Look at the chart of flowers sold in a month. What is the probability that a person will buy each?

Roses __48 in 76 ($\frac{12}{19}$)__

Tulips __10 in 76 ($\frac{5}{38}$)__

Violets __11 in 76 ($\frac{11}{76}$)__

Orchids __7 in 76 ($\frac{7}{76}$)__

Flowers	Number Sold
Roses	48
Tulips	10
Violets	11
Orchids	7
Total	76

How would probability help a flower store owner keep the correct quantity of each flower in the store?

Answers will vary

Likely and Unlikely

The probability of an event happening can be written as a fraction between 0 and 1.

Example:

Certain if the probability is 1.   The probability of spinning red, blue, or green is $\frac{4}{4}$ or 1.

More likely if its probability is greater than another.   It is more likely to spin green ($\frac{2}{4}$) than red ($\frac{1}{4}$).

Less likely if its probability is less than another.   It is less likely to spin blue ($\frac{1}{4}$) than red ($\frac{1}{4}$).

Equally likely if the probabilities are the same.   It is equally likely to spin red or blue ($\frac{1}{4}$) or green ($\frac{2}{4}$).

Impossible if the probability is 0.   It is impossible to spin white ($\frac{0}{4}$ = 0).

Look at the spinner. Write the probability for each event below. Write certain or impossible, where appropriate.

spinning a 6 $\frac{0}{10}$: __impossible__   spinning a 4 $\frac{3}{10}$

spinning a 2 $\frac{1}{10}$ spinning a 4 or 5 $\frac{5}{10}$

spinning an even number $\frac{4}{10}$ spinning a prime number $\frac{10}{}$

spinning a number < 10 $\frac{10}{10}$: __certain__   spinning a zero $\frac{0}{10}$: __impossible__

Look at the spinner to find which is **more likely**, **less likely**, or **equally likely**.

Spinning a 4 is __more likely__ than spinning a 5.

Spinning a 4 is __equally likely__ than spinning a 1.

Spinning an even number is __less likely__ than spinning an odd number.

Bar Graphs

Another way to organize information is a **bar graph**. The bar graph in the example compares the number of students in 4 elementary schools. Each bar stands for 1 school. You can easily see that School A has the most students and School C has the least. The numbers along the left show how many students attend each school.

Example:

Directions: Complete the following exercises.

1. This bar graph will show how many calories are in 1 serving of 4 kinds of cereal. Draw the bars the correct height and label each with the name of the cereal. After completing the bar graph, answer the questions. Data: Korn Kernals—150 calories; Oat Floats—160 calories; Rite Rice—110 calories; Sugar Shapes—200 calories.

a. Which cereal is the best to eat if you're trying to lose weight? __Rite Rice__
b. Which cereal has nearly the same number of calories as Oat Floats? __Korn Kernals__

2. On another sheet, draw your own graph, showing the number of TV commercials in 1 week for each of the 4 cereals in the graph above. After completing the graph, answer the questions. Data: Oat Floats—27 commercials; Rite Rice—15; Sugar Shapes—35; Korn Kernals—28.

a. Which cereal is most heavily advertised? __Sugar Shapes__
b. What similarities do you notice between the graph of calories and the graph of TV commercials? __Sugar Shapes is highest in sugar and advertisements__

Picture Graphs

Newspapers and textbooks often use **pictures** in graphs instead of bars. Each picture stands for a certain number of objects. Half a picture means half the number. The picture graph in the example indicates the number of games each team won. The Astros won 7 games, so they have 3 balls.

Example:

Games Won				
Astros				
Orioles				
Bluebirds				
Sluggers				

(1 ball = 2 games)

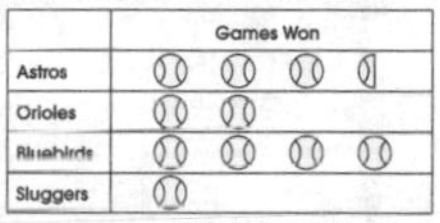

Directions: Complete the following exercises.

Finish this picture graph, showing the number of students who have dogs in 4 sixth-grade classes. Draw simple dogs in the graph, letting each drawing stand for 2 dogs.

Data: Class 1—12 dogs; Class 2—16 dogs; Class 3—22 dogs; Class 4—12 dogs. After completing the graph, answer the questions.

Dogs Owned by Students	
Class 1	OOOOOO
Class 2	OOOOOOOO
Class 3	OOOOOOOOOOO
Class 4	OOOOOO

(One dog drawing = 2 students' dogs)

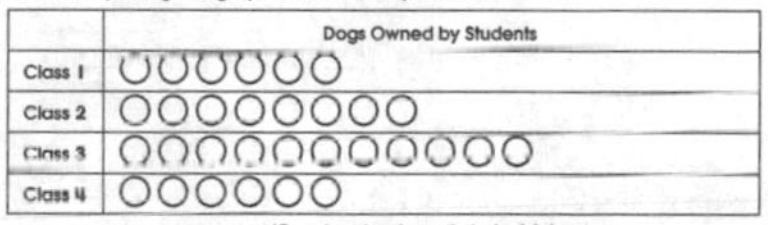

1. Why do you think newspapers use picture graphs? __Answers will vary. It simplifies information and is easier to read.__

2. Would picture graphs be appropriate to show exact number of dogs living in America? Why or why not? __There are too many!__

Line Graphs

Still another way to display information is a **line graph**. The same data can often be shown in both a bar graph and a line graph. Nevertheless, line graphs are especially useful in showing changes over a period of time.

The line graph in the example shows changes in the number of students enrolled in a school over a 5-year period. Enrollment was highest in 2000 and has decreased gradually each year since then. Notice how labeling the years and enrollment numbers make the graph easy to understand.

Example:

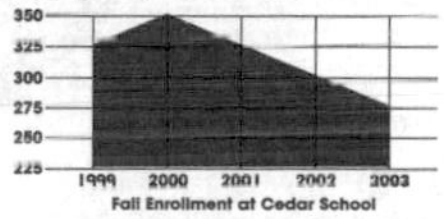

Fall Enrollment at Cedar School

Directions: Complete the following exercises.

1. On another sheet of paper, draw a line graph that displays the growth of a corn plant over a 6-week period. Mark the correct points, using the data below, and connect them with a line. After completing the graph, answer the questions. Data: week 1—3.5 in.; week 2—4.5 in.; week 3—5 in.; week 4—5.5 in.; week 5—5.75 in.; week 6—6 in.

a. Between which weeks was the growth fastest? __1 and 2__
b. Between which weeks was the growth slowest? __4 and 5; 5 and 6__

2. On another sheet of paper draw a line graph to show how the high temperature varied during one week. Then answer the questions. Data: Sunday—high of 53 degrees; Monday—51; Tuesday—56; Wednesday—60; Thursday—58; Friday—67; Saturday—73. Don't forget to label the numbers.

a. In general, did the days get warmer or cooler? __warmer__
b. Do you think this data would have been as clear in a bar graph? __No__
Explain your answer. __Line graphs show a trend up and down across the graph.__

Circle Graphs

Circle graphs are useful in showing how something is divided into parts. The circle graph in the example shows how Carly spent her $10 allowance. Each section is a fraction of her whole allowance. For example, the movie tickets section is $\frac{3}{10}$ of the circle, showing that she spent $\frac{3}{10}$ of her allowance, or $3, on movie tickets.

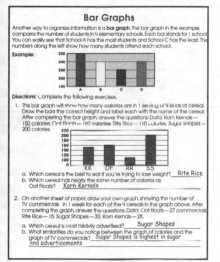

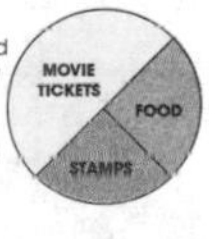

Directions: Complete the following exercises.

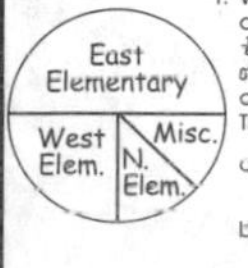

1. When the middle school opened last fall, $\frac{1}{2}$ of the students came from East Elementary, $\frac{1}{4}$ came from West Elementary, $\frac{1}{8}$ came from North Elementary, and the remaining students moved into the town from other cities. Make a circle graph showing these proportions. Label each section. Then answer the questions.

a. What fraction of students at the new school moved into the area from other cities? __$\frac{1}{8}$__

b. If the new middle school has 450 students enrolled, how many used to go to East Elementary? __225__

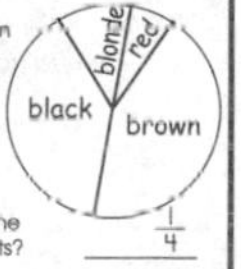

2. This circle graph will show the hair color of 24 students in one class. Divide the circle into 4 sections to show this data: black hair—8 students; brown hair—10 students; blonde hair—4 students; red hair—2 students. (Hint: 8 students are $\frac{8}{24}$ or $\frac{1}{3}$ of the class.) Be sure to label each section by hair color. Then answer the questions.

a. Looking at your graph, what fraction of the class is the combined group of blonde- and red-haired students? __$\frac{1}{4}$__

b. Which two fractions of hair color combine to total half the class? __red/brown__

Length in Customary Units

The **customary** system of measurement is the most widely used in the United States. It measures length in inches, feet, yards, and miles.

Examples:

12 inches (in.) = 1 foot (ft.)
3 ft. (36 in.) = 1 yard (yd.)
5,280 ft. (1,760 yds.) = 1 mile (mi.)

To change to a larger unit, divide. To change to a smaller unit, multiply.

Examples:
To change inches to feet, divide by 12.   24 in. = 2 ft.   27 in. = 2 ft. 3 in.
To change feet to inches, multiply by 12.   3 ft. = 36 in.   4 ft. = 48 in.
To change inches to yards, divide by 36.   108 in. = 3 yd.   80 in. = 2 yd. 8 in.
To change feet to yards, divide by 3.   12 ft. = 4 yd.   11 ft. = 3 yd. 2 ft.

Sometimes in subtraction you have to borrow units.

Examples:

Directions: Solve the following problems.

1. 108 in. = __3__ ft.   2. 68 in. = 5 ft. __8__ in.

3. 8 ft. = __3__ yd. __2__ ft.   4. 8,020 yd. = __2__ mi.

5. What form of measurement (inches, feet, yards or miles) would you use for each item below?

a. pencil __inches__   b. vacation trip __miles__

c. playground __yards or feet__   d. wall __feet or yards__

6. One side of a square box is 2 ft. 4 in. What is the perimeter of the box? __9 ft. 6 in.__

7. Jason is 5 ft. tall. Kent is 4 ft. 1 in. tall. Who is taller and by how much? __Kent, 2 in.__

8. Karen bought a doll 2 ft. 8 in. tall for her little sister. She found a box that is 24 in. long. Will the doll fit in that box? __No__

9. Dan's dog likes to go out in the backyard, which is 85 ft. wide. The dog's chain is 17 ft. 6 in. long. If Dan attaches one end of the chain to a pole in the middle of the yard, will his dog be able to leave the yard? __No__

Length in Metric Units

The **metric system** measures length in meters, centimeters, millimeters, and kilometers.

Examples:
A **meter** (m) is about 40 inches or 3.3 feet.
A **centimeter** (cm) is $\frac{1}{100}$ of a meter or 0.4 inches.
A **millimeter** (mm) is $\frac{1}{1000}$ of a meter or 0.04 inches.
A **kilometer** (km) is 1,000 meters or 0.6 miles.

As before, divide to find a larger unit and multiply to find a smaller unit.

Examples:
To change m to mm, multiply by 10.
10 change cm to meters, divide by 100.
To change mm to meters, divide by 1,000.
To change km to meters, multiply by 1,000.

Directions: Solve the following problems.

1. 600 cm = __6__ m   2. 12 cm = __1.2__ mm   3. 117 m = __470__ cm   4. 3 km = __3,000__

5. In the sentences below, write the missing unit: m, cm, mm, or km.

a. A fingernail is about 1 __mm__ thick.
b. An average car is about 5 __m__ long.
c. Someone could walk 1 __km__ in 10 minutes.
d. A finger is about 7 __cm__ long.
e. A street could be 3 __km__ long.
f. The Earth is about 40,000 __km__ around at the equator.
g. A pencil is about 17 __cm__ long.
h. A noodle is about 4 __mm__ wide.
i. A teacher's desk is about 1 __m__ wide.

6. A nickel is about 1 mm thick. How many nickels would be in a stack 1 cm high? __10__

7. Is something 25 cm long closer to 10 inches or 10 feet? __10 inches__

8. Is something 18 mm wide closer to 0.7 inch or 7 inches? __0.7 inch__

9. Would you get more exercise running 4 km or 500 m? __4 km__

10. Which is taller, something 40 m or 350 cm? __40 m__

Page 71

Weight in Customary Units

Here are the main ways to measure weight in customary units:

16 ounces (oz.) = 1 pound (lb.)
2,000 lb. = 1 ton (tn.)
To change ounces to pounds, divide by 16.
To change pounds to ounces, multiply by 16.

As with measurements of length, you may have to borrow units in subtraction.

> **BRIDGE UNSAFE FOR TRUCKS OVER 2 TONS**

Example:
```
  4 lb.  5 oz.  = 3 lb. 21 oz.
- 2 lb. 10 oz.   - 2 lb. 10 oz.
                   1 lb. 11 oz.
```

Directions: Solve the following problems.

1. 48 oz. = __3__ lb.　2. 39 oz. = __2.44__ lb.　3. 4 lb. = __64__ oz.　4. 1.25 tn. = __2,500__ lb.

5. What form of measurement would you use for each of these: ounces, pounds, or tons?
a. pencil __ounces__　b. elephant __tons__　c. person __pounds__

6. Which is heavier, 0.25 ton or 750 pounds? — __750 lbs.__

7. Twenty-two people, each weighing an average of 150 lb., want to take an elevator that can carry up to 1.5 tons. How many of them should wait for the next elevator? — __2 people__

8. A one ton truck is carrying 14 boxes that weigh 125 lb. each. It comes to a small bridge with a sign that says, "Bridge unsafe for trucks over 2 tons." Is it safe for the truck and the boxes to cross the bridge? — __Yes__

9. A large box of Oat Boats contains 2 lb. 3 oz. of cereal, while a box of Honey Hunks contains 1 lb. 14 oz. How many more ounces are in the box of Oat Boats? — __5 oz.__

10. A can of Peter's Powdered Drink Mix weighs 2 lb. 5 oz. A can of Petunia's Powdered Drink Mix weighs 40 oz. Which one is heavier? — __Petunia's__

11. A can of Peter's Drink Mix is 12 cents an ounce. How much does it cost? — __$4.44__

12. How many 5-oz. servings could you get from a fish that weighs 3 lb. 12 oz.? — __12__

Page 72

Weight in Metric Units

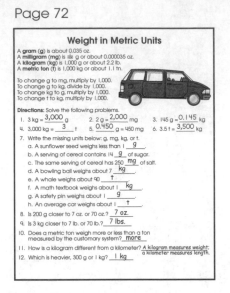

A **gram** (g) is about 0.035 oz.
A **milligram** (mg) is 1/1000 g or about 0.000035 oz.
A **kilogram** (kg) is 1,000 g or about 2.2 lb.
A **metric ton** (t) is 1,000 kg or about 1.1 tn.

To change g to mg, multiply by 1,000.
To change g to kg, divide by 1,000.
To change kg to g, multiply by 1,000.
To change t to kg, multiply by 1,000.

Directions: Solve the following problems.

1. 3 kg = __3,000__ g　2. 2 g = __2,000__ mg　3. 145 g = __0.145__ kg
4. 3,000 kg = __3__ t　5. __0.450__ g = 450 mg　6. 3.5 t = __3,500__ kg

7. Write the missing units below: g, mg, kg, or t.
a. A sunflower seed weighs less than 1 __g__.
b. A serving of cereal contains 14 __g__ of sugar.
c. The same serving of cereal has 250 __mg__ of salt.
d. A bowling ball weighs about 7 __kg__.
e. A whale weighs about 90 __t__.
f. A math textbook weighs about 1 __kg__.
g. A safety pin weighs about 1 __g__.
h. An average car weighs about 1 __t__.

8. Is 200 g closer to 7 oz. or 70 oz.? __7 oz.__

9. Is 3 kg closer to 7 lb. or 70 lb.? __7 lb.__

10. Does a metric ton weigh more or less than a ton measured by the customary system? __more__

11. How is a kilogram different from a kilometer? __A kilogram measures weight; a kilometer measures length.__

12. Which is heavier, 300 g or 1 kg? __1 kg__

Page 73

Capacity in Customary Units

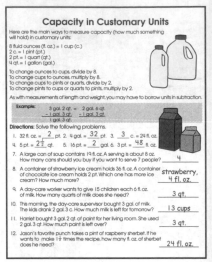

Here are the main ways to measure capacity (how much something will hold) in customary units:

8 fluid ounces (fl. oz.) = 1 cup (c.)
2 c. = 1 pint (pt.)
2 pt. = 1 quart (qt.)
4 qt. = 1 gallon (gal.)

To change ounces to cups, divide by 8.
To change cups to ounces, multiply by 8.
To change cups to pints or quarts, divide by 2.
To change pints to cups or quarts to pints, multiply by 2.

As with measurements of length and weight, you may have to borrow units in subtraction.

Example:
```
  3 gal. 2 qt. = 2 gal. 6 qt.
- 1 gal. 3 qt.  - 1 gal. 3 qt.
                  1 gal. 3 qt.
```

Directions: Solve the following problems.

1. 32 fl. oz. = __2__ c.　2. 4 gal. = __32__ pt.　3. __3__ c. = 24 fl. oz.
4. 5 pt. = __2½__ qt.　5. 16 pt. = __2__ gal.　6. 3 pt. = __48__ fl. oz.

7. A large can of soup contains 19 fl. oz. A serving is about 8 oz. How many cans should you buy if you want to serve 7 people? — __4__

8. A container of strawberry ice cream holds 36 fl. oz. A container of chocolate ice cream holds 2 pt. Which one has more ice cream? How much more? — __strawberry, 4 fl. oz.__

9. A day-care worker wants to give 15 children each 6 fl. oz. of milk. How many quarts of milk does she need? — __3 qt.__

10. This morning, the day-care supervisor bought 3 gal. of milk. The kids drank 2 gal. 3 c. How much milk is left for tomorrow? — __13 cups__

11. Harriet bought 3 gal. 2 qt. of paint for her living room. She used 2 gal. 3 qt. How much paint is left over? — __3 qt.__

12. Jason's favorite punch takes a pint of raspberry sherbet. If he wants to make 1½ times the recipe, how many fl. oz. of sherbet does he need? — __24 fl. oz.__

Page 74

Capacity in Metric Units

A **liter** (L) is a little over 1 quart.
A **milliliter** (mL) is 1/1000 of a liter or about 0.03 oz.
A **kiloliter** (kL) is 1,000 liters or about 250 gallons.

Directions: Solve the following problems.

1. 5,000 mL = __5__ L
2. 2,000 L = __2__ kL
3. 3 L = __3,000__ mL
4. Write the missing unit: L, mL, or kL.
a. A swimming pool holds about 100 __kL__ of water.
b. An eyedropper is marked for 1 and 2 __mL__.
c. A pitcher could hold 1 or 2 __L__ of juice.
d. A teaspoon holds about 5 __mL__ of medicine.
e. A birdbath might hold 5 __L__ of water.
f. A tablespoon holds about 15 __mL__ of salt.
g. A bowl holds about 250 __mL__ of soup.
h. We drank about 4 __L__ of punch at the party.

5. Which is more, 3 L or a gallon? — __gallon__
6. Which is more, 400 mL or 40 oz.? — __40 oz.__
7. Which is more, 1 kL or 500 L? — __1 kL__
8. Is 4 L closer to a quart or a gallon? — __gallon__
9. Is 480 mL closer to 2 cups or 2 pints? — __2 cups__
10. Is a mL closer to 4 drops or 4 teaspoonsful? — __4 drops__
11. How many glasses of juice containing 250 mL each could you pour from a 1-L jug? — __4 glasses__
12. How much water would you need to water an average-sized lawn, 1 kL or 1 L? — __1 kL__

Page 75

Temperature in Customary and Metric Units

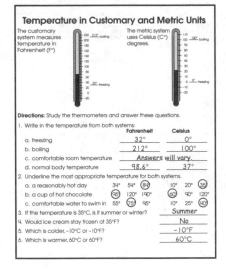

The customary system measures temperature in Fahrenheit (F°)

The metric system uses Celsius (C°) degrees.

Directions: Study the thermometers and answer these questions.

1. Write in the temperature from both systems:

	Fahrenheit	Celsius
a. freezing	32°	0°
b. boiling	212°	100°
c. comfortable room temperature	Answers will vary.	
d. normal body temperature	98.6°	37°

2. Underline the most appropriate temperature for both systems.
a. a reasonably hot day　34°　54°　(84°)　10°　20°　(35°)
b. a cup of hot chocolate　(96°)　120°　190°　(60°)　90°　120°
c. comfortable water to swim in　55°　(75°)　95°　10°　25°　(40°)

3. If the temperature is 35°C, is it summer or winter? __Summer__
4. Would ice cream stay frozen at 35°F? __No__
5. Which is colder, -10°C or -10°F? __-10°F__
6. Which is warmer, 60°C or 60°F? __60°C__

Page 76

Review

Directions: Write the best unit to measure each item: inch, foot, yard, mile, ounce, pound, ton, fluid ounce, cup, pint, quart, or gallon.

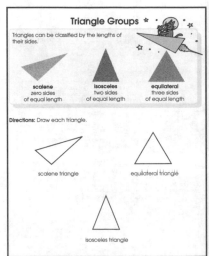

distance from New York to Chicago	__miles__
weight of a goldfish	__ounces__
height of a building	__feet__
water in a large fish tank	__gallons__
glass of milk	__ounces__
weight of a whale	__tons__
length of a pencil	__inches__
distance from first base to second base	__feet__
distance traveled by a space shuttle	__miles__
length of a soccer field	__yards__
amount of paint needed to cover a house	__gallons__
material needed to make a dress	__yards__

Page 77

Geometric Figures

Example	Description	Symbol	Read
Point	A point is an end of a line segment (an exact location in space).	A	point A
Line	A line is a collection of points in a straight path that extends in two directions without end.	$\overleftrightarrow{DE}$	line DE
Line Segment	A line segment is part of a line with two endpoints.	$\overline{RS}$	segment RS
Ray	A ray is part of a line having only one endpoint.	$\overrightarrow{BC}$	ray BC
Angle	An angle is two rays having a common endpoint.	∠CDE	angle CDE
Plane	A plane is an endless flat surface.	plane STU	plane STU

Use the figure to write the symbol for each.

1. 1 ray _____

2. a plane _____

3. 3 point _____ _Answers will vary._

4. 2 lines _____

5. 3 angles _____ , _____ , _____

6. 3 line segments _____ , _____ , _____

Page 78

Figuring Angles

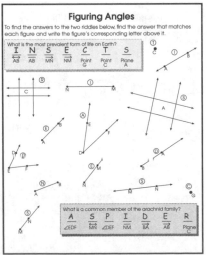

To find the answers to the two riddles below, find the answer that matches each figure and write the figure's corresponding letter above it.

What is the most prevalent form of life on Earth?

I	N	S	E	C	T	S
$\overrightarrow{AB}$	$\overrightarrow{AB}$	$\overline{MN}$	$\overline{NM}$	Point G	Point G	Plane A

What is a common member of the arachnid family?

A	S	P	I	D	E	R
∠EDF	$\overline{MN}$	∠DEF	$\overline{NM}$	$\overline{BA}$	$\overrightarrow{AB}$	Plane C

Page 79

Triangle Groups

Triangles can be classified by the lengths of their sides.

scalene
zero sides of equal length

isosceles
two sides of equal length

equilateral
three sides of equal length

Directions: Draw each triangle.

scalene triangle

equilateral triangle

isosceles triangle

Page 80

Classifying Triangles

The sum of the angles in any triangle is 180°.

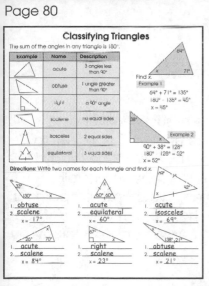

Example	Name	Description
	acute	3 angles less than 90°
	obtuse	1 angle greater than 90°
	right	a 90° angle
	scalene	no equal sides
	isosceles	2 equal sides
	equilateral	3 equal sides

Find x.
Example 1
64° + 71° = 135°
180° – 135° = 45°
x = 45°

Example 2
90° + 38° = 128°
180° – 128° = 52°
x = 52°

Directions: Write two names for each triangle and find x.

1. obtuse scalene x = 17°
2. acute equilateral x = 60°
3. acute isosceles x = 69°
4. acute scalene x = 84°
5. right scalene x = 23°
6. obtuse scalene x = 21°

Page 81

Perimeter

Perimeter is the distance around an area.

Directions: Find the perimeter of each figure.

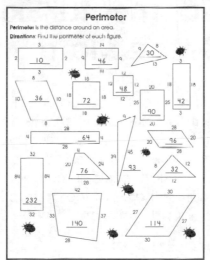

10, 46, 30, 36, 72, 48, 42, 90, 64, 96, 32, 76, 93, 232, 76, 140, 114

Page 82

Perimeter Formula

The perimeter of some polygons can be given as a formula.

Examples:
The sides of a square are the same length.
The perimeter equals 4 times the length of a side (s).
Perimeter of a square: s + s + s + s = 4 x s or 4s

The opposite sides of a rectangle are the same length. The perimeter equals 2 times the length (l) plus 2 times the width (w).
Perimeter of a rectangle: 2l + 2w

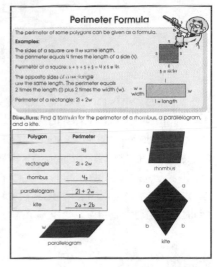

Directions: Find a formula for the perimeter of a rhombus, a parallelogram, and a kite.

Polygon	Perimeter
square	4s
rectangle	2l + 2w
rhombus	4s
parallelogram	2l + 2w
kite	2a + 2b

Page 83

The Circle Game

The perimeter of a circle is called the **circumference**. There is a formula for finding the circumference of a circle. The formula uses this special number **3.14**. We call this number **pi** (π). To find the circumference of a circle, use this formula:

Circumference = π x diameter
Circumference = πd
or
Circumference = π x 2 x radius
Circumference = 2πr

Examples:
C = πd   C = 2πr
C = 3.14 x 4 C = 2 x 3.14 x 2
C = 12.56   C = 12.56

Directions: Find the circumference for each circle.

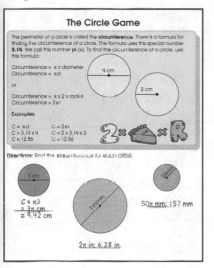

C = π3 = 3π cm ≈ 9.42 cm
50π mm; 157 mm
2π in; 6.28 in.

Page 84

Formula One

To find the **area** of a square or rectangle, multiply the length by the width.

Example:

Area = 2 in. x 3 in.
= 6 square in.
= 6 in.²

Area of a square = side x side = s x s = s²
Area of a rectangle = length x width = l x w = lw

Directions: Find the area of each shape.

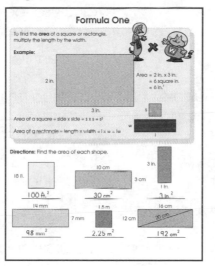

100 ft.², 30 cm², 3 in.², 98 mm², 2.25 m², 192 cm²

Page 85

Area: Squares and Rectangles

The **area** is the number of square units that covers a certain space. To find the area, multiply the length by the width. The answer is in square units, shown by adding a superscript 2 (²) to the number.

Examples:

For the rectangle, use this formula: A = l x w
A = 8 x 5
A = 40 in.²

For the square formula, s stands for side: A = s x s (or s²)
A = 3 x 3 (or 3²)
A = 9 ft.²

Directions: Find the area of each shape below.

1. Find the area of a room which is 12 feet long and 7 feet wide. A = 84 ft.²
2. A farmer's field is 32 feet on each side. How many square feet does he have to plow? 1,024 ft.²
3. Steve's bedroom is 10 feet by 12 feet. How many square feet of carpeting would cover the floor? 120 ft.²
4. Two of Steve's walls are 7.5 feet high and 12 feet long. The other two are the same height and 10 feet long. How many square feet of wallpaper would cover all four walls?
Square feet for 12-foot wall = 90 ft.² x 2 = 180 ft.²
Square feet for 10-foot wall = 75 ft.² x 2 = 150 ft.²
5. A clothes shop moved from a store that was 35 by 22 feet to a new location that was 53 by 32 feet. How many more square feet does the store have now?
Square feet for first location = 770 ft.²
Square feet for new location = 1,696 ft.²   Difference = 926 ft.²
6. A school wanted to purchase a climber for the playground. The one they selected would need 98 square feet of space. The only space available on the playground was 12 feet long and 8 feet wide. Will there be enough space for the climber? No

Page 86

Volume of Prisms

Volume is measured in cubic units.

Volume of a nonrectangular prism = base area • height

Volume of a rectangular prism = l • w • h

V = b • h
V = (½ • 4 • 6) • 12
V = 144 in³

V = 8 • 5 • 3
V = 120 m³

Directions: Find the volume of each prism.

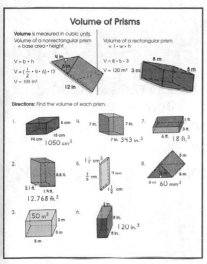

1. 1050 cm³
2. 343 in.³
3. 18 ft.³
4. 12.768 ft.³
5.
6. 60 mm³
7. 50 m³
8. 120 in.³

Page 87

Geometric Patterns

Geometric patterns can be described in several ways. **Similar shapes** have the same shape but in differing sizes. **Congruent shapes** have the same geometric pattern but may be facing in different directions. **Symmetrical shapes** are identical when divided in half.

Directions: Use the terms **similar**, **congruent**, or **symmetrical** to describe the following patterns.

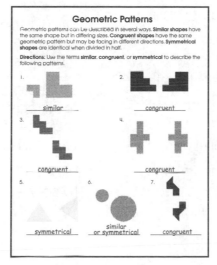

1. similar
2. congruent
3. congruent
4. congruent
5. symmetrical
6. similar or symmetrical
7. congruent

Developmental Skills for Sixth Grade Math Success

Parents and educators alike know that the School Specialty name ensures outstanding educational experience and content. *Summer Link Math* was designed to help your child retain those skills learned during the past school year. With *Summer Link Math*, your child will be ready to review and master new material with confidence when he or she returns to school in the fall.

Use this checklist—compiled from state curriculum standards—to help your child prepare for proficiency testing. Place a check mark in the box if the appropriate skill has been mastered. If your child needs more work with a particular skill, place an "R" in the box and come back to it for review.

Math Skills

❑ Uses place value to read, write, compare, and order whole numbers and decimals.

❑ Uses problem-solving strategies—such as rounding, regrouping, using multiple operations, and Venn diagrams—to solve numerical and word problems.

❑ Reads, writes, and identifies any decimals, fractions, or percents.

❑ Selects the appropriate operation to solve problems. Adds, subtracts, multiplies, divides, compares, and orders whole numbers, decimals, and fractions, including mixed numbers.

❑ Translates word problems into number sentences, solves, and explains solutions.

❑ Solves problems involving units of measure and converts answers to either the metric or customary system. Estimates measurements in real-world situations.

❑ Creates, analyzes, and interprets graphs, tables, equations, and inequalities.

❑ Uses algebraic problem-solving strategies, variables, and equations to solve problems.

❑ Describes, draws, identifies, and analyzes two- and three-dimensional shapes.

❑ Identifies and distinguishes between similar, congruent, and symmetric figures. Visualizes and illustrates ways in which shapes can be combined, subdivided, and changed.

❑ Calculates perimeter and area of triangles, parallelograms, and circles. Determines the circumference of a circle using pi (π).

❑ Uses logical thinking and problem solving skills to analyze problems by identifying relationships, distinguishing relevant from irrelevant information, identifying missing information, sequencing, breaking a problem into simpler parts, and finding solutions.

❑ Makes predictions and uses statistical methods to make inferences and valid arguments about problems and real-world situations.

❑ Uses inductive and deductive reasoning to solve problems.

SUMMER LINK
READING

Summer Before Grade 6
Recommended Reading

- **Anne of Green Gables** — L.M. Montgomery
- **The Borning Room; Dateline Troy;**
  Joyful Noise: Poems for Two Voices — Paul Fleischman
- **Castle in the Attic** — Elizabeth Winthrop
- **The Children's Atlas of World History** — Neil DeMarco
- **Dress Sense Series** — Christine Hatt
- **The Foxman; Hatchet** — Gary Paulsen
- **Freckle Juice** — Judy Blume
- **From the Mixed Up Files of Mrs. Basil E. Frankweiler** — E.L. Konigsburg
- **The Giver** — Lois Lowry
- **Heroes, Gods and Emperors from Roman Mythology** — Kerry Usher
- **Holes; Sixth Grade Secrets** — Louis Sachar
- **Hope Was Here** — Joan Bauer
- **The House of the Scorpion** — Nancy Farmer
- **I am the Cheese** — Robert Cormier
- **Island of the Blue Dolphins** — Scott O'Dell
- **Jacob Have I Loved** — Katherine Paterson
- **The Lion, the Witch, and the Wardrobe** — C.S. Lewis
- **Maniac Magee** — Jerry Spinelli
- **The Moon and I** — Betsy Byars
- **On the Far Side of the Mountain** — Jean Craighead George
- **The Phantom Tollbooth** — Norton Juster
- **Pink and Say** — Patricia Polacco
- **The Secret Garden** — Frances Hodgson Burnett
- **Shiloh** — Phyllis Reynolds Naylor
- **A Single Shard** — Linda Sue Park
- **Sixth Grade Can Really Kill You** — Barthe Declements
- **Surviving the Applewhites** — Stephanie S. Tolan
- **Tuck Everlasting** — Natalie Babbit
- **The 20th Century Children's Poetry Treasury** — Jack Prelutsky
- **The Van Gogh Café** — Cynthia Rylant
- **Walk Two Moons** — Sharon Creech
- **White Fang** — Jack London
- **A Wrinkle in Time** — Madeline L'Engle

Nouns

A **noun** is a word that names a person, place, or thing.

Examples:
    person — friend
    place — home
    thing — desk

Nouns are used many ways in sentences. They can be the subjects of sentences.

Example: Noun as subject: Your high-topped **sneakers** look great with that outfit.

Nouns can be direct objects of a sentence. The **direct object** follows the verb and completes its meaning. It answers the question **who** or **what**.

Example: Noun as direct object: Shelly's family bought a new **car**.

Nouns can be indirect objects. An **indirect object** comes between the verb and the direct object and tells **to whom** or **for whom** something was done.

Example: Noun as indirect object: She gave **Tina** a big hug.

Directions: Underline all the nouns. Write **S** above the noun if it is a subject, **DO** if it is a direct object, or **IO** if it is an indirect object. The first one has been done for you.

       S   DO
1. Do <u>alligators</u> eat <u>people</u>?

2. James hit a home run, and our team won the game.

3. The famous actor gave Susan his autograph.

4. Eric loaned Keith his bicycle.

5. The kindergarten children painted cute pictures.

6. Robin sold David some chocolate chip cookies.

7. The neighbors planned a going-away party and bought a gift.

8. The party and gift surprised Kurt and his family.

9. My scout leader told our group a funny joke.

10. Karen made her little sister a clown costume.

Verbs

A **verb** is the action word in a sentence. It tells what the subject does (**build, laugh, express, fasten**) or that it exists (**is, are, was, were**).

Examples: Randy **raked** the leaves into a pile.
I **was** late to school today.

Directions: In the following sentences, write verbs that make sense.

1. The quarterback _____ the ball to the receiver.

2. My mother _____ some cookies yesterday.

3. John _____ newspapers to make extra money.

4. The teacher _____ the instructions on the board.

5. Last summer, our family _____ a trip to Florida to visit relatives.

Sometimes, a verb can be two or more words. Verbs used to "support" other verbs are called **helping verbs.**

Examples: We **were** listening to music in my room.
Chris **has been** studying for over 2 hours.

Directions: In the following sentences, write helping verbs along with the correct form of the given verbs. The first one has been done for you.

1. Michelle (write) ___*is writing*___ a letter to her grandmother right now.

2. My brother (have) _____ trouble with his math homework.

3. When we arrived, the movie (start) _____ already.

4. My aunt (live) _____ in the same house for 30 years.

5. Our football team (go) _____ to win the national championship this year.

6. My sister (talk) _____ on the phone all afternoon!

7. I couldn't sleep last night because the wind (blow)_____ so hard.

8. Last week, Pat was sick, but now he (feel) _____ much better.

9. Tomorrow, our class (have) _____ a bake sale.

10. Mr. Smith (collect) _____ stamps for 20 years.

Irregular Verbs

Irregular verbs change completely in the past tense. Unlike regular verbs, the past tense forms of irregular verbs are not formed by adding **ed**.

Examples:
Chung **eats** the cookies.
Chung **ate** them yesterday.
Chung **has eaten** them for weeks.

Present Tense	Past Tense	Past Participle
begin	began	has/have/had begun
speak	spoke	has/have/had spoken
drink	drank	has/have/had drunk
know	knew	has/have/had known
eat	ate	has/have/had eaten
wear	wore	has/have/had worn

Directions: Rewrite these sentences once using the past tense and again using the past participle of each verb.

1. Todd begins football practice this week.

   _____

   _____

2. She wears her hair in braids.

   _____

   _____

3. I drink two glasses of milk.

   _____

   _____

4. The man is speaking to us.

   _____

   _____

5. The dogs are eating.

   _____

   _____

Irregular Verbs

The past participle form of an irregular verb needs a helping verb.

Examples:

Present	Past	Past Participle
begin	began	has/have/had begun
drive	drove	has/have/had driven

present, past and past participle

Directions: Write the past and past participle form of these irregular verbs. Use a dictionary if you need help.

Present	Past	Past Participle
1. speak		
2. break		
3. beat		
4. dream		
5. tear		
6. forget		
7. lead		
8. stand		
9. sting		
10. freeze		
11. grow		
12. lose		
13. run		
14. meet		
15. sit		
16. do		

Verb Tenses

Verbs have different forms to show whether something already happened, is happening right now or will happen.

Examples:
   Present tense: I walk.
   Past tense: I walked.
   Future tense: I will walk.

Directions: Write **PAST** if the verb is past tense, **PRES** for present tense, or **FUT** for future tense. The first one has been done for you.

<u>PRES</u> 1. My sister Sara works at the grocery store.

_____ 2. Last year, she worked in an office.

_____ 3. Sara is going to college, too.

_____ 4. She will be a dentist some day.

_____ 5. She says studying is difficult.

_____ 6. Sara hardly studied at all in high school.

_____ 7. I will be ready for college in a few years.

_____ 8. Last night, I read my history book for 2 hours.

Directions: Complete these sentences using verbs in the tenses listed. The first one has been done for you.

9. take: future tense   My friends and I __will take__ a trip.

10. talk: past tense   We _____ for a long time about where to go.

11. want: present tense Pam _____ to go to the lake.

12. want: past tense   Jake _____ to go with us.

13. say: past tense   His parents _____ no.

14. ride: future tense   We _____ our bikes.

15. pack: past tense   Susan and Jared already _____ lunches for us.

Adverbs

Adverbs modify verbs. Adverbs tell **when**, **where**, or **how**. Many, but not all adverbs, end in **ly**.

Adverbs of time answer the questions **how often** or **when**.

Examples:

The dog escapes its pen **frequently**.
Smart travelers **eventually** will learn to use travelers' checks.

Adverbs of place answer the question **where**.

Example: The police pushed bystanders **away** from the accident scene.

Adverbs of manner answer the questions **how** or **in what manner**.

Example: He **carefully** replaced the delicate vase.

Directions: Underline the verb in each sentence. Circle the adverb. Write the question each adverb answers on the line.

1. My grandmother walks gingerly to avoid falls.

   _____

2. The mice darted everywhere to escape the cat.

   _____

3. He decisively moved the chess piece.

   _____

4. Our family frequently enjoys a night at the movies.

   _____

5. Later, we will discuss the consequences of your behavior.

   _____

6. The audience glanced up at the balcony where the noise originated.

   _____

7. The bleachers are already built for the concert.

   _____

8. My friend and I study daily for the upcoming exams.

   _____

Adverbs

Like adjectives, adverbs have types of comparison. They are positive, comparative, and superlative.

Examples:

Positive	**Comparative**	**Superlative**
expertly	more expertly	most expertly
soon	sooner	soonest

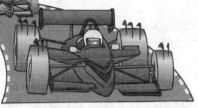

Directions: Underline the adverb in each sentence. Then write the type of comparison on the line.

1. The car easily won the race. _____

2. Our class most eagerly awaited the return of our test. _____

3. My ice cream melted more quickly than yours. _____

4. Frances awoke early the first day of school. _____

5. He knows well the punishment for disobeying his parents. _____

6. There is much work to be done on the stadium project. _____

7. The child played most happily with the building blocks. _____

8. This article appeared more recently than the other. _____

Directions: Write the comparative and superlative forms of these adverbs.

Positive	Comparative	Superlative
9. hard	_____	_____
10. impatiently	_____	_____
11. anxiously	_____	_____
12. suddenly	_____	_____
13. far	_____	_____
14. long	_____	_____

Simple Predicates

The **simple predicate** of a sentence tells what the subject does, is doing, did, or will do. The simple predicate is always a verb.

Example:
My mom **is turning** forty this year.
"Is turning" is the simple predicate.

Directions: Underline the simple predicate in each sentence. Include all helping verbs.

1. I bought school supplies at the mall.

2. The tiger chased its prey.

3. Mark will be arriving shortly.

4. The hamburgers are cooking now.

5. We will attend my sister's wedding.

6. The dental hygienist cleaned my teeth.

7. My socks are hanging on the clothesline.

8. Where are you going?

9. The dog is running toward its owner.

10. Ramos watched the tornado in fear.

11. Please wash the dishes after dinner.

12. My dad cleaned the garage yesterday.

13. We are going hiking at Yellowstone today.

14. The picture shows our entire family at the family picnic.

15. Our coach will give us a pep talk before the game.

Conjunctions

The conjunctions **and, or, but**, and **nor** can be used to make a compound subject, a compound predicate, or a compound sentence.

Examples:
   Compound subject: My friend **and** I will go to the mall.
   Compound predicate: We ran **and** jumped in gym class.
   Compound sentence: I am a talented violinist,
                           but my father is better.

Directions: Write two sentences of your own in each section.

Compound subject:

1. _____

_____

2. _____

_____

Compound predicate:

1. _____

_____

2. _____

_____

Compound sentence:

1. _____

_____

2. _____

_____

Prepositions

A **preposition** is a word that comes before a noun or pronoun and shows the relationship of that noun or pronoun to some other word in the sentence.

The **object of a preposition** is the noun or pronoun that follows a preposition and adds to its meaning.

A **prepositional phrase** includes the preposition, the object of the preposition, and all modifiers.

Example:
She gave him a pat **on his back.**
On is the preposition.
Back is the object of the preposition.
His is a possessive pronoun.

Common Prepositions			
about	down	near	through
above	for	of	to
across	from	off	up
at	in	on	with
behind	into	out	within
by	like	past	without

Directions: Underline the prepositional phrases. Circle the prepositions. Some sentences have more than one prepositional phrase. The first one has been done for you.

1. He claimed he felt (at) home only (on) the West Coast.

2. She went up the street, then down the block.

3. The famous poet was near death.

4. The beautiful birthday card was from her father.

5. He left his wallet at home.

6. Her speech was totally without humor and boring as well.

7. I think he's from New York City.

8. Kari wanted to go with her mother to the mall.

Dangling Modifiers

A **dangling modifier** is a word or group of words that does not modify what it is supposed to modify. To correct dangling modifiers, supply the missing words to which the modifiers refer.

Examples:
  Incorrect: While doing the laundry, the dog barked.
  Correct: While I was doing the laundry, the dog barked.

In the **incorrect** sentence, it sounds as though the dog is doing the laundry. In the **correct** sentence, it's clear that **I** is the subject of the sentence.

Directions: Rewrite the sentences to make the subject of the sentence clear and eliminate dangling modifiers. The first one has been done for you.

1. While eating our hot dogs, the doctor called.

   <u>While we were eating our hot dogs, the doctor called.</u>

2. Living in Cincinnati, the ball park is nearby.

   _____

3. While watching the movie, the TV screen went blank.

   _____

4. While listening to the concert, the lights went out.

   _____

5. Tossed regularly, anyone can make great salad.

   _____

6. While working, something surprised him.

   _____

Appositives

An **appositive** is a noun or pronoun placed after another noun or pronoun to further identify or rename it. An appositive and the words that go with it are usually set off from the rest of the sentence with commas. Commas are not used if the appositive tells "which one."

Example: Angela's mother, **Ms. Glover**, will visit our school.

Commas are needed because **Ms. Glover** renames Angela's mother.

Example: Angela's neighbor Joan will visit our school.

Commas are not needed because the appositive "Joan" tells **which** neighbor.

Directions: Write the appositive in each sentence in the blank. The first one has been done for you.

_____Tina_____ 1. My friend Tina wants a horse.

_____ 2. She subscribes to the magazine *Horses.*

_____ 3. Her horse is the gelding "Brownie."

_____ 4. We rode in her new car, a convertible.

_____ 5. Her gift was jewelry, a bracelet.

_____ 6. Have you met Ms. Abbott, the senator?

_____ 7. My cousin Karl is very shy.

_____ 8. Do you eat the cereal Oaties?

_____ 9. Kiki's cat, Samantha, will eat only tuna.

_____ 10. My last name, Jones, is very common.

Parts of Speech

Directions: Play the following game with a partner. In the story below, some of the words are missing. Without letting your partner see the story, ask him or her to provide a word for each blank. Each word should be a noun, verb, adjective, or adverb, as shown. Then read the story aloud. It might not make sense, but it will make you laugh!

Last night, as I was _____ through the _____ ,
                         (verb + ing)   (noun)

a _____ _____ fell from the ceiling and landed
    (adjective)   (noun)

on my head! "Yikes!" I shrieked. I _____ _____ through
                              (past-tense verb)   (adverb)

the _____ , trying to get rid of the thing. Finally, it fell off, and it
    (noun)

started _____ around the _____ . I tried to hit it with
        (verb + ing)   (noun)

a _____ , but it was too _____ . I _____ managed
  (noun)   (adjective)   (adverb)

to _____ it out of the house, where it quickly climbed the
  (verb)

nearest _____ .
    (noun)

Parts of Speech

Directions: Write each word from the box in the column that names its part of speech. Some words can be listed in two columns.

                            ADJ   ADV
Example: a chair **behind** me   he was walking **behind** me

code	young	slowly	today	finally	screen
thirsty	praise	loan	broken	decrease	slowly
nearby	twenty	Monday	town	faithful	red
coax	goal	bathe	release	cheat	there

Noun	**Verb**	**Adjective**	**Adverb**
_____	_____	_____	_____
_____	_____	_____	_____
_____	_____	_____	_____
_____	_____	_____	_____
_____	_____	_____	_____

Directions: Write four sentences, using at least three words from the box in each one. Mark each word as a noun (**N**), verb (**V**), adjective (**ADJ**), or adverb (**ADV**).

               ADJ   ADV   N
Example: Twenty people **slowly** walked through the **town**.

_____

_____

_____

_____

Parts of Speech

Directions: Identify the part of speech of the words in bold. The first one has been done for you.

1. The dog ran **across** the field. _____preposition_____

2. My **parents** allow me to stay up until 10:00 P.M. _____

3. Our cat **is** long-haired. _____

4. Matt will wash the **dirty** dishes. _____

5. Joseph washed the **car** on Saturday. _____

6. The waterfall crashed **over** the cliff. _____

7. What will you give **her**? _____

8. The car **rolled** to a stop. _____

9. He **slowly** finished his homework. _____

10. My **nephew** will be 12 years old on Sunday. _____

11. The news program discussed the **war**. _____

12. Our **family** portrait was taken in the gazebo. _____

13. I **would like** to learn to fly a plane. _____

14. **My** hair needs to be trimmed. _____

15. **Strawberry** jam is her favorite. _____

16. The horse **quickly** galloped across the field. _____

17. **What** will you do next? _____

18. Please stand **and** introduce yourself. _____

19. My neighbor takes **great** pride in her garden. _____

20. She sang **well** tonight. _____

21. My grandmother is from **Trinidad**. _____

Identifying Sentence Parts

Directions: Write **S** for subject, **P** for predicate, **ADJ** for adjective, or **ADV** for adverb above the appropriate words in these sentences.

1. The large cat pounced on the mouse ferociously.

2. Did you remember your homework?

3. My mother is traveling to New York tomorrow.

4. I play basketball on Monday and Friday afternoons.

5. The old, decrepit house sat at the end of the street.

6. Several tiny rabbits nibbled at the grass at the edge of the field.

7. The lovely bride wore a white dress with a long train.

8. We packed the clothes for the donation center in a box.

9. The telephone rang incessantly.

10. The lost child cried helplessly.

11. What will we do with these new puppies?

12. Lauren reads several books each week.

13. The picture hung precariously on the wall.

14. I purchased many new school supplies.

15. Computers have changed the business world.

Metaphors

A **metaphor** makes a direct comparison between two unlike things. A noun must be used in the comparison. The words **like** and **as** are not used.

Examples:
   Correct: The exuberant puppy was a **bundle of energy.**
   Incorrect: The dog is **happy. (Happy** is an adjective.)

Directions: Circle the two objects being compared.

1. The old truck was a heap of rusty metal.

2. The moon was a silver dollar in the sky.

3. Their vacation was a nightmare.

4. That wasp is a flying menace.

5. The prairie was a carpet of green.

6. The flowers were jewels on stems.

7. This winter, our pond is glass.

8. The clouds were marshmallows.

Directions: Complete the metaphor in each sentence.

9. The ruby was _____.

10. The hospital is _____.

11. The car was _____.

12. This morning when I awoke, I was _____.

13. When my brother is grumpy, he is _____.

14. Her fingers on the piano keys were _____.

Similes

A **simile** is a comparison of two things that have something in common but are really very different. The words **like** and **as** are used in similes.

Examples:
    The baby was **as** happy **as** a lark.
    She is **like** a ray of sunshine to my tired eyes.

Directions: Choose a word from the box to complete each comparison. The first one has been done for you.

tack	grass	fish	mule	ox	rail	hornet	monkey

1. as stubborn as a _____mule_____
2. as strong as an _____
3. swims like a _____
4. as sharp as a _____
5. as thin as a _____
6. as mad as a _____
7. climbs like a _____
8. as green as _____

Directions: Use your own words to complete these similes.

9. as _____ as a tack
10. _____ like a bird
11. as hungry as a _____
12. as white as _____

13. as light as a _____
14. as _____ as honey
15. _____ like a snake
16. as cold as _____

Directions: Use your own similes to complete these sentences.

17. Our new puppy sounded _____.
18. The clouds were _____.
19. Our new car is _____.
20. The watermelon tasted _____.

Common Similes

There are many similes that are used often in the English language. For example, "as frightened as a mouse" is a very common simile. Can you think of others?

Directions: Match the first part of each common simile to the second part. The first one has been done for you.

as slippery as	a mule
as smart as	a statue
as sly as	a rock
as still as	a bee
as quick as	an eel
as slow as	a pancake
as busy as	a whip
as cold as	a turtle
as flat as	a fox
as stubborn as	lIghtning
as hungry as	ice
as hard as	a bear

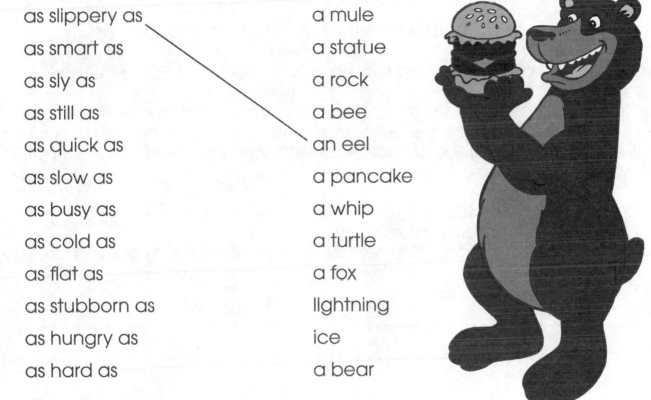

Directions: Write sentences using these common similes.

1. eats like a bird

_____

2. fits like a glove

_____

3. sits there like a bump on a log

_____

4. like a bull in a china shop

_____

5. works like a charm

_____

Similes and Metaphors

Using **similes** and **metaphors** makes writing interesting. They are ways of describing things. **Similes** are comparisons that use **like** or **as**.

Examples: She looked like a frightened mouse.
She looked as frightened as a mouse.

Metaphors are direct comparisons that do not use **like** or **as**.

Example: She was a frightened mouse.

Directions: Rewrite each sentence two different ways to make them more interesting. In the first sentence (a), add at least one adjective and one adverb. In the second sentence (b), compare something in the sentence to something else, using a simile or metaphor.

Example: The baby cried.
a. The sick baby cried softly all night.
b. The baby cried louder and louder, like a storm gaining strength.

1. The stranger arrived.

   a. _____

   b. _____

2. The dog barked.

   a. _____

   b. _____

3. The children danced.

   a. _____

   b. _____

4. The moon rose.

   a. _____

   b. _____

Similes and Metaphors in Poetry

Many poems use similes and metaphors to create a more interesting description of what the poem is about.

Directions: Read the following poems and underline any similes or metaphors you see.

Flint

An emerald is as green as grass,
    A ruby red as blood;
A sapphire shines as blue as heaven;
    A flint lies in the mud.

A diamond is a brilliant stone,
    To catch the world's desire;
An opal holds a fiery spark;
    But a flint holds fire.

                    —Christina Rossettl

The Night Is a Big Black Cat

The night is a big black cat
    The moon is her topaz eye,
The stars are the mice she hunts at night,
    In the field of the sultry sky.

                    —G. Orr Clark

Directions: Now, write your own poem, using at least one simile and one metaphor.

_____

_____

_____

_____

_____

_____

_____

_____

_____

_____

Analogies

Directions: Write your own words on the blanks to complete each analogy. The first one has been done for you.

1. Fuse is to firecracker as wick is to _____ .

2. Wheel is to steering as _____ is to stopping.

3. Scissors are to _____ as needles are to sew.

4. Water is to skiing as rink is to _____ .

5. Steam shovel is to dig as tractor is to _____ .

6. Stick is to hockey as _____ is to baseball.

7. Watch is to television as _____ is to radio.

8. _____ are to goose as children are to child.

9. Multiply is to multiplication as _____ is to subtraction.

10. Milk is to cow as egg is to _____ .

11. Yellow is to banana as _____ is to tomato.

12. _____ is to slow as day is to night.

13. Pine is to tree as _____ is to flower.

14. Zipper is to jacket as _____ is to shirt.

15. Museum is to painting as library is to _____ .

16. Petal is to flower as branch is to _____ .

17. Cow is to barn as car is to _____ .

18. Dresser is to bedroom as _____ is to kitchen.

19. Teacher is to _____ as doctor is to patient.

20. Ice is to cold as fire is to _____ .

Analogies

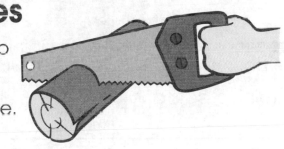

An **analogy** is a way of comparing objects to show how they relate.

Example: Nose is to smell as tongue is to taste.

Directions: Write the correct word on the blank to fill in the missing part of each analogy. The first one has been done for you.

1. <u>Scissors</u> are to paper as saw is to wood.   fold   scissors   thin

2. Man is to boy as woman is to _____ .   mother   girl   lady

3. _____ is to cellar as sky is to ground.   down   attic   up

4. Rag is to dust as _____ is to sweep.   floor   straw   broom

5. Freezer is to cold as stove is to _____ .   cook   hot   recipe

6. Car is to _____ as book is to bookshelf.   ride   gas   garage

7. Window is to _____ as car is to metal.   glass   clear   house

8. Eyes are to seeing as feet are to _____ .   legs   walking   shoes

9. Gas is to car as _____ is to lamp.   electricity   plug   cord

10. Refrigerator is to food as _____ is to clothes.   fold   material   closet

11. Floor is to down as ceiling is to _____ .   high   over   up

12. Pillow is to soft as rock is to _____ .   dirt   hard   hurt

13. Carpenter is to house as poet is to _____ .   verse   novel   writing

14. Lamp is to light as clock is to _____ .   time   hands   numbers

15. _____ is to hand as sole is to foot.   wrist   finger   palm

Idioms

Directions: Use the following idioms in a sentence of your own. Then tell what the phrase means in your own words.

1. raining cats and dogs

   a. _____

   b. _____

2. going to the dogs

   a. _____

   b. _____

3. barking up the wrong tree

   a. _____

   b. _____

4. hit the nail on the head

   a. _____

   b. _____

5. went out on a limb

   a. _____

   b. _____

6. all in the same boat

   a. _____

   b. _____

7. keep up with the Joneses

   a. _____

   b. _____

Direct Objects

A **direct object** is a word or words that follow a transitive verb and complete its meaning. It answers the question **whom** or **what**. Direct objects are always nouns or pronouns.

Examples:
We built a **doghouse. Doghouse** is the direct object. It tells **what** we built.
I called **Mary. Mary** is the direct object. It tells **whom** I called.

Directions: Underline the direct objects.

1. Jean drew a picture of the doghouse.

2. Then we bought some wood at the store.

3. Erin measured each board.

4. Who will saw the wood into boards?

5. Chad hammered nails into the boards.

6. He accidentally hit his thumb with the hammer.

7. Kirsten found some paint in the basement.

8. Should we paint the roof?

9. Will you write Sparky's name above the door?

10. Spell his name correctly.

Directions: Write direct objects to complete these sentences.

11. Will Sparky like _____?

12. When we were finished, we put away _____.

13. We washed out _____.

14. We threw away _____.

15. Then, to celebrate, we ate _____.

Indirect Objects

An **indirect object** is a word or words that come between the verb and the direct object. An indirect object tells **to whom** or **for whom** something has been done. Indirect objects are always nouns or pronouns.

Examples:

She cooked **me** a great dinner. **Me** is the indirect object. It tells **for whom** something was cooked.

Give the **photographer** a smile. **Photographer** is the indirect object. It tells **to whom** the smile should be given.

Directions: Circle the indirect objects. Underline the direct objects.

1. Marla showed me her drawing.

2. The committee had given her an award for it.

3. The principal offered Marla a special place to put her drawing.

4. While babysitting, I read Timmy a story.

5. He told me the end of the story.

6. Then I fixed him some hot chocolate.

7. Timmy gave me a funny look.

8. Why didn't his mother tell me?

9. Hot chocolate gives Timmy a rash.

10. Will his mom still pay me three dollars for watching him?

Directions: Write indirect objects to complete these sentences.

11. I will write _____ a letter.

12. I'll give _____ part of my lunch.

13. Show _____ your model.

14. Did you send _____ a card?

15. Don't tell _____ my secret.

Direct and Indirect Objects

Directions: Underline the direct objects. Circle the indirect objects.

1. Please give him a note card.

2. My father told me a secret.

3. I carefully examined the dinosaur bones.

4. Joseph decorated the banquet hall for the wedding.

5. Every night, I telephone my grandmother.

6. The head of the company offered my father a new position.

7. Too much pizza can give you a stomachache.

8. Will you draw me a picture?

9. This new computer gives me a headache!

10. Thomas discovered a new entrance to the cave.

11. He showed me the rare penny.

12. While watching television, I wrote Marla a letter.

13. Mrs. Fetters will pay me ten dollars for shoveling her sidewalk this winter.

14. The teacher handed her class a surprise quiz.

15. I like to drink iced tea on summer days.

16. Mom bought Sharon new school supplies for kindergarten.

17. I had to pay the library a fine for overdue books.

18. My family enjoys playing football.

19. Each night my mom reads me one chapter of a novel.

20. The teacher gave us our report cards.

"All Right," "All Ready," and "Already"

All right means "well enough" or "very well." Sometimes **all right** is incorrectly spelled. **Alright** is not a word.

Example:
    Correct: We'll be all right when the rain stops.
    Incorrect: Are you feeling **alright** today?

All ready is an adjective meaning "completely ready."

Already is an adverb meaning "before this time" or "by this time."

Examples:
    Are you **all ready** to go?
    He was **already** there when I arrived.

Directions: Write the correct words to complete these sentences.

_____ 1. The children are (all ready/already) for the picnic.

_____ 2. Ted was (all ready/already) late for the show.

_____ 3. Is your sister going to be (all right/alright)?

_____ 4. I was (all ready/already) tired before the race began.

_____ 5. Joan has (all ready/already) left for the dance.

_____ 6. Will you be (all right/alright) by yourself?

_____ 7. We are (all ready/already) for our talent show.

_____ 8. I (all ready/already) read that book.

_____ 9. I want to be (all ready/already) when they get here.

_____ 10. Dad was sick, but he's (all right/alright) now.

_____ 11. The dinner is (all ready/already) to eat.

_____ 12. Cathy (all ready/already) wrote her report.

"Lie" and "Lay"

Lie is a verb meaning "to rest." Lie is an intransitive verb that doesn't need a direct object.

Lay is a verb meaning "to place or put something down." Lay is a transitive verb that requires a direct object.

Examples:
> **Lie** here for a while. (**Lie** has no direct object; **here** is an adverb.)
> **Lay** the book here. (**Lay** has a direct object: **book**.)

Lie and lay are especially tricky because they are both irregular verbs. Notice the past tense of lie is lay!

Present tense	ing form	Past tense	Past participle
lie	lying	lay	has/have/had lain
lay	laying	laid	has/have/had laid

Examples:

I **lie** here today.
I **lay** here yesterday.
I **was lying** there for three hours.

I **lay** the baby in her bed.
I will be **laying** her down in a minute.
I **laid** her in her bed last night, too.

Directions: Write the correct words to complete these sentences.

_____ 1. Shelly (lies/lays) a blanket on the grass.

_____ 2. Then she (lies/lays) down in the sun.

_____ 3. Her dog (lies/lays) there with her.

_____ 4. Yesterday, Shelly (lay/laid) in the sun for an hour.

_____ 5. The workers are (lying/laying) bricks for a house.

_____ 6. Yesterday, they (lay/laid) a ton of them.

_____ 7. They (lie/lay) one brick on top of the other.

_____ 8. The bricks just (lie/lay) in a pile until the workers are ready for them.

_____ 9. At lunchtime, some workers (lie/lay) down for a nap.

_____10. Would you like to (lie/lay) bricks?

_____11. Last year, my uncle (lay/laid) bricks for his new house.

_____12. He was so tired every day that he (lay/laid) down as soon as he finished.

"Amount" and "Number"

Amount indicates quantity, bulk, or mass.

Example: She carried a large **amount** of money in her purse.

Number indicates units.

Example: What **number** of people volunteered to work?

Directions: Write **amount** or **number** in the blanks to complete these sentences correctly. The first one has been done for you.

number   1. She did not (amount/number) him among her closest friends.

_____ 2. What (amount/number) of ice cream should we order?

_____ 3. The (amount/number) of cookies on her plate was three.

_____ 4. His excuses did not (amount/number) to much.

_____ 5. Her contribution (amounted/numbered) to half the money raised.

_____ 6. The (amount/number) of injured players rose every day.

_____ 7. What a huge (amount/number) of cereal!

_____ 8. The (amount/number) of calories in the diet was low.

_____ 9. I can't tell you the (amount/number) of friends she has!

_____ 10. The total (amount/number) of money raised was incredible!

_____ 11. The (amount/number) of gadgets for sale was amazing.

_____ 12. He was startled by the (amount/number) of people present.

_____ 13. He would not do it for any (amount/number) of money.

_____ 14. She offered a great (amount/number) of reasons for her actions.

_____ 15. Can you guess the (amount/number) of beans in the jar?

"Among" and "Between"

Among is a preposition that applies to more than two people or things.

Example: The group divided the cookies **among** themselves.

Between is a preposition that applies to only two people or things.

Example: The cookies were divided **between** Jeremy and Sara.

Directions: Write **between** or **among** in the blanks to complete these sentences correctly. The first one has been done for you.

between   1. The secret is (between/among) you and Jon.

_____ 2. (Between/Among) the two of them, whom do you think is nicer?

_____ 3. I must choose (between/among) the cookies, candy and pie.

_____ 4. She threaded her way (between/among) the kids on the playground.

_____ 5. She broke up a fight (between/among) Josh and Sean.

_____ 6. "What's come (between/among) you two?" she asked.

_____ 7. "I'm (between/among) a rock and a hard place," Josh responded.

_____ 8. "He has to choose (between/among) all his friends," Sean added.

_____ 9. "Are you (between/among) his closest friends?" she asked Sean.

_____ 10. "It's (between/among) another boy and me," Sean replied.

_____ 11. "Can't you settle it (between/among) the group?"

_____ 12. "No," said Josh. "This is (between/among) Sean and me."

_____ 13. "I'm not sure he's (between/among) my closest friends."

_____ 14. Sean, Josh, and Andy began to argue (between/among) themselves.

_____ 15. I hope Josh won't have to choose (between/among) the two!

Denotations and Connotations

Sometimes two words can be similar, yet you would not substitute one for the other because they each suggest different feelings.

Denotation means the literal or dictionary definition of a word.

Connotation is the meaning of a word including all the emotions associated with it.

For example, **job** and **chore** are synonyms, but because of their connotations, anyone would choose to do a job instead of a chore.

Directions: Circle the word in each group with the most positive connotation.

Example:

task	old	retort
(job)	mature	respond
chore	antiquated	react

remainder	haughty	conversational
remnants	cheeky	wordy
residue	proud	talkative

excessively	relaxed	shack
grossly	lazy	hovel
abundantly	inactive	hut

curious	swift	scamp
prying	hasty	rascal
nosy	speedy	hoodlum

"Affect" and "Effect"

Affect means to act upon or influence. It is usually a verb.

Example: Studying will **affect** my test grade.

Effect means a result or an impression. It is usually a noun.

Example: The **effect** of her smile was immediate!

I HOPE ALL THIS STUDYING AFFECTS MY GRADE!

Directions: Write **affect** or **effect** in the blanks to complete these sentences correctly. The first one has been done for you.

affects   1.   Your behavior (affects/effects) how others feel about you.

_____   2.   His (affect/effect) on her was amazing.

_____   3.   The (affect/effect) of his jacket was striking.

_____   4.   What you say won't (affect/effect) me!

_____   5.   There's a relationship between cause and (affect/effect).

_____   6.   The (affect/effect) of her behavior was positive.

_____   7.   The medicine (affected/effected) my stomach.

_____   8.   What was the (affect/effect) of the punishment?

_____   9.   Did his behavior (affect/effect) her performance?

_____   10. The cold (affected/effected) her breathing.

_____   11. The (affect/effect) was instantaneous!

_____   12. Your attitude will (affect/effect) your posture.

_____   13. The (affect/effect) on her posture was major.

_____   14. The (affect/effect) of the colored lights was calming.

_____   15. She (affected/effected) his behavior.

"All Together" and "Altogether"

All together is a phrase meaning everyone or everything in the same place.

Example: We put the eggs **all together** in the bowl.

Altogether is an adverb that means entirely, completely, or in all.

Example: The teacher gave **altogether** too much homework.

THE EGGS ARE ALL TOGETHER

Directions: Write **altogether** or **all together** in the blanks to complete these sentences correctly. The first one has been done for you.

__altogether__ 1. "You ate (altogether/all together) too much food."

_____ 2. The girls sat (altogether/all together) on the bus.

_____ 3. (Altogether/All together) now: one, two, three!

_____ 4. I am (altogether/all together) out of ideas.

_____ 5. We are (altogether/all together) on this project.

_____ 6. "You have on (altogether/all together) too much makeup!"

_____ 7. They were (altogether/all together) on the same team.

_____ 8. (Altogether/All together), we can help stop

        pollution (altogether/all together).

_____ 9. He was not (altogether/all together) happy with his grades.

_____ 10. The kids were (altogether/all together) too loud.

_____ 11. (Altogether/All together), the babies cried gustily.

_____ 12. She was not (altogether/all together) sure what to do.

_____ 13. Let's sing the song (altogether/all together).

_____ 14. He was (altogether/all together) too pushy for her taste.

_____ 15. (Altogether/All together), the boys yelled the school cheer.

"Irritate" and "Aggravate"

Irritate means to cause impatience, to provoke, or annoy.

Example: His behavior **irritated** his father.

Aggravate means to make a condition worse.

Example: Her sunburn was **aggravated** by additional exposure to the sun.

Directions: Write **aggravate** or **irritate** in the blanks to complete these sentences correctly. The first one has been done for you.

aggravated 1. The weeds (aggravated/irritated) his hay fever.

_____ 2. Scratching the bite (aggravated/irritated) his condition.

_____ 3. Her father was (aggravated/irritated) about her low grade in math.

_____ 4. It (aggravated/Irritated) him when she switched TV channels.

_____ 5. Are you (aggravated/irritated) when the cat screeches?

_____ 6. Don't (aggravate/irritate) me like that again!

_____ 7. He was in a state of (aggravation/irritation).

_____ 8. Picking at the scab (aggravates/irritates) a sore.

_____ 9. Whistling (aggravates/irritates) the old grump.

_____ 10. She was (aggravated/irritated) when she learned about it.

_____ 11. "Please don't (aggravate/irritate) your mother," Dad warned.

_____ 12. His asthma was (aggravated/irritated) by too much stress.

_____ 13. Sneezing is sure to (aggravate/irritate) his allergies.

_____ 14. Did you do that just to (aggravate/irritate) me?

_____ 15. Her singing always (aggravated/irritated) her brother.

"Rise" and "Raise"

Rise is a verb meaning "to get up" or "to go up." Rise is an intransitive verb that doesn't need a direct object.

Raise is a verb meaning "to lift" or "to grow." Raise is a transitive verb that requires a direct object.

Examples:
The curtain **rises**.
The girl **raises** her hand.

Raise is a regular verb. Rise is irregular.

Present tense	Past tense	Past participle
rise	rose	has/have/had risen
raise	raised	has/have/had raised

Examples:
The sun **rose** this morning.
The boy **raised** the window higher.

Directions: Write the correct words to complete these sentences.

_____ 1. This bread dough (rises/raises) in an hour.

_____ 2. The landlord will (rise/raise) the rent.

_____ 3. The balloon (rose/raised) into the sky.

_____ 4. My sister (rose/raised) the seat on my bike.

_____ 5. The baby (rose/raised) the spoon to his mouth.

_____ 6. The eagle (rose/raised) out of sight.

_____ 7. The farmer (rises/raises) pigs.

_____ 8. The scouts (rose/raised) the flag.

_____ 9. When the fog (rose/raised), we could see better.

_____ 10. The price of ice cream (rose/raised) again.

_____ 11. The king (rose/raised) the glass to his lips.

_____ 12. (Rise/Raise) the picture on that wall higher.

"Teach" and "Learn"

Teach is a verb meaning "to explain something."
Teach is an irregular verb. Its past tense is **taught**.

Learn is a verb meaning "to gain information."

Examples:

Carrie will **teach** me how to play the piano.
Yesterday, she **taught** me "Chopsticks."

I will **learn** a new song every week.
Yesterday, I **learned** to play "Chopsticks."

Directions: Write the correct words to complete these sentences.

_____ 1. My brother (taught/learned) me how to ice skate.

_____ 2. With his help, I (taught/learned) in three days.

_____ 3. First, I tried to (teach/learn) skating from a book.

_____ 4. I couldn't (teach/learn) that way.

_____ 5. You have to try it before you can really (teach/learn) how to do it.

_____ 6. Now I'm going to (teach/learn) my cousin.

_____ 7. My cousin already (taught/learned) how to roller skate.

_____ 8. I shouldn't have any trouble (teaching/learning) her how to ice skate.

_____ 9. Who (taught/learned) you how to skate?

_____ 10. My brother (taught/learned) Mom how to skate, too.

_____ 11. My mother took longer to (teach/learn) it than I did.

_____ 12. Who will he (teach/learn) next?

_____ 13. Do you know anyone who wants to (teach/learn) how to ice skate?

_____ 14. My brother will (teach/learn) you for free.

_____ 15. You should (teach/learn) how to ice skate in the wintertime, though. The ice is a little thin in the summer!

Quotation Marks

Quotation marks are used to enclose a speaker's exact words. Use commas to set off a direct quotation from other words in the sentence.

Examples:
   Kira smiled and said, "Quotation marks come in handy."
   "Yes," Josh said, "I'll take two."

Directions: If quotation marks and commas are used correctly, write **C** in the blank. If they are used incorrectly, write an **X** in the blank. The first one has been done for you.

___C___ 1. "I suppose," Elizabeth remarked, "that you'll be there on time."

_____ 2. "Please let me help! insisted Mark.

_____ 3. I'll be ready in 2 minutes!" her father said.

_____ 4. "Just breathe slowly," the nurse said, "and calm down."

_____ 5. "No one understands me" William whined.

_____ 6. "Would you like more milk?" Jasmine asked politely.

_____ 7. "No thanks, her grandpa replied, "I have plenty."

_____ 8. "What a beautiful morning!" Jessica yelled.

_____ 9. "Yes, it certainly is" her mother agreed.

_____ 10. "Whose purse is this?" asked Andrea.

_____ 11. It's mine" said Stephanie. "Thank you."

_____ 12. "Can you play the piano?" asked Heather.

_____ 13. "Music is my hobby." Jonathan replied.

_____ 14. Great!" yelled Harry. Let's play some tunes."

_____ 15. "I practice a lot," said Jayne proudly.

"This is exactly what I'm saying! You can tell by my quotation marks!"

Name _____

Quotation Marks

Directions: Use quotation marks and commas to punctuate these sentences correctly.

"Remember: quotation marks are used to enclose a speaker's exact words."

1. No Ms. Elliot replied you may not go.

2. Watch out! yelled the coach.

3. Please bring my coat called Renee.

4. After thinking for a moment, Paul said I don't believe you.

5. Dad said Remember to be home by 9:00 P.M.

6. Finish your projects said the art instructor.

7. Go back instructed Mom and comb your hair.

8. I won't be needing my winter coat anymore replied Mei-ling.

9. He said How did you do that?

10. I stood and said My name is Rosalita.

11. No said Misha I will not attend.

12. Don't forget to put your name on your paper said the teacher.

13. Pay attention class said our history teacher.

14. As I came into the house, Mom called Dinner is almost ready!

15. Jake, come when I call you said Mother.

16. How was your trip to France Mrs. Shaw? asked Deborah.

Dashes

Dashes (—) are used to indicate sudden changes of thought.

Examples:
I want milk—no, make that soda—with my lunch.
Wear your old clothes—new ones would get spoiled.

Directions: If the dash is used correctly in the sentence, write **C** in the blank. If the dash is missing or used incorrectly, draw an **X** in the blank. The first one has been done for you.

___C___ 1. No one—not even my dad—knows about the surprise.

_____ 2. Ask—him—no I will to come to the party.

_____ 3. I'll tell you the answer oh, the phone just rang!

_____ 4. Everyone thought—even her brother—that she looked pretty.

_____ 5. Can you please—oh, forget it!

_____ 6. Just stop it I really mean it!

_____ 7. Tell her that I'll—never mind—I'll tell her myself!

_____ 8. Everyone especially Anna is overwhelmed.

_____ 9. I wish everyone could—forgive me—I'm sorry!

_____ 10. The kids—all six of them—piled into the backseat.

Directions: Write two sentences of your own that include dashes.

11. _____

_____

12. _____

_____

Apostrophes

Use an **apostrophe** (') in a contraction to show that letters have been left out. A **contraction** is a shortened form of two words, usually a pronoun and a verb.

Add an **apostrophe** and **s** to form the **possessive** of singular nouns. **Plural possessives** are formed two ways. If the noun ends in **s**, simply add an apostrophe at the end of the word. If the noun does not end in **s**, add an apostrophe and **s**.

Examples:
   Contraction: He **can't** button his sleeves.
   Singular possessive: The **boy's** sleeves are too short.
   Plural noun ending in s: The **ladies'** voices were pleasant.
   Plural noun not ending in s: The **children's** song was long.

Directions: Use apostrophes to punctuate the sentences correctly. The first one has been done for you.

1. I can't understand that child's game.
2. The farmers wagons were lined up in a row.
3. She didnt like the chairs covers.
4. Our parents beliefs are often our own.
5. Sandys mothers aunt isnt going to visit.
6. Two ladies from work didnt show up.
7. The citizens group wasnt very happy.
8. The colonists demands werent unreasonable.
9. The mothers babies cried at the same time.
10. Our parents generation enjoys music.

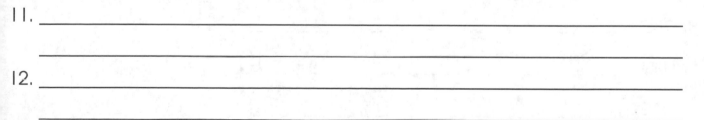

Directions: Write two sentences of your own that include apostrophes.

11. _____

   _____

12. _____

   _____

Singular Possessives

Directions: Write the singular possessive form of each word. Then, add a noun to show possession. The first one has been done for you.

1. spider ___ **spider's web** _____

2. clock _____

3. car _____

4. book _____

5. Mom _____

6. boat _____

7. table _____

8. baby _____

9. woman _____

10. writer _____

11. mouse _____

12. fan _____

13. lamp _____

14. dog _____

15. boy _____

16. house _____

Contractions

Examples:
   he will = **he'll**
   she is = **she's**
   they are = **they're**
   can not = **can't**

Contraction Chart

Pronoun		Verb		Contraction
I	+	am	=	I'm
we, you, they	+	are	=	we're, you're, they're
he, she, it	+	is	=	he's, she's, it's
I, we, you, they	+	have	=	I've, we've, you've, they've
I, you, we, she, he, they	+	would	=	I'd, you'd, we'd, she'd, he'd, they'd
I, you, we, she, he, they	+	will	=	I'll, you'll, we'll, she'll, he'll, they'll

Directions: Write a sentence using a contraction. The first one has been done for you.

1. I will   <u>I'll see you tomorrow!</u> _____

2. they are _____

3. we have _____

4. she would _____

5. you are _____

6. they will _____

7. she is _____

8. he would _____

9. they are _____

10. I am _____

Commas

A **comma** tells a reader where to pause when reading a sentence. Use commas when combining two or more *complete* sentences with a joining word.

Examples: **We raked the leaves,** and **we put them into bags**.
Brian dressed quickly, but **he still missed the school bus**.

Do not use commas if you are not combining complete sentences.

Examples: We raked the leaves and put them into bags.
Brian dressed quickly but still missed the school bus.

If either part of the sentence does not have both a subject and a verb, do not use a comma.

Directions: Read each sentence below and decide whether or not it needs a comma. If it does, rewrite the sentence, placing the comma correctly. If it doesn't, write **O.K.** on the line.

1. The cat stretched lazily and walked out of the room.

   _____

2. I could use the money to buy a new shirt or I could go to the movies.

   _____

3. My sister likes pizza but she doesn't like spaghetti.

   _____

4. Mom mixed the batter and poured it into the pan.

   _____

5. The teacher passed out the tests and she told us to write our names on them.

   _____

6. The car squealed its tires and took off out of the parking lot.

   _____

7. The snow fell heavily and we knew the schools would be closed the next day.

   _____

8. The batter hit the ball and it flew over the fence.

   _____

Punctuation

Directions: Add commas where needed. Put the correct punctuation at the end of each sentence.

1. My friend Jamie loves to snowboard

2. Winter sports such as hockey skiing and skating are fun

3. Oh what a lovely view

4. The map shows the continents of Asia Africa Australia and Antarctica

5. My mother a ballet dancer will perform tonight

6. What will you do tomorrow

7. When will the plane arrive at the airport

8. Jason do you know what time it is

9. Friends of ours the Watsons are coming for dinner

10. Margo look out for that falling rock

11. The young child sat reading a book

12. Who wrote this letter

13. My sister Jill is very neat

14. The trampoline is in our backyard

15. We will have chicken peas rice and salad for dinner

16. That dog a Saint Bernard looks dangerous

Proofreading

Proofreading or "proofing" means to carefully look over what has been written, checking for spelling, grammar, punctuation, and other errors. At a newspaper, this is the job of a copyeditor. All good writers carefully proofread and correct their own work before turning it in to a copyeditor—or a teacher.

Here are three common proofreading marks:

Correct spelling   ~~doi~~ dog

Replace with lower-case letter X̷

Replace with upper-case letter a̲

Directions: Carefully read the following paragraphs. Use proofreading marks to mark errors in the second paragraph. Correct all errors. The first sentence has been done for you.

A six-~~alurm~~ alarm fire at 2121 w̲indsor Terrace on the

northeast side awoke apartment R̷esidents at 3 A.M.

yesterday morning. Elven people were in the biulding.

No one was hurt in the blase, which caused $200,000

of property damage.

Proporty manager Jim smith credits a perfectly Functioning smoke

alurm system for waking residents so they could get out safely. A

springkler system were also in plase. "There was No panick," Smith

said proudly. "Everone was calm and Orderly."

Editing

Directions: Draw a line from the editing mark on the left to its meaning on the right.

coɱplain

Close up a word

The two boys came to class,
The girls, though,

Insert an apostrophe

¶This is the best pie ever.

Insert a comma

~~this~~

Delete a word

copy editor

Transpose words

We went zoo to the,

Transpose letters

There#were two of us in the house.

Insert a space

Once upon a time,there were

Capitalize

leonardo da vinci

Move text down to line below

T/homas was the best.

Change letter to lower-case

The two girls came to class. The two boys never came back until the principal left.

Start a new paragraph

Now I will end the story⊙

Move text up to line above

My mother the best lady I know
was

Insert a period

This is my mother's hat.

Insert a word

Joining Sentences

Conjunctions are words that join sentences, words, or ideas. When two sentences are joined with **and**, they are more or less equal.

Example: Julio is coming, **and** he is bringing cookies.

When two sentences are joined with **but**, the second sentence contradicts the first one.

Example: Julio is coming, **but** he will be late.

When two sentences are joined with **or**, they name a choice.

Example: Julio might bring cookies, **or** he might bring a cake.

When two sentences are joined with **because**, the second one names the reason for the first one.

Example: I'll bring cookies, too, **because** Julio might forget his.

When two sentences are joined with **so**, the second one names a result of the first one.

Example: Julio is bringing cookies, **so** we will have a snack.

Directions: Complete each sentence. The first one has been done for you.

1. We could watch TV, or **we could play a game.** _____

2. I wanted to seize the opportunity, but _____

3. You had better not deceive me, because _____

4. My neighbor was on vacation, so _____

5. Veins take blood back to your heart, and _____

6. You can't always yield to your impulses, because _____

7. I know that is your belief, but _____

8. It could be reindeer on the roof, or _____

9. Brent was determined to achieve his goal, so _____

10. Brittany was proud of her height, because _____

11. We painted the ceiling, and _____

Descriptive Sentences

Descriptive sentences give readers a vivid image and enable them to imagine a scene clearly.

Example:
   Nondescriptive sentence: There were grapes in the bowl.
   Descriptive sentence: The plump purple grapes in the bowl looked tantalizing.

Directions: Rewrite these sentences using descriptive language.

1. The dog walked in its pen.

   _____

2. The turkey was almost done.

   _____

3. I became upset when my computer wouldn't work.

   _____

4. Jared and Michelle went to the ice-cream parlor.

   _____

5. The telephone kept ringing.

   _____

6. I wrote a story.

   _____

7. The movie was excellent.

   _____

8. Dominique was upset that her friend was ill.

   _____

Combining Sentences

When the subjects are the same, sentences can be combined by using appositives.

Examples:

Tony likes to play basketball. Tony is my neighbor.
Tony, **my neighbor**, likes to play basketball.

Ms. Herman was sick today. Ms. Herman is our math teacher.
Ms. Herman, **our math teacher**, was sick today.

Appositives are set off from the rest of the sentence with commas.

Directions: Use commas and appositives to combine the pairs of sentences.

1. Julie has play practice today. Julie is my sister.

   _____

2. Greg fixed my bicycle. Greg is my cousin.

   _____

3. Mr. Scott told us where to meet. Mr. Scott is our coach.

   _____

4. Tiffany is moving to Detroit. Tiffany is my neighbor.

   _____

5. Kyle has the flu. Kyle is my brother.

   _____

6. My favorite football team is playing tonight.   Houston is my favorite team.

   _____

7. Bonnie Pryor will be at our school next week. Bonnie Pryor is a famous author.

   _____

8. Our neighborhood is having a garage sale. Our neighborhood is the North
   End._____

Statements and Questions

A **statement** is a sentence that tells something. It ends with a period (.).

A **question** is a sentence that asks something. It ends with a question mark (?).

Examples:
    Statement: Shari is walking to school today.
    Question: Is Shari walking to school today?

In some questions, the subject comes between two parts of the verb. In the examples below, the subjects are underlined. The verbs and the rest of the predicates are bold.

Examples:
    Is <u>Steve</u> **coming with us**?
    <u>Who</u> **will be there**?
    Which one did <u>you</u> **select**?

To find the predicate, turn a question into a statement.

Example: Is Steve coming with us? Steve is coming with us.

Directions: Write **S** for statement or **Q** for question. Put a period after the statements and a question mark after the questions.

_____ 1. Today is the day for our field trip.

_____ 2. How are we going to get there?

_____ 3. The bus will take us.

_____ 4. Is there room for everyone?

_____ 5. Who forgot to bring a lunch?

_____ 6. I'll save you a seat.

Directions: Circle the subjects and underline all parts of the predicates.

7. Do you like field trips?

8. Did you bring your coat?

9. Will it be cold there?

10. Do you see my gloves anywhere?

11. Is anyone sitting with you?

12. Does the bus driver have a map?

13. Are all the roads this bumpy?

Facts and Opinions

A **fact** is a statement based on truth. It can be proven. **Opinions** are the beliefs of an individual that may or may not be true.

Examples:
 Fact: Alaska is a state.
 Opinion: Alaska is the most magnificent state.

Directions: Write **F** if the statement is a fact. Write **O** if the statement is an opinion.

1. _____ The Grand Canyon is the most scenic site in the United States.

2. _____ Dinosaurs roamed Earth millions of years ago.

3. _____ Scientists have discovered how to clone sheep.

4. _____ All people should attend this fair.

5. _____ Purebreds are the best dogs to own because they are intelligent.

6. _____ Nobody likes being bald.

7. _____ Students should be required to get straight A's to participate in extracurricular activities.

8. _____ Reading is an important skill that is vital in many careers.

9. _____ Snakes do not make good pets.

10. _____ Many books have been written about animals.

11. _____ Thomas Edison invented the lightbulb.

12. _____ Most people like to read science fiction.

13. _____ Insects have three body parts.

Facts and Opinions

A **fact** is information that can be proved.

Example: Hawaii is a state.

An **opinion** is a belief. It tells what someone thinks. It cannot be proved.

Example: Hawaii is the prettiest state.

Directions: Write **f** (fact) or **o** (opinion) on the line by each sentence. The first one has been done for you.

f 1. Hawaii is the only island state.

_____ 2. The best fishing is in Michigan.

_____ 3. It is easy to find a job in Wyoming.

_____ 4. Trenton is the capital of New Jersey.

_____ 5. Kentucky is nicknamed the Bluegrass State.

_____ 6. The friendliest people in the United States live in Georgia.

_____ 7. The cleanest beaches are in California.

_____ 8. Summers are most beautiful in Arizona.

_____ 9. Only one percent of North Dakota is forest or woodland.

_____ 10. New Mexico produces almost half of the nation's uranium.

_____ 11. The first shots of the Civil War were fired in South Carolina on April 12, 1861.

_____ 12. The varied geographical features of Washington include mountains, deserts, a rainforest, and a volcano.

_____ 13. In 1959, Alaska and Hawaii became the 49th and 50th states admitted to the Union.

_____ 14. Wyandotte Cave, one of the largest caves in the United States, is in Indiana.

Directions: Write one fact and one opinion about your own state.

Fact: _____

_____

Opinion: _____

_____

Cause and Effect

Directions: Complete the chart by listing the cause and effect of each weather phenomenon.

	Cause	Effect
Thunderstorms		
Hurricanes		
Tornadoes		
Rainbows		
Precipitation		
Drought		

Venn Diagrams

A **Venn diagram** is used to chart information that shows similarities and differences between two things. The outer part of each circle shows the differences. The intersecting part of the circles shows the similarities.

Example:

Basketball

Played on a court

Points scored through baskets

Five players on a team

Played with a ball

Two teams

Professional sport

Played on a diamond

Points scored through runs

Nine players on a team

Baseball

Directions: Complete the Venn diagram below. Think of at least three things to write in the outer part of each circle (differences) and at least three things to write in the intersecting part (similarities).

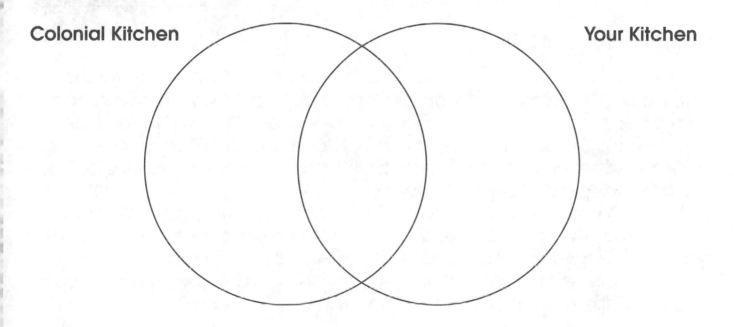

Colonial Kitchen   **Your Kitchen**

Venn Diagrams

You can use a Venn diagram as an organizational tool before writing a compare/contrast essay.

Directions: Review the completed Venn diagram and the compare/contrast essay below.

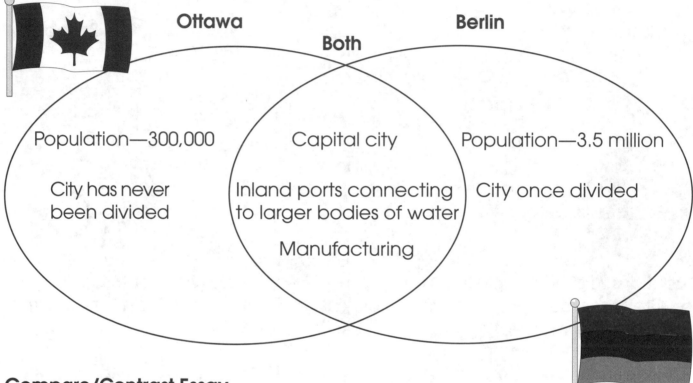

Ottawa

Both

Berlin

Population—300,000

City has never been divided

Capital city

Inland ports connecting to larger bodies of water

Manufacturing

Population—3.5 million

City once divided

Compare/Contrast Essay

Ottawa, Canada, and Berlin, Germany share important characteristics. Ottawa and Berlin are both capital cities in their countries. This means that both cities house the country's federal government. Ottawa has access to Lake Ontario through the Rideau Canal. Inland Harbor in Berlin provides that city's access to the Baltic Sea. Finally, both Ottawa and Berlin are sites for major manufacturing industries that help the economy.

Although Ottawa and Berlin are alike in some ways, in other ways, they are very different. The most obvious difference is in population. Ottawa has 300,000 people, while over 3 million reside in Berlin. Also, Berlin was once divided into East and West sections after World War II, with separate governments and facilities. Ottawa has never been divided.

Following Directions

Directions: Read and follow the directions.

1. Draw a vertical line from the top mid-point of the square to the bottom mid-point of the square.
2. Draw a diagonal line from top left to bottom right of the square.
3. In each of the two triangles, draw a heart.
4. Draw a picture of a cat's face below the square.
5. Draw a horizontal line from the left mid-point to the right mid-point of the square.
6. Draw two intersecting lines in each of the two smaller squares so they are equally divided into four quadrants.
7. Draw a triangle-shaped roof on the square.
8. Draw a circle next to each heart.
9. Write your name in the roof section of your drawing.

Maps

Directions: Read the information about planning a map.

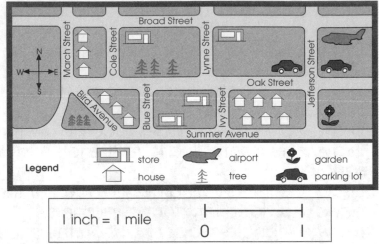

Maps have certain features that help you to read them. A **compass rose** points out directions. Color is often used so you can easily see where one area (such as a county, state, or country) stops and the next starts.

To be accurate, a map must be drawn to scale. The **scale** of a map shows how much area is represented by a given measurement. The scale can be small: one inch = one mile; or large: one inch = 1,000 miles.

Symbols are another map tool. An airplane may represent an airport. Sometimes a symbol does not look like what it represents. Cities are often represented by dots. A map **legend** tells what each symbol means.

One of the best ways to learn about maps is to make one of your own. You may be surprised at how much you learn about your neighborhood, too. You will need a large piece of paper, a ruler, a pencil and colored pencils.

You will need to choose the area you want to map out. It is important to decide on the scale for your map. It could be small: one inch = three feet, if you are mapping out your own backyard. Be sure to include symbols, like a picnic table to represent a park or a flag to represent a school. Don't forget to include the symbols and other important information in your legend.

Directions: Number in order the steps to making your own map.

_____ Figure out the scale that will work best for your map.

_____ Obtain a large piece of paper, ruler, pencil, and colored pencils.

_____ Make a legend explaining the symbols you used.

_____ Draw your map!

_____ Draw symbols to represent features of the area you are mapping.

_____ Decide on the area you want to map out.

Maps

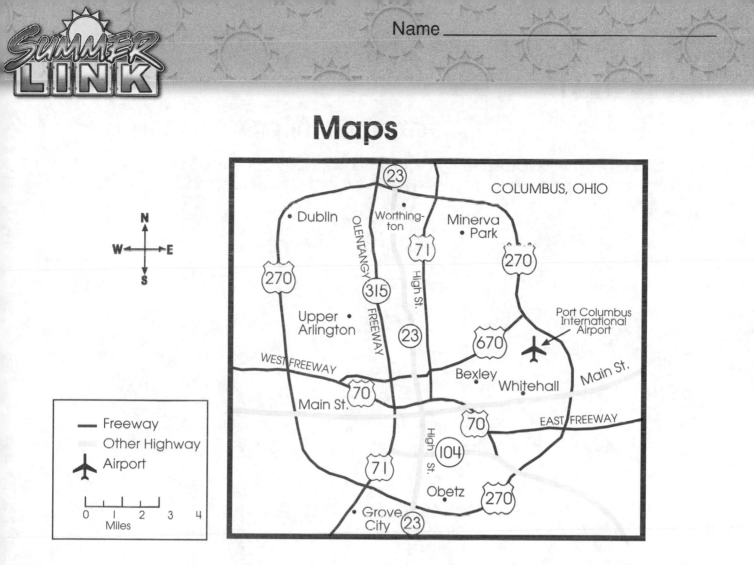

Directions: Use this map of Columbus, Ohio, to answer the questions.

1. Does Highway 104 run east and west or north and south?

_____

2. What is the name of the freeway numbered 315?

_____

3. Which is farther south, Bexley or Whitehall?

_____

4. What two freeways join near the Port Columbus International Airport?

_____

5. Which two suburbs are farther apart, Dublin and Upper Arlington or Dublin and Worthington?_____

6. In which direction would you be traveling if you drove from Grove City to Worthington?_____

Creating a Map

Directions: In the space below, draw a map of your street or town. Be sure to include a compass rose, scale, symbols, and a map legend.

It's Your Opinion

Your opinion is how you feel or think about something. Although other people may have the same opinion, their reasons could not be exactly the same because of their individuality.

When writing an opinion paragraph, it is important to first state your opinion. Then, in at least three sentences, support your opinion. Finally, end your paragraph by restating your opinion in different words.

Example:

   I believe dogs are excellent pets. For thousands of years, dogs have guarded and protected their owners. Dogs are faithful and have been known to save the lives of those they love. Dogs offer unconditional love as well as company for the quiet times in our lives. For these reasons, I feel that dogs make wonderful pets.

Directions: Write an opinion paragraph on whether you would or would not like to have lived in Colonial America. Be sure to support your opinion with at least three reasons.

_____

_____

_____

_____

_____

_____

Writing Checklist

Reread your paragraph carefully.

☐ My paragraph makes sense.   ☐ I have a good opening and ending.

☐ There are no jumps in ideas.   ☐ I used correct spelling.

☐ I used correct punctuation.   ☐ My paragraph is well-organized.

                    ☐ My paragraph is interesting.

Recalling Details: The Earth's Atmosphere

The most important reason that life can exist on Earth is its atmosphere—the air around us. Without it, plant and animal life could not have developed. There would be no clouds, weather, or even sounds, only a deathlike stillness and an endlessly black sky. Without the protection of the atmosphere, the sun's rays would roast the Earth by day. At night, with no blanketing atmosphere, the stored heat would escape into space, dropping the temperature of the planet hundreds of degrees.

Held captive by Earth's gravity, the atmosphere surrounds the planet to a depth of hundreds of miles. However, all but 1 percent of the atmosphere is in a layer about 20 miles deep just above the surface of the Earth. It is made up of a mixture of gases and dusts. About 78 percent of it is a gas called nitrogen, which is very important as food for plants. Most of the remaining gas, 21 percent, is oxygen, which all people and animals depend on for life. The remaining 1 percent is made up of a blend of other gases—including carbon dioxide, argon, ozone and helium—and tiny dust particles. These particles come from ocean salt crystals, bits of rocks and sand, plant pollen, volcanic ash and even meteor dust.

You may not think of air as matter, as something that can be weighed. In fact, the Earth's air weighs billions and billions of tons. Near the surface of the planet, this "air pressure" is greatest. Right now, about 10 tons of air is pressing in on you. Yet, like the fish living near the floor of the ocean, you don't notice this tremendous weight because your body is built to withstand it.

Directions: Answer these questions about the Earth's atmosphere.

1. What is the atmosphere? _____

2. Of what is the atmosphere made? _____

3. What is the most abundant gas in the atmosphere? _____

4. Which of the atmosphere's gases is most important to humans and animals?

   _____

5. What is air pressure? _____

Recalling Details: Clothing in Colonial Times

The clothing of the colonists varied from the north to the south, accounting for the differences not only in climate, but also in the religions and ancestries of the settlers. The clothes seen most often in the early New England colonies where the Puritans settled were very plain and simple. The materials—wool and linen—were warm and sturdy.

The Puritans had strict rules about clothing. There were no bright colors, jewelry, ruffles, or lace. A Puritan woman wore a long-sleeved gray dress with a big white collar, cuffs, apron, and cap. A Puritan man wore long woolen stockings and baggy leather "breeches," which were knee-length trousers. Adults and children dressed in the same style of clothing.

In the middle colonies, the clothing ranged from the simple clothing of the Quakers to the colorful, loose-fitting outfits of the Dutch colonists. Dutch women wore more colorful outfits than Puritan women, with many petticoats and fur trim. The men had silver buckles on their shoes and wore big hats decked with curling feathers.

In the southern colonies, where there were no religious restrictions against fancy clothes, wealthy men wore brightly colored breeches and coats of velvet and satin sent from England. The women's gowns also were made of rich materials and were decorated with ruffles, ribbons, and lace. The poorer people wore clothes similar to the simple dress of the New England Puritans.

Directions: Answer these questions about clothing in colonial times.

1. Why did the clothing of the colonists vary from the north to the south?

   _____

2. Why did the Puritans wear very plain clothing?

   _____

3. What was the nationality of many settlers in the middle colonies?

   _____

4. From what country did wealthy southern colonists obtain their clothing?

   _____

Making Inferences: Cairo

- Cairo is the capital of Egypt.
- Cairo is the largest city of not only Egypt but all of Africa and the Middle East.
- The population of Cairo is almost 7 million people.
- Cairo is the cultural center for the Islamic religion.
- Cairo is a major industrial site for Egypt.
- Cairo is a port on the Nile River near the head of the Nile delta.
- Interesting sites include the Egyptian Museum, the Sphinx, the pyramids, and the City of the Dead.

Directions: Answer these questions about Cairo.

1. All the major cities discussed so far, including Cairo, have a seaport. Historically speaking, what is the importance of having access to the sea?

_____

_____

_____

2. Cairo has a population of almost 7 million people. What are three problems which could arise from having such a large population?

1) _____

2) _____

3) _____

3. Would you like to visit Cairo? Why or why not? _____

_____

_____

_____

Making Inferences: Ottawa

- Ottawa is the capital of Canada and is located in Ontario.
- The federal government employs most people in the city. Manufacturing is another large employer.
- The Rideau Canal connects Ottawa to Lake Ontario.
- The population of Ottawa is over 300,000 people.
- Points of interest include the Peace Tower, Parliament Buildings, the Royal Canadian Mint and the Canadian Museum of Nature.

Directions: Answer these questions about Ottawa.

1. Who employs the most people in Ottawa, Canada?_____
_____

2. What body of water connects Ottawa to Lake Ontario?_____

3. In order from largest to smallest, list the six cities you have read about and their populations.

_____   _____

_____   _____

_____   _____

_____   _____

_____   _____

_____   _____

4. Canada is the United States' neighbor to the north. What problems could arise due to a shared border?

_____

_____

_____

_____

_____

Comprehension: Rainbows

Although there are some violent, frightening aspects of the weather, there is, of course, considerable beauty, too. The rainbow is one simple, lovely example of nature's atmospheric mysteries.

You usually can see a rainbow when the sun comes out after a rain shower or in the fine spray of a waterfall or fountain. Although sunlight appears to be white, it is actually made up of a mixture of colors— all the colors in the rainbow. We see a rainbow because thousands of tiny raindrops act as mirrors and prisms on the sunlight. Prisms are objects that bend light, splitting it into bands of color.

The bands of color form a perfect semicircle. From the top edge to the bottom, the colors are always in the same order—red, orange, yellow, green, blue, indigo, and violet. The brightness and width of each band may vary from one minute to the next. You also may notice that the sky framed by the rainbow is lighter than the sky above. This is because the light that forms the blue and violet bands is more bent and spread out than the light that forms the top red band.

You will always see morning rainbows in the west, with the sun behind you. Afternoon rainbows, likewise, are always in the east. To see a rainbow, the sun can be no higher than 42 degrees—nearly halfway up the sky. Sometimes, if the sunlight is strong and the water droplets are very small, you can see a double rainbow. This happens because the light is reflected twice in the water droplets. The color bands are fainter and in reverse order in the second band.

Directions: Answer these questions about rainbows.

1. Check the statement that is the main idea.

☐ Although there are violent, frightening aspects of weather, there is considerable beauty, too.

☐ The rainbow is one simple, lovely example of nature's atmospheric mysteries.

2. What is the correct definition for semicircle?

☐ colored circle ☐ diameter of a circle ☐ half circle

3. What is a prism?_____

4. In which direction would you look to see an afternoon rainbow? _____

Name _____

Comprehension: Causes/Effects of Weather

The behavior of the atmosphere, which we experience as weather and climate, affects our lives in many important ways. It is the reason no one lives on the South Pole. It controls when a farmer plants the food we will eat, which crops will be planted and also whether those crops will grow. The weather tells you what clothes to wear and how you will play after school. Weather is the sum of all the conditions of the air that may affect the Earth's surface and its living things. These conditions include the temperature, air pressure, wind and moisture. Climate refers to these conditions but generally applies to larger areas and longer periods of time, such as the annual climate of South America rather than today's weather in Oklahoma City.

Climate is influenced by many factors. It depends first and foremost on latitude. Areas nearest the equator are warm and wet, while the poles are cold and relatively dry. The poles also have extreme seasonal changes, while the areas at the middle latitudes have more moderate climates, neither as cold as the poles nor as hot as the equator. Other circumstances may alter this pattern, however. Land near the oceans, for instance, is generally warmer than inland areas.

Elevation also plays a role in climate. For example, despite the fact that Africa's highest mountain, Kilimanjaro, is just south of the equator, its summit is perpetually covered by snow. In general, high land is cooler and wetter than nearby low land.

Directions: Check the answers to these questions about the causes and effects of weather.

1. What is the correct definition for **atmosphere**?

   ☐ the clouds   ☐ the sky   ☐ where weather occurs

2. What is the correct definition for **foremost**?

   ☐ most important   ☐ highest number   ☐ in the front

3. What is the correct definition for **circumstances**?

   ☐ temperatures   ☐ seasons   ☐ conditions

4. What is the correct definition for **elevation**?

   ☐ height above Earth ☐ nearness to equator ☐ snow covering

5. What is the correct definition for **perpetually**?

   ☐ occasionally   ☐ rarely   ☐ always

Poetry: Free Verse

Poems that do not rhyme and do not have a regular rhythm are called **free verse**. They often use adjectives, adverbs, similes, and metaphors to create word pictures.

My Old Cat
Curled on my bed at night,
Quietly happy to see me,
Soft, sleepy, relaxed,
A calm island in my life.

Directions: Write your own free verse. Use the guidelines for each poem.

1. Write a two-line free verse poem about a feeling. Compare it to some kind of food. For example, anger could be a tangle of spaghetti. Give your poem a title.

   _____

   _____

   _____

2. Think of how someone you know is like a color, happy like yellow, for example. Write a two-line free verse poem on this topic without naming the person. Don't forget a title.

   _____

   _____

   _____

3. Write a four-line free verse poem, like "My Old Cat," that creates a word picture of a day at school

   _____

   _____

   _____

   _____

   _____

Poetry: Haiku

Haiku is a type of unrhymed Japanese poetry with three lines. The first line has five syllables. The second line has seven syllables. The third line has five syllables.

Example:

Katie

Katie is my dog.
She likes to bark and chase balls.
Katie is my friend.

Directions: Write a haiku about a pet and another about a hobby you enjoy.

Be sure to write a title on the first line.

Pet   _____

_____

_____

_____

_____

Hobby   _____

_____

_____

Persuasive Writing

Writing is usually more persuasive if written from the reader's point of view.

If you made cookies to sell at a school fair, which of these sentences would you write on your sign?
1. I spent a lot of time making these cookies.
2. These cookies taste delicious!

If you were writing to ask your school board to start a gymnastics program, which sentence would be more persuasive?
1. I really am interested in gymnastics.
2. Gymnastics would be good for our school because both boys and girls can participate, and it's a year-round sport we can do in any weather.

In both situations, the second sentence is more persuasive because it is written from the reader's point of view. People care how the cookies taste, not how long it took you to make them. The school board wants to provide activities for all the students, not just you.

Directions: Write **R** if the statement is written from the reader's point of view or **W** if it's written from the writer's point of view.

_____ 1. If you come swimming with me, you'll be able to cool off.

_____ 2. Come swimming with me. I don't want to go alone.

_____ 3. Please write me a letter. I really like to get mail.

_____ 4. Please write me a letter. I want to hear from you.

Directions: Follow these steps to write an "invitation" on another sheet of paper to persuade people to move to your town or city.

1. Think about reasons someone would want to live in your town. Make a list of all the good things there, like the schools, parks, annual parades, historic buildings, businesses where parents could work, scout groups, Little League, and so on. You might also describe your town's population, transportation, restaurants, celebrations, or even holiday decorations.
2. Now, select three or four items from your list. Write a sentence (or two) about each one from the reader's point of view. For example, instead of writing "Our Little League team won the championship again last year," you could tell the reader, "You could help our Little League team win the championship again this year."
3. Write a topic sentence to begin your invitation, and put your support sentences in order after it.
4. Read your invitation out loud to another person. Make any needed changes, and copy the invitation onto a clean sheet of paper.

Creative Writing: Washington, D.C.

- Washington, D.C. is the capital of the United States.
- The population of Washington, D.C. is over 600,000 people in the city itself. Many people who work in Washington, D.C. reside in suburbs of the city in Virginia and Maryland.
- One-third of the people employed in Washington, D.C. work for the federal government.
- The Potomac and Anacostia Rivers join in Washington, D.C.
- Interesting sites include the White House, the Vietnam Veterans Memorial, the Lincoln Memorial, the Washington Monument, and the United States Capitol Building.

Directions: Using the above information, create a tourist article describing Washington, D.C. Do some research and add other interesting information.

_____

_____

_____

_____

_____

When you think of Washington, D.C., what comes to mind?_____

_____

_____

Would you like to visit Washington, D.C.? Why or why not?_____

_____

_____

Writing From a Prompt

Directions: Write an opinion essay in response to the prompt.

Writing Prompt: Think about rainforests. What is the importance of preserving the rainforests of the world? What problems could arise if there were no longer any rainforest areas? What problems could arise for humans due to the preservation of rainforests? How do rainforests affect you?

_____

_____

_____

_____

_____

_____

_____

_____

_____

_____

Directions: When you finish writing, reread your essay. Use this checklist to help make corrections.

☐ I have used correct spelling, grammar, and punctuation.

☐ I have no sentence fragments.

☐ My essay makes sense.

☐ I wrote complete sentences.

☐ I have no run-on sentences.

☐ I answered the prompt.

Writing: Just the Facts

Some forms of writing, such as reports and essays, contain opinions that are supported by the writer. In other kinds of writing, however, it is important to stick to the facts. Newspaper reporters, for example, must use only facts when they write their stories.

Directions: Read the following newspaper story about a fire, and underline the sentences or parts of sentences that are opinions. Then rewrite the story in your own words, giving only the facts.

At around 10:30 p.m. last night, a fire broke out in a house at 413 Wilshire Boulevard. The house is in a very nice neighborhood, surrounded by beautiful trees. The family of four who lives in the house was alerted by smoke alarms, and they all exited the house safely, although they must have been very frightened. Firefighters arrived on the scene at approximately 10:45 p.m., and it took them over 3 hours to extinguish the blaze. The firefighters were very courageous. The cause of the fire has not yet been determined, although faulty electric wiring is suspected. People should have their electric wiring checked regularly. The family is staying with relatives until repairs to their home can be made, and they are probably very anxious to move back into their house.

_____

_____

_____

_____

_____

_____

_____

_____

_____

_____

_____

Friendly Letters

Directions: Study the format for writing a letter to a friend. Then answer the questions.

your return address

date

123 Waverly Road
Cincinnati, Ohio 45241
June 23, 1999

greeting

Dear Josh,

body

How is your summer going? I am enjoying mine so far. I have been swimming twice already this week, and it's only Wednesday! I am glad there is a pool near our house.

My parents said that you can stay overnight when your family comes for the 4th of July picnic. Do you want to? We can pitch a tent in the back yard and camp out. It will be a lot of fun!

Please write back to let me know if you can stay over on the 4th. I will see you then!

closing
signature

Your friend,
Michael

your return address

Michael Delaney
123 Waverly Road
Cincinnati, Ohio 45241

main address

Josh Sommers
2250 West First Ave.
Columbus, OH 43212

1. What words are in the greeting? _____

2. What words are in the closing?_____

3. On what street does the writer live? _____

Friendly Letters

Directions: Write a friendly letter. Then address the envelope.

Newswriting: Inverted Pyramid Style

Newspaper reporters organize their news stories in what is called the **inverted pyramid** style. The inverted pyramid places the most important facts at the beginning of the story—called the lead (LEED)—and the least important facts at the end.

There are two practical reasons for this approach:

1) If the story must be shortened by an editor, he or she simply cuts paragraphs from the end of the story rather than rewriting the entire story.

2) Because newspapers contain so much information, few people read every word of every newspaper story. Instead, many readers skim headlines and opening paragraphs. The inverted pyramid style of writing enables readers to quickly get the basics of what the story is about without reading the entire story.

Directions: Read the news story. Then answer the questions.

> Cleveland—Ohio State University student John Cook is within one 36-hole match of joining some of amateur golf's top performers. The 21-year-old Muirfield Village Golf Club representative will try for his second straight U.S. Amateur championship Sunday against one of his California golf buddies, Mark O'Meara, over the 6,837-yard Canterbury Golf Club course. Starting times are 8 a.m. and 12:30 p.m.
>
> "Winning the U.S. Amateur once is a great thrill," said Cook after Saturday's breezy 5-3 semifinal decision over Alabama's Cecil Ingram III. "But winning the second time is something people don't very often do."

1. Who is the story about? _____

2. The "dateline" at the beginning of a news article tells where the event happened and where the reporter wrote the story. Where was the story about John Cook written?

   _____

3. What is Cook trying to accomplish? _____

   _____

4. Who did Cook beat on Saturday? _____

5. Which of the above paragraphs could be cut by an editor? _____

Writing: You're the Reporter

Directions: Now, write your own short newspaper story about an interesting event that occurred at your school or in your neighborhood. Find out who and what the story Is about, where and when it happened, and why and how it happened. Take some notes, interview some of the people involved, and write your story. Give your story a title, and remember to stick to the facts! In the box, draw a picture (or "photo") to go with your story.

_____

_____

_____

_____

_____

_____

_____

_____

_____

_____

_____

_____

_____

_____

_____

_____

_____

Personal Narratives

A **narrative** is a spoken or written account of an actual event. A **personal narrative** tells about your own experience. It can be written about any event in your life and may be serious or comical.

When writing a personal narrative, remember to use correct sentence structure and punctuation. Include important dates, sights, sounds, smells, tastes, and feelings to give your reader a clear picture of the event.

Directions: Write a personal narrative about an event in your life that was funny.

_____

_____

_____

_____

_____

_____

_____

_____

_____

_____

_____

_____

_____

_____

_____

_____

Complete the Story

Directions: Read the beginning of this story. Then complete the story with your own ideas.

It was a beautiful summer day in June when my family and I set off on vacation. We were headed for Portsmouth, New Hampshire. There we planned to go on a whale-watching ship and perhaps spy a humpback whale or two. However, there were many miles between our home and Portsmouth.

We camped at many lovely parks along the way to New Hampshire. We stayed in the Adirondack Mountains for a few days and then visited the White Mountains of Vermont before crossing into New Hampshire.

My family enjoys tent camping. My dad says you can't really get a taste of the great outdoors in a pop-up camper or RV. I love sitting by the fire at night, gazing at the stars and listening to the animal noises.

The trip was going well, and everyone was enjoying our vacation. We made it to Portsmouth and were looking forward to the whale-watching adventure. We arrived at the dock a few minutes early. The ocean looked rough, but we had taken seasickness medication. We thought we were prepared for any kind of weather.

_____

_____

_____

_____

_____

_____

_____

_____

Glossary of Reading and Language Arts Terms

adjective: a describing word that tells more about a noun

adverb: tells when, where, or how about the verb of a sentence

antonym: words with opposite, or nearly opposite, meanings

articles: any one of the words *a*, *an*, or *the* used to modify a noun

autobiography: a written account of your life

base word (also called root word): the word left after you take off a prefix or a suffix

character: a person, animal, or object that a story is about

climax: the most thrilling part of the story where the problem will or will not be solved

compound word: a word formed by two or more words

conclusion: a final decision about something, or the part of a story that tells what happens to the characters

conjunction: words that join other words, phrases, and sentences

contraction: shortened forms of two words often using an apostrophe to show where letters are missing

dialogue: a conversation between two or more people

digraph: two consonants pronounced as one sound

diphthongs: two vowels together that make a new sound

fact: something known to be true

fiction: stories that are made up

homophone: a word with the same pronunciation as another, but with a different meaning, and often a different spelling, such as son–sun

idiom: a figure of speech or phrase that means something different than what the words actually say, such as "He changed his bad habits and *turned over a new leaf*"

metaphor: a direct comparison that does not use *like* or *as*

mood: the atmosphere one gets from strong, descriptive language

nonfiction: stories that are true

noun: a word that names a person, place, or thing

opinion: a belief based on what a person thinks instead of what is known to be true

paraphrasing: restating something in your own words

plot: explains the events in a story that create a problem

plural: a form of a word that names or refers to more than one person or thing

point of view: the attitude a person has about a particular topic

prefix: a part that is added to the beginning of a word that changes the word's meaning

preposition: a word that comes before a noun or pronoun, showing the relationship of that noun or pronoun to another word in the sentence

pronoun: a word that is used in place of a noun

proofreading: reading to find and correct errors

punctuation: the marks that qualify sentences, such as a period, comma, question mark, exclamation point, and apostrophe

reading strategies: main idea, supporting details, context clues, fact/opinion

resolution: tells how the characters solve the story problem

setting: the place and time that a story happens

simile: a comparison using *like* or *as*

suffix: a part added to the end of a word to change the word's meaning

synonym: words that mean the same, or almost the same, thing

theme: a message or central idea ot the story

variable: a letter used to represent a number value in an expression or an equation

verb: a word that can show action

verb tense: tells whether the action is happening in the past, present, or future

Nouns

A **noun** is a word that names a person, place, or thing.

Examples:
person — friend
place — home
thing — desk

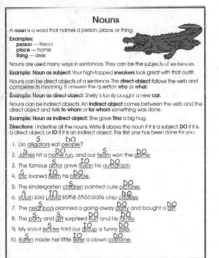

Nouns are used many ways in sentences. They can be the subjects of sentences.

Example: Noun as subject: Your high-topped **sneakers** look great with that outfit.

Nouns can be direct objects of a sentence. The **direct object** follows the verb and completes its meaning. It answers the question who or what.

Example: Noun as direct object: Shelly's family bought a new **car**.

Nouns can be indirect objects. An **indirect object** comes between the verb and the direct object and tells to whom or for whom something was done.

Example: Noun as indirect object: She gave **Tina** a big hug.

Directions: Underline all the nouns. Write **S** above the noun if it is a subject, **DO** if it is a direct object, or **IO** if it is an indirect object. The first one has been done for you.

1. Do alligators eat people?
2. James hit a home run, and our team won the game.
3. The famous actor gave Susan his autograph.
4. Eric loaned Keith his bicycle.
5. The kindergarten children painted cute pictures.
6. Robin sold Olivia some chocolate chip cookies.
7. The neighbors planned a going-away party and bought a gift.
8. The party and gift surprised Kurt and his family.
9. My scout leader told our group a funny joke.
10. Karen made her little sister a clown costume.

Verbs

A **verb** is the action word in a sentence. It tells what the subject does (build, laugh, express, fasten) or that it exists (is, are, was, were).

Examples: Randy raked the leaves into a pile.
I was late to school today.

Answers may include:

Directions: In the following sentences, write verbs that make sense.

1. The quarterback **threw** the ball to the receiver.
2. My mother **baked** some cookies yesterday.
3. John **sold** newspapers to make extra money.
4. The teacher **wrote** the instructions on the board.
5. Last summer, our family **took** a trip to Florida to visit relatives.

Sometimes, a verb can be two or more words. Verbs used to "support" other verbs are called **helping verbs**.

Examples: We **were** listening to music in my room.
Chris **has been** studying for over 2 hours.

Directions: In the following sentences, write helping verbs along with the correct form of the given verbs. The first one has been done for you.

1. Michelle (write) **is writing** a letter to her grandmother right now.
2. My brother (have) **is having** trouble with his math homework.
3. When we arrived, the movie (start) **had started** already.
4. My aunt (live) **has lived** in the same house for 30 years.
5. Our football team (go) **is going** to win the national championship this year.
6. My sister (talk) **has been talking** on the phone all afternoon!
7. I couldn't sleep last night because the wind (blow) **was blowing** so hard.
8. Last week, Pat was sick, but now he (feel) **is feeling** much better.
9. Tomorrow, our class (have) **will have** a bake sale.
10. Mr. Smith (collect) **has collected** stamps for 20 years.

Irregular Verbs

Irregular verbs change completely in the past tense. Unlike regular verbs, the past tense forms of irregular verbs are not formed by adding **ed**.

Examples:
Chung **eats** the cookies.
Chung **ate** them yesterday.
Chung **has eaten** them for weeks.

Present Tense	Past Tense	Past Participle
begin	began	has/have/had begun
speak	spoke	has/have/had spoken
drink	drank	has/have/had drunk
know	knew	has/have/had known
eat	ate	has/have/had eaten
wear	wore	has/have/had worn

Directions: Rewrite these sentences once using the past tense and again using the past participle of each verb.

1. Todd begins football practice this week.
Todd began football practice this week.
Todd has begun football practice this week.
2. She wears her hair in braids.
She wore her hair in braids.
She had worn her hair in braids.
3. I drink two glasses of milk.
I drank two glasses of milk.
I have drunk two glasses of milk.
4. The man is speaking to us.
The man spoke to us.
The man has spoken to us.
5. The dogs are eating.
The dogs ate.
The dogs have eaten.

Irregular Verbs

The past participle form of an irregular verb needs a helping verb.

present, past and past participle

Examples:
Present	Past	Past Participle
begin	began	has/have/had begun
drive	drove	has/have/had driven

Directions: Write the past and past participle form of these irregular verbs. Use a dictionary if you need help.

	Present	Past	Past Participle
1.	speak	spoke	has/have/had spoken
2.	break	broke	has/have/had broken
3.	beat	beat	has/have/had beaten
4.	dream	dreamed	has/have/had dreamed
5.	tear	tore	has/have/had torn
6.	forget	forgot	has/have/had forgotten
7.	lead	led	has/have/had led
8.	stand	stood	has/have/had stood
9.	sting	stung	has/have/had stung
10.	freeze	froze	has/have/had frozen
11.	grow	grew	has/have/had grown
12.	lose	lost	has/have/had lost
13.	run	ran	has/have/had run
14.	meet	met	has/have/had met
15.	sit	sat	has/have/had sat
16.	do	did	has/have/had done

Verb Tenses

Verbs have different forms to show whether something already happened, is happening right now or will happen.

Examples:
Present tense: I walk.
Past tense: I walked.
Future tense: I will walk.

Directions: Write **PAST** if the verb is past tense, **PRES** for present tense, or **FUT** for future tense. The first one has been done for you.

PRES 1. My sister Sara works at the grocery store.
PAST 2. Last year, she worked in an office.
PRES 3. Sara is going to college, too.
FUT 4. She will be a dentist some day.
PRES 5. She says studying is difficult.
PAST 6. Sara hardly studied at all in high school.
FUT 7. I will be ready for college in a few years.
PAST 8. Last night, I read my history book for 2 hours.

Directions: Complete these sentences using verbs in the tenses listed. The first one has been done for you.

9. take: future tense   My friends and I **will take** a trip.
10. talk: past tense   We **talked** for a long time about where to go.
11. want: present tense   Pam **wants** to go to the lake.
12. want: past tense   Jake **wanted** to go with us.
13. say: past tense   His parents **said** no.
14. ride: future tense   We **will ride** our bikes.
15. pack: past tense   Susan and Jared already **packed** lunches for us.

Adverbs

Adverbs modify verbs. Adverbs tell **when**, **where**, or **how**. Many, but not all adverbs, end in **ly**.

Adverbs of time answer the questions how often or when.

Examples:
The dog escapes its pen **frequently**.
Smart travelers **eventually** will learn to use travelers' checks.

Adverbs of place answer the question **where**.

Example: The police pushed bystanders **away** from the accident scene.

Adverbs of manner answer the questions how or in what manner.

Example: He **carefully** replaced the delicate vase.

Directions: Underline the verb in each sentence. Circle the adverb. Write the question each adverb answers on the line.

1. My grandmother walks gingerly to avoid falls.
how or in what manner
2. The mice darted everywhere to escape the cat.
where
3. He decisively moved the chess piece.
how or in what manner
4. Our family frequently enjoys a night at the movies.
how often or when
5. Later, we will discuss the consequences of your behavior.
when
6. The audience glanced up at the balcony where the noise originated.
where
7. The bleachers are already built for the concert.
when
8. My friend and I study daily for the upcoming exams.
how often or when

Adverbs

Like adjectives, adverbs have types of comparison. They are positive, comparative, and superlative.

Examples:
Positive	Comparative	Superlative
expertly	more expertly	most expertly
soon	sooner	soonest

Directions: Underline the adverb in each sentence, then write the type of comparison on the line.

1. The car easily won the race. **positive**
2. Our class most eagerly awaited the return of our test. **superlative**
3. My ice cream melted more quickly than yours. **comparative**
4. Frances awoke early the first day of school. **positive**
5. He knows well the punishment for disobeying his parents. **positive**
6. There is much work to be done on the stadium project. **positive**
7. The child played most happily with the building blocks. **superlative**
8. This article appeared more recently than the other. **comparative**

Directions: Write the comparative and superlative forms of these adverbs.

	Positive	Comparative	Superlative
9.	hard	harder	hardest
10.	impatiently	more impatiently	most impatiently
11.	anxiously	more anxiously	most anxiously
12.	suddenly	more suddenly	most suddenly
13.	far	farther	farthest
14.	long	longer	longest

Simple Predicates

The **simple predicate** of a sentence tells what the subject does, is doing, did or will do. The simple predicate is always a verb.

Example:
My mom is turning forty this year.
"Is turning" is the simple predicate.

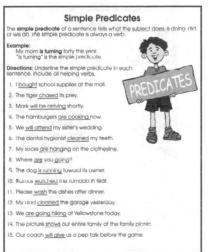

Directions: Underline the simple predicate in each sentence. Include all helping verbs.

1. I bought school supplies at the mall.
2. The tiger chased its prey.
3. Mark will be arriving shortly.
4. The hamburgers are cooking now.
5. We will attend my sister's wedding.
6. The dental hygienist cleaned my teeth.
7. My socks are hanging on the clothesline.
8. Where are you going?
9. The dog is running toward its owner.
10. Rufus watched the tornado in fear.
11. Please wash the dishes after dinner.
12. My dad cleaned the garage yesterday.
13. We are going hiking at Yellowstone today.
14. The picture shows our entire family at the family picnic.
15. Our coach will give us a pep talk before the game.

Conjunctions

The conjunctions **and**, **or**, **but**, and **nor** can be used to make a compound subject, a compound predicate, or a compound sentence.

Examples:
Compound subject: My friend **and** I will go to the mall.
Compound predicate: We ran **and** jumped in gym class.
Compound sentence: I am a talented violinist, **but** my flute is better.

Directions: Write two sentences of your own in each section.

Compound subject:
1. _____
2. _____

Compound predicate:
1. _____
2. _____

Answers Will Vary.

Compound sentence:
1. _____
2. _____

Page 110

Prepositions

A **preposition** is a word that comes before a noun or pronoun and shows the relationship of that noun or pronoun to some other word in the sentence.

The **object of a preposition** is the noun or pronoun that follows a preposition and adds to its meaning.

A **prepositional phrase** includes the preposition, the object of the preposition, and all modifiers.

Example:
She gave him a pat **on his back.**
On is the preposition.
Back is the object of the preposition.
His is a possessive pronoun.

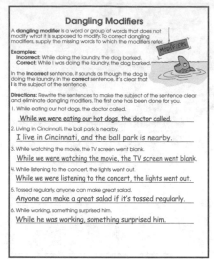

Common Prepositions			
about	down	near	through
above	for	of	to
across	from	off	up
at	in	on	with
behind	into	out	within
by	like	past	without

Directions: Underline the prepositional phrases. Circle the prepositions. Some sentences have more than one prepositional phrase. The first one has been done for you.

1. He claimed he felt (at) home only (on) the West Coast.
2. She went (up) the street, then (down) the block.
3. The famous poet was (near) death.
4. The beautiful birthday card was (from) her father.
5. He left his wallet (at) home.
6. Her speech was totally (without) humor and boring as well.
7. I think he's (from) New York City.
8. Karl wanted (to) go (with) her mother (to) the mall.

Page 111

Dangling Modifiers

A **dangling modifier** is a word or group of words that does not modify what it is supposed to modify. To correct dangling modifiers, supply the missing words to which the modifiers refer.

Examples:
Incorrect: While doing the laundry, the dog barked.
Correct: While I was doing the laundry, the dog barked.

In the **incorrect** sentence, it sounds as though the dog is doing the laundry. In the **correct** sentence, it's clear that I is the subject of the sentence.

Directions: Rewrite the sentences to make the subject of the sentence clear and eliminate dangling modifiers. The first one has been done for you.

1. While eating our hot dogs, the doctor called.
   While we were eating our hot dogs, the doctor called.
2. Living in Cincinnati, the ball park is nearby.
   I live in Cincinnati, and the ball park is nearby.
3. While watching the movie, the TV screen went blank.
   While we were watching the movie, the TV screen went blank.
4. While listening to the concert, the lights went out.
   While we were listening to the concert, the lights went out.
5. Tossed regularly, anyone can make great salad.
   Anyone can make a great salad if it's tossed regularly.
6. While working, something surprised him.
   While he was working, something surprised him.

Page 112

Appositives

An **appositive** is a noun or pronoun placed after another noun or pronoun to further identify or rename it. An appositive and the words that go with it are usually set off from the rest of the sentence with commas. Commas are not used if the appositive tells "which one."

Example: Angela's mother, Ms. Glover, will visit our school.

Commas are needed because **Ms. Glover** renames Angela's mother.

Example: Angela's neighbor Joan will visit our school.

Commas are not needed because the appositive "Joan" tells **which** neighbor.

Directions: Write the appositive in each sentence in the blank. The first one has been done for you.

Tina	1. My friend Tina wants a horse.
Horses	2. She subscribes to the magazine *Horses*.
"Brownie"	3. Her horse is the gelding "Brownie."
convertible	4. We rode in her new car, a convertible.
bracelet	5. Her gift was jewelry, a bracelet.
senator	6. Have you met Ms. Abbott, the senator?
Karl	7. My cousin Karl is very shy.
Oaties	8. Do you eat the cereal Oaties?
Samantha	9. Kiki's cat, Samantha, will eat only tuna.
Jones	10. My last name, Jones, is very common.

Page 113

Parts of Speech

Directions: Play the following game with a partner. In the story below, some of the words are missing. Without letting your partner see the story, ask him or her to provide a word for each blank. Each word should be a noun, verb, adjective, or adverb, as shown. Then read the story aloud. It might not make sense, but it will make you laugh!

Last night, as I was _____ (verb + ing) through the _____ (noun), a _____ (adjective) _____ and landed on my head! "Yikes!" I shr_____ _____ through the _____ (noun) _____ (verb) to get rid of the thing. Finally, it fell off, and it started _____ (verb + ing) around the _____ (noun). I tried to hit it with a _____ (noun), but it was too _____ (adjective) and _____ (adverb). I managed to _____ (verb) it out of the house, where it quickly climbed the nearest _____ (noun).

Answers will vary.

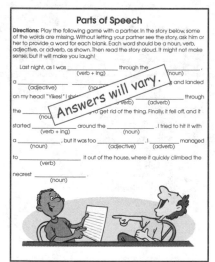

Page 114

Parts of Speech

Directions: Write each word from the box in the column that names its part of speech. Some words can be listed in two columns.

Example: a chair **behind** me — ADJ   he was walking **behind** me — ADV

code	young	slowly	today	finally	screen
thirsty	praise	loan	broken	decrease	slowly
nearby	twenty	Monday	town	faithful	red
coax	goal	bathe	release	cheat	there

Answers will vary but may include:

Noun	Verb	Adjective	Adverb
code	coax	thirsty	nearby
goal	praise	young	slowly
loan	cheat	twenty	today
Monday	bathe	broken	finally
screen	release	red	slowly
town	decrease	faithful	there

Directions: Write four sentences, using at least three words from the box in each one. Mark each word as a noun (**N**), verb (**V**), adjective (**ADJ**), or adverb (**ADV**).

Example: **Twenty** people **slowly** walked through the **town**.
               ADJ   ADV   N

Sentences will vary.

Page 115

Parts of Speech

Directions: Identify the part of speech of the words in bold. The first one has been done for you.

1. The dog ran **across** the field.	preposition
2. My **parents** allow me to stay up until 10:00 PM.	noun as subject
3. Our cat **is** long-haired.	verb
4. Matt will wash the **dirty** dishes.	adjective
5. Joseph washed the **car** on Saturday.	noun as direct object
6. The waterfall crashed **over** the cliff.	preposition
7. What will you give **her**?	personal pronoun
8. The car **rolled** to a stop.	verb
9. He **slowly** finished his homework.	adverb
10. My **nephew** will be 12 years old on Sunday.	noun as subject
11. The news program discussed the **war**.	noun as direct object
12. Our **family** portrait was taken in the gazebo.	adjective
13. I would **like** to learn to fly a plane.	verb
14. **My** hair needs to be trimmed.	possessive pronoun
15. **Strawberry** jam is her favorite.	adjective
16. The horse **quickly** galloped across the field.	adverb
17. **What** will you do next?	interrogative pronoun
18. Please stand **and** introduce yourself.	conjunction
19. My neighbor takes **great** pride in her garden.	adjective
20. She sang **well** tonight.	adverb
21. My grandmother is from **Trinidad**.	noun as object of preposition

Page 116

Identifying Sentence Parts

Directions: Write **S** for subject, **P** for predicate, **ADJ** for adjective, or **ADV** for adverb above the appropriate words in these sentences.

1. The large cat pounced on the mouse ferociously. (ADJ S P ADV)
2. Did you remember your homework? (P S P)
3. My mother is traveling to New York tomorrow. (S P ADV)
4. I play basketball on Monday and Friday afternoons. (S P ADJ ADJ)
5. The old, decrepit house sat at the end of the street. (ADJ ADJ S P)
6. Several tiny rabbits nibbled at the grass at the edge of the field. (ADJ ADJ S P)
7. The lovely bride wore a white dress with a long train. (ADJ S P ADJ ADJ)
8. We packed the clothes for the donation center in a box. (S P ADJ)
9. The telephone rang incessantly. (S P ADV)
10. The lost child cried helplessly. (ADJ S P ADV)
11. What will we do with these new puppies? (P S P ADJ ADJ)
12. Lauren reads several books each week. (S P ADJ ADV)
13. The picture hung precariously on the wall. (S P ADV)
14. I purchased many new school supplies. (S P ADJ)
15. Computers have changed the business world. (S P ADJ)

Page 117

Metaphors

A **metaphor** makes a direct comparison between two unlike things. A noun must be used in the comparison. The words **like** and **as** are not used.

Examples:
Correct: The exuberant puppy was a **bundle of energy**.
Incorrect: The dog is **happy**. (Happy is an adjective.)

Directions: Circle the two objects being compared.

1. (The old truck) was (a heap of rusty metal).
2. (The moon) was (a silver dollar in the sky).
3. (Their vacation) was (a nightmare).
4. (That wasp) is (a flying menace).
5. (The prairie) was (a carpet of green).
6. (The flowers) were (jewels on stems).
7. This winter, (our pond) is (glass).
8. (The clouds) were (marshmallows).

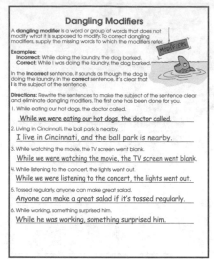

Directions: Complete the metaphor in each sentence.

9. The ruby was _____
10. The hospital is _____
11. The car was _____
12. This morn_____ _____
13. When my _____ grumpy, he is _____
14. Her fingers on the piano keys were _____

Answers will vary.

Page 118

Similes

A **simile** is a comparison of two things that have something in common but are really very different. The words **like** and **as** are used in similes.

Examples:
The baby was **as** happy **as** a lark.
She is **like** a ray of sunshine to my tired eyes.

Directions: Choose a word from the box to complete each comparison. The first one has been done for you.

tack	grass	fish	mule	ox	rail	hornet	monkey

1. as stubborn as a   mule
2. as strong as an   ox
3. swims like a   fish
4. as sharp as a   tack
5. as thin as a   rail
6. as mad as a   hornet
7. climbs like a   monkey
8. as green as   grass

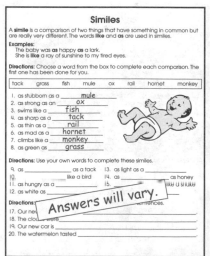

Directions: Use your own words to complete these similes.

9. as _____ as a tack
10. _____ like a bird
11. as hungry as a _____
12. as white as _____
13. as light as a _____
14. as _____ as free
15. _____ like a snake

Answers will vary.

Directions: _____ sentences.

17. Our new _____
18. The clou____ _____
19. Our new car is _____
20. The watermelon tasted _____

Answers will vary.

Page 119

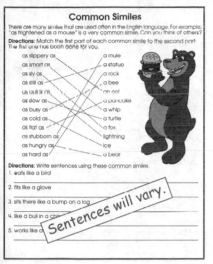

Common Similes

There are many similes that are used often in the English language. For example, "as frightened as a mouse" is a very common simile. Can you think of others?

Directions: Match the first part of each common simile to the second part. The first one has been done for you.

as slippery as	a mule
as smart as	a statue
as sly as	a rock
as still as	a bee
as quick as	an eel
as slow as	a pancake
as busy as	a whip
as cold as	a turtle
as flat as	a fox
as stubborn as	lightning
as hungry as	ice
as hard as	a bear

Directions: Write sentences using these common similes.

1. eats like a bird

2. fits like a glove

3. sits there like a bump on a log

4. like a bull in a chi___

5. works like a ___

Sentences will vary.

Page 120

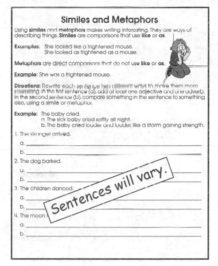

Similes and Metaphors

Using **similes** and **metaphors** makes writing interesting. They are ways of describing things. **Similes** are comparisons that use **like** or **as**.

Example: She looked like a frightened mouse.
She looked as frightened as a mouse.

Metaphors are direct comparisons that do not use **like** or **as**.

Example: She was a frightened mouse.

Directions: Rewrite each sentence two different ways to make them more interesting. In the first sentence (a), add at least one adjective and one adverb. In the second sentence (b), compare something in the sentence to something else, using a simile or metaphor.

Example: The baby cried.
a. The sick baby cried softly all night.
b. The baby cried louder and louder, like a storm gaining strength.

1. The stranger arrived.
a.
b.

2. The dog barked.
a.
b.

3. The children danced.
a.
b.

4. The moon
a.
b.

Sentences will vary.

Page 121

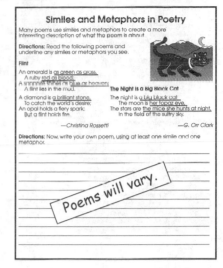

Similes and Metaphors in Poetry

Many poems use similes and metaphors to create a more interesting description of what the poem is about.

Directions: Read the following poems and underline any similes or metaphors you see.

Flint

An emerald is as green as grass,
A ruby red as blood;
A sapphire shines as blue as heaven;
A flint lies in the mud.

A diamond is a brilliant stone,
To catch the world's desire;
An opal holds a fiery spark;
But a flint holds fire.

—Christina Rossetti

The Night is a Big Black Cat

The night is a big black cat
The moon is her topaz eye,
The stars are the mice she hunts at night,
In the field of the sultry sky.

—G. Orr Clark

Directions: Now, write your own poem, using at least one simile and one metaphor.

Poems will vary.

Page 122

Analogies

Directions: Write your own words on the blanks to complete each analogy. The first one has been done for you.

Answers will vary. Examples given.

1. Fuse is to firecracker as wick is to ___candle___.
2. Wheel is to steering as ___brake___ is to stopping.
3. Scissors are to ___cut___ as needles are to sew.
4. Water is to skiing as rink is to ___skating___.
5. Steam shovel is to dig as tractor is to ___plow___.
6. Stick is to hockey as ___bat___ is to baseball.
7. Watch is to television as ___listen___ is to radio.
8. ___Geese___ are to goose as children are to child.
9. Multiply is to multiplication as ___subtract___ is to subtraction.
10. Milk is to cow as egg is to ___hen___.
11. Yellow is to banana as ___red___ is to tomato.
12. ___Fast___ is to slow as day is to night.
13. Pine is to tree as ___daisy___ is to flower.
14. Zipper is to jacket as ___button___ is to shirt.
15. Museum is to painting as library is to ___book___.
16. Petal is to flower as branch is to ___tree___.
17. Cow is to barn as car is to ___garage___.
18. Dresser is to bedroom as ___stove___ is to kitchen.
19. Teacher is to ___student___ as doctor is to patient.
20. Ice is to cold as fire is to ___hot___.

Page 123

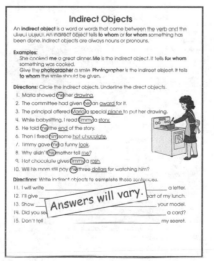

Analogies

An **analogy** is a way of comparing objects to show how they relate.

Example: Nose is to smell as tongue is to taste.

Directions: Write the correct word on the blank to fill in the missing part of each analogy. The first one has been done for you.

1. Scissors are to paper as saw is to wood.		fold	(scissors)	thin
2. Man is to boy as woman is to ___girl___.		mother	(girl)	lady
3. ___Attic___ is to cellar as sky is to ground.		down	(attic)	up
4. Rag is to dust as ___broom___ is to sweep.		floor	(broom)	straw
5. Freezer is to cold as stove is to ___hot___.		cook	(hot)	recipe
6. Car is to ___garage___ as book is to bookshelf.		ride	car	(garage)
7. Window is to ___glass___ as car is to metal.		(glass)	clear	house
8. Eyes are to seeing as feet are to ___walking___.		legs	(walking)	shoes
9. Gas is to car as ___electricity___ is to lamp.		(electricity)	plug	cord
10. Refrigerator is to food as ___closet___ is to clothes.		fold	material	(closet)
11. Floor is to down as ceiling is to ___up___.		high	over	(up)
12. Pillow is to soft as rock is to ___hard___.		dirt	(hard)	hurt
13. Carpenter is to house as poet is to ___verse___.		(verse)	novel	writing
14. Lamp is to light as clock is to ___time___.		(time)	hands	numbers
15. ___Palm___ is to hand as sole is to foot.		wrist	finger	(palm)

Page 124

Idioms

Directions: Use the following idioms in a sentence of your own. Then tell what the phrase means in your own words.

Sentences will vary.

1. raining cats and dogs
a.
b. raining very hard

2. going to the dogs
a.
b. getting run down, deteriorating

3. barking up the wrong tree
a.
b. asking the wrong person, searching in the wrong place

4. hit the nail on the head
a.
b. got the exact right idea

5. went out on a limb
a.
b. took a chance

6. all in the same boat
a.
b. all in the same situation

7. keep up with the Joneses
a.
b. keep up with the people around you

Page 125

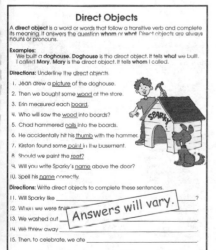

Direct Objects

A **direct object** is a word or words that follow a transitive verb and complete its meaning. It answers the question **whom** or **what**. Direct objects are always nouns or pronouns.

Examples:
We built a **doghouse**. Doghouse is the direct object. It tells **what** we built.
I called **Mary**. Mary is the direct object. It tells **whom** I called.

Directions: Underline the direct objects.

1. Jean drew a picture of the doghouse.
2. Then we bought wood at the store.
3. Erin measured each board.
4. Who will saw the wood into boards?
5. Chad hammered nails into the boards.
6. He accidentally hit his thumb with the hammer.
7. Kirsten found some paint in the basement.
8. Should we paint the roof?
9. Will you write Sparky's name above the door?
10. Spell his name correctly.

Directions: Write direct objects to complete these sentences.

Answers will vary.

11. Will Sparky like ___?
12. When we were finished, we ___.
13. We washed out ___.
14. We threw away ___.
15. Then, to celebrate, we ate ___.

Page 126

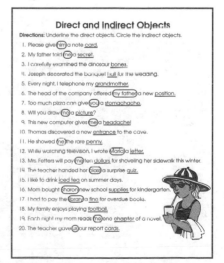

Indirect Objects

An **indirect object** tells **to whom** or **for whom** something has been done. Indirect objects are always nouns or pronouns.

Examples:
She cooked **me** a great dinner. Me is the indirect object. It tells **for whom** something was cooked.
Give the **photographer** a smile. Photographer is the indirect object. It tells **to whom** the smile should be given.

Directions: Circle the indirect objects. Underline the direct objects.

1. Maria showed (her) her drawing.
2. The committee had given (her) an award for it.
3. The principal offered (Maria) a special place to put her drawing.
4. While babysitting, I read (Timmy) a story.
5. He told (me) the end of the story.
6. Then I fixed (him) some hot chocolate.
7. Timmy gave (me) a funny look.
8. Why didn't (his) mother tell (me)?
9. Hot chocolate gives (Timmy) a rash.
10. Will his mom still pay (me) three dollars for watching him?

Directions: Write indirect objects to complete these sentences.

11. I will write ___ a letter.
12. I'll give ___ part of my model.
13. Show ___.
14. Did you se ___ a card?
15. Don't tell ___ my secret.

Answers will vary.

Page 127

Direct and Indirect Objects

Directions: Underline the direct objects. Circle the indirect objects.

1. Please give (him) a note card.
2. My father told (me) a secret.
3. I carefully examined the dinosaur bones.
4. Joseph decorated the banquet hall for the wedding.
5. Every night, I telephone my grandmother.
6. The head of the company offered (my father) a new position.
7. Too much pizza can give (you) a stomachache.
8. Will you draw (me) a picture?
9. This new computer gives (me) a headache.
10. Thomas discovered a new entrance to the cave.
11. He showed (me) the rare penny.
12. While watching television, I wrote (Maria) a letter.
13. Mrs. Fetters will pay (me) ten dollars for shoveling her sidewalk this winter.
14. The teacher handed her class a surprise quiz.
15. I like to drink iced tea on summer days.
16. Mom bought (Sharon) new school supplies for kindergarten.
17. I had to pay the library a fine for overdue books.
18. My family enjoys playing football.
19. Each night my mom reads (me) one chapter of a novel.
20. The teacher gave (us) our report cards.

Summer Link Super Edition Grade 6

Summer Link

Page 128

"All Right," "All Ready," and "Already"

All right means "well enough" or "very well." Sometimes **all right** is incorrectly spelled. **Alright** is not a word.

Example:
Correct: We'll be **all right** when the rain stops.
Incorrect: Are you feeling **alright** today?

All ready is an adjective meaning "completely ready."

Already is an adverb meaning "before this time" or "by this time."

Examples:
Are you **all ready** to go?
He was **already** there when I arrived.

Directions: Write the correct words to complete these sentences.

all ready 1. The children are (all ready/already) for the picnic.
already 2. Ted was (all ready/already) late for the show.
all right 3. Is your sister going to be (all right/alright)?
already 4. I was (all ready/already) tired before the race began.
already 5. Joan has (all ready/already) left for the dance.
all right 6. Will you be (all right/alright) by yourself?
all ready 7. We are (all ready/already) for our talent show.
already 8. I (all ready/already) read that book.
all ready 9. I want to be (all ready/already) when they get here.
all right 10. Dad was sick, but he's (all right/alright) now.
all ready 11. The dinner is (all ready/already) to eat.
already 12. Cathy (all ready/already) wrote her report.

Page 129

"Lie" and "Lay"

Lie is a verb meaning "to rest." Lie is an intransitive verb that doesn't need a direct object.

Lay is a verb meaning "to place or put something down." Lay is a transitive verb that requires a direct object.

Examples:
Lie here for a while. (**Lie** has no direct object; **here** is an adverb.)
Lay the book here. (**Lay** has a direct object: **book**.)

Lie and lay are especially tricky because they are both irregular verbs. Notice the past tense of lie is lay!

Present tense	Ing form	Past tense	Past participle
lie	lying	lay	has/have/had lain
lay	laying	laid	has/have/had laid

Examples:
I **lie** here today. I **lay** the baby in her bed.
I **lay** here yesterday. I will be **laying** her down in a minute.
I **was lying** there for three hours. I **laid** her in her bed last night, too.

Directions: Write the correct words to complete these sentences.

lays 1. Shelly (lies/lays) a blanket on the grass.
lies 2. Then she (lies/lays) down in the sun.
lies 3. Her dog (lies/lays) there with her.
laid 4. Yesterday, Shelly (lay/laid) in the sun for an hour.
laying 5. The workers are (lying/laying) bricks for a house.
laid 6. Yesterday, they (lay/laid) a ton of them.
lay 7. They (lie/lay) one brick on top of the other.
lay 8. The bricks just (lie/lay) in a pile until the workers are ready for them.
lie 9. At lunchtime, some workers (lie/lay) down for a nap.
lay 10. Would you like to (lie/lay) bricks?
laid 11. Last year, my uncle (lay/laid) bricks for his new house.
laid 12. He was so tired every day that he (lay/laid) down as soon as he finished.

Page 130

"Amount" and "Number"

Amount indicates quantity, bulk, or mass.

Example: She carried a large **amount** of money in her purse.

Number indicates units.

Example: What **number** of people volunteered to work?

Directions: Write **amount** or **number** in the blanks to complete these sentences correctly. The first one has been done for you.

number 1. She did not (amount/number) him among her closest friends.
amount 2. What (amount/number) of ice cream should we order?
number 3. The (amount/number) of cookies on her plate was three.
amount 4. His excuses did not (amount/number) to much.
amounted 5. Her contribution (amounted/numbered) to half the money raised.
number 6. The (amount/number) of injured players rose every day.
amount 7. What a huge (amount/number) of cereal!
number 8. The (amount/number) of calories in the diet was low.
number 9. I can't tell you the (amount/number) of friends she has!
amount 10. The total (amount/number) of money raised was incredible!
number 11. The (amount/number) of gadgets for sale was amazing.
number 12. He was startled by the (amount/number) of people present.
amount 13. He would not do it for any (amount/number) of money.
number 14. She offered a great (amount/number) of reasons for her actions.
number 15. Can you guess the (amount/number) of beans in the jar?

Page 131

"Among" and "Between"

Among is a preposition that applies to more than two people or things.

Example: The group divided the cookies **among** themselves.

Between is a preposition that applies to only two people or things.

Example: The cookies were divided **between** Jeremy and Sara.

Directions: Write **between** or **among** in the blanks to complete these sentences correctly. The first one has been done for you.

between 1. The secret is (between/among) you and Jon.
Between 2. (Between/Among) the two of them, whom do you think is nicer?
among 3. I must choose (between/among) the cookies, candy and pie.
among 4. She threaded her way (between/among) the kids on the playground.
between 5. She broke up a fight (between/among) Josh and Sean.
between 6. "What's come (between/among) you two?" she asked.
between 7. "I'm (between/among) a rock and a hard place," Josh responded.
among 8. "He has to choose (between/among) all his friends," Sean added.
among 9. "Are you (between/among) his closest friends?" she asked Sean.
between 10. "It's (between/among) another boy and me," Sean replied.
among 11. "Can't you settle it (between/among) the group?"
between 12. "No," said Josh. "This is (between/among) Sean and me."
among 13. "I'm not sure he's (between/among) my closest friends."
among 14. Sean, Josh, and Andy began to argue (between/among) themselves.
between 15. I hope Josh won't have to choose (between/among) the two!

Page 132

Denotations and Connotations

Sometimes two words can be similar, yet you would not substitute one for the other because they each suggest different feelings.

Denotation means the literal or dictionary definition of a word.

Connotation is the meaning of a word including all the emotions associated with it.

For example, **job** and **chore** are synonyms, but because of their connotations, anyone would choose to do a job instead of a chore.

Directions: Circle the word in each group with the most positive connotation.

Example:

task	old	retort
(job)	(mature)	(respond)
chore	antiquated	react
(remainder)	haughty	(conversational)
remnants	cheeky	wordy
residue	(proud)	talkative
excessively	(relaxed)	shack
grossly	lazy	hovel
(abundantly)	inactive	(hut)
(curious)	(swift)	(scamp)
prying	hasty	rascal
nosy	speedy	hoodlum

Page 133

"Affect" and "Effect"

Affect means to act upon or influence. It is usually a verb.

Example: Studying will **affect** my test grade.

Effect means a result or an impression. It is usually a noun.

Example: The **effect** of her smile was immediate!

Directions: Write **affect** or **effect** in the blanks to complete these sentences correctly. The first one has been done for you.

affects 1. Your behavior (affects/effects) how others feel about you.
effect 2. His (affect/effect) on her was amazing.
effect 3. The (affect/effect) of his jacket was striking.
affect 4. What you say won't (affect/effect) me!
effect 5. There's a relationship between cause and (affect/effect).
effect 6. The (affect/effect) of her behavior was positive.
affected 7. The medicine (affected/effected) my stomach.
effect 8. What was the (affect/effect) of the punishment?
affect 9. Did his behavior (affect/effect) her performance?
affected 10. The cold (affected/effected) her breathing.
effect 11. The (affect/effect) was instantaneous!
affect 12. Your attitude will (affect/effect) your posture.
effect 13. The (affect/effect) on her posture was major.
effect 14. The (affect/effect) of the colored lights was calming.
affected 15. She (affected/effected) his behavior.

Page 134

"All Together" and "Altogether"

All together is a phrase meaning everyone or everything in the same place.

Example: We put the eggs **all together** in the bowl.

Altogether is an adverb that means entirely, completely, or in all.

Example: The teacher gave **altogether** too much homework.

Directions: Write **altogether** or **all together** in the blanks to complete these sentences correctly. The first one has been done for you.

altogether 1. "You ate (altogether/all together) too much food."
all together 2. The girls sat (altogether/all together) on the bus.
All together 3. (Altogether/All together) now: one, two, three!
altogether 4. I am (altogether/all together) out of ideas.
all together 5. We are (altogether/all together) on this project.
altogether 6. "You have on (altogether/all together) too much makeup!"
all together 7. They were (altogether/all together) on the same team.
All together 8. (Altogether/All together), we can help stop pollution (altogether/all together).
altogether
altogether 9. He was not (altogether/all together) happy with his grades.
altogether 10. The kids were (altogether/all together) too loud.
All together 11. (Altogether/All together), the babies cried gustily.
altogether 12. She was not (altogether/all together) sure what to do.
all together 13. Let's sing the song (altogether/all together).
altogether 14. He was (altogether/all together) too pushy for her taste.
All together 15. (Altogether/All together), the boys yelled the school cheer.

Page 135

"Irritate" and "Aggravate"

Irritate means to cause impatience, to provoke, or annoy.

Example: His behavior **irritated** his father.

Aggravate means to make a condition worse.

Example: Her sunburn was **aggravated** by additional exposure to the sun.

Directions: Write **aggravate** or **irritate** in the blanks to complete these sentences correctly. The first one has been done for you.

aggravated 1. The weeds (aggravated/irritated) his hay fever.
aggravated 2. Scratching the bite (aggravated/irritated) his condition.
irritated 3. Her father was (aggravated/irritated) about her low grade in math.
irritated 4. It (aggravated/irritated) him when she switched TV channels.
irritated 5. Are you (aggravated/irritated) when the cat screeches?
irritate 6. Don't (aggravate/irritate) me like that again!
irritation 7. He was in a state of (aggravation/irritation).
aggravates 8. Picking at the scab (aggravates/irritates) a sore.
irritates 9. Whistling (aggravates/irritates) the old grump.
irritated 10. She was (aggravated/irritated) when she learned about it.
irritate 11. "Please don't (aggravate/irritate) your mother," Dad warned.
aggravated 12. His asthma was (aggravated/irritated) by too much stress.
aggravate 13. Sneezing is sure to (aggravate/irritate) his allergies.
irritate 14. Did you do that just to (aggravate/irritate) me?
irritated 15. Her singing always (aggravated/irritated) her brother.

Page 136

"Rise" and "Raise"

Rise is a verb meaning "to get up" or "to go up." Rise is an intransitive verb that doesn't need a direct object.

Raise is a verb meaning "to lift" or "to grow." Raise is a transitive verb that requires a direct object.

Examples:
The curtain **rises**.
The girl **raises** her hand.

Raise is a regular verb. Rise is irregular.

Present tense	Past tense	Past participle
rise	rose	has/have/had risen
raise	raised	has/have/had raised

Examples:
The sun **rose** this morning.
The boy **raised** the window higher.

Directions: Write the correct words to complete these sentences.

rises 1. This bread dough (rises/raises) in an hour.
raise 2. The landlord will (rise/raise) the rent.
rose 3. The balloon (rose/raised) into the sky.
raised 4. My sister (rose/raised) the seat on my bike.
raised 5. The baby (rose/raised) the spoon to his mouth.
rose 6. The eagle (rose/raised) out of sight.
raises 7. The farmer (rises/raises) pigs.
raised 8. The scouts (rose/raised) the flag.
rose 9. When the fog (rose/raised), we could see better.
rose 10. The price of ice cream (rose/raised) again.
raised 11. The king (rose/raised) the glass to his lips.
Raise 12. (Rise/Raise) the picture on that wall higher.

Page 137

"Teach" and "Learn"

Teach is a verb meaning "to explain something."
Teach is an irregular verb. Its past tense is **taught**.

Learn is a verb meaning "to gain information."

Examples:
Carrie will **teach** me how to play the piano.
Yesterday, she **taught** me "Chopsticks."

I will **learn** a new song every week.
Yesterday, I **learned** to play "Chopsticks."

Directions: Write the correct words to complete these sentences.

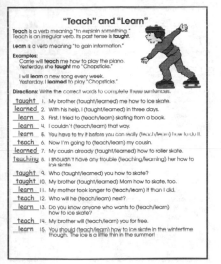

1. _taught_ My brother (taught/learned) me how to ice skate.
2. _learned_ With his help, I (taught/learned) in three days.
3. _learn_ First, I tried to (teach/learn) skating from a book.
4. _learn_ I couldn't (teach/learn) that way.
5. _learn_ You have to try it before you can really (teach/learn) how to do it.
6. _teach_ Now I'm going to (teach/learn) my cousin.
7. _learned_ My cousin already (taught/learned) how to roller skate.
8. _teaching_ I shouldn't have any trouble (teaching/learning) her how to ice skate.
9. _taught_ Who (taught/learned) you how to skate?
10. _taught_ My brother (taught/learned) Mom how to skate, too.
11. _learn_ My mother took longer to (teach/learn) it than I did.
12. _teach_ Who will he (teach/learn) next?
13. _learn_ Do you know anyone who wants to (teach/learn) how to ice skate?
14. _teach_ My brother will (teach/learn) you for free.
15. _learn_ You should (teach/learn) how to ice skate in the wintertime though. The ice is a little thin in the summer!

Page 138

Quotation Marks

Quotation marks are used to enclose a speaker's exact words. Use commas to set off a direct quotation from other words in the sentence.

Examples:
Kira smiled and said, "Quotation marks come in handy."
"Yes," Josh said, "I'll take two."

Directions: If quotation marks and commas are used correctly, write **C** in the blank. If they are used incorrectly, write an **X** in the blank. The first one has been done for you.

_C_ 1. "I suppose," Elizabeth remarked, "that you'll be there on time."
_X_ 2. "Please let me help! insisted Mark.
_X_ 3. I'll be ready in 2 minutes!" her father said.
_C_ 4. "Just breathe slowly," the nurse said, "and calm down."
_X_ 5. "No one understands me" William whined.
_C_ 6. "Would you like more milk?" Jasmine asked politely.
_X_ 7. No thanks, her grandpa replied. "I have plenty."
_C_ 8. "What a beautiful morning!" Jessica yelled.
_X_ 9. "Yes, it certainly is" her mother agreed.
_C_ 10. "Whose purse is this?" asked Andrea.
_X_ 11. "It's mine" said Stephanie. "Thank you."
_C_ 12. "Can you play the piano?" asked Heather.
_X_ 13. "Music is my hobby." Jonathan replied.
_X_ 14. Great!" yelled Harry. Let's play some tunes."
_C_ 15. "I practice a lot," said Jayne proudly.

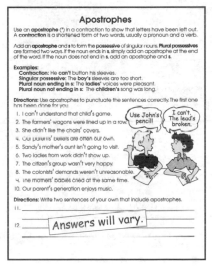

"This is exactly what I'm saying! You can tell by my quotation marks!"

Page 139

Quotation Marks

Directions: Use quotation marks and commas to punctuate these sentences correctly.

"Remember: quotation marks are used to enclose a speaker's exact words."

1. "No," Ms. Elliot replied, "you may not go."
2. "Watch out!" yelled the coach.
3. "Please bring my coat," called Renee.
4. After thinking for a moment, Paul said, "I don't believe you."
5. Dad said, "Remember to be home by 9:00 PM."
6. "Finish your projects," said the art instructor.
7. "Go back," instructed Mom, "and comb your hair."
8. "I won't be needing my winter coat anymore," replied Mei-ling.
9. He said, "How did you do that?"
10. I stood and said, "My name is Rosalita."
11. "No," said Misha, "I will not attend."
12. "Don't forget to put your name on your paper," said the teacher.
13. "Pay attention, class," said our history teacher.
14. As I came into the house, Mom called, "Dinner is almost ready!"
15. "Jake, come when I call you," said Mother.
16. "How was your trip to France, Mrs. Shaw?" asked Deborah.

Page 140

Dashes

Dashes (—) are used to indicate sudden changes of thought.

Examples:
I want milk—no, make that soda—with my lunch.
Wear your old clothes—new ones would get spoiled.

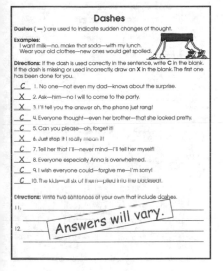

Directions: If the dash is used correctly in the sentence, write **C** in the blank. If the dash is missing or used incorrectly, draw an **X** in the blank. The first one has been done for you.

_C_ 1. No one—not even my dad—knows about the surprise.
_X_ 2. Ask—him—no I will to come to the party.
_X_ 3. I'll tell you the answer oh, the phone just rang!
_C_ 4. Everyone thought—even her brother—that she looked pretty.
_C_ 5. Can you please—oh, forget it!
_X_ 6. Just stop it I really mean it!
_C_ 7. Tell her that I'll—never mind—I'll tell her myself!
_X_ 8. Everyone especially Anna is overwhelmed.
_C_ 9. I wish everyone could—forgive me—I'm sorry!
_C_ 10. The kids—all six of them—piled into the backseat.

Directions: Write two sentences of your own that include dashes.

11.
12.

Answers will vary.

Page 141

Apostrophes

Use an **apostrophe** (') in a contraction to show that letters have been left out. A **contraction** is a shortened form of two words, usually a pronoun and a verb.

Add an **apostrophe** and s to form the **possessive** of singular nouns. **Plural possessives** are formed two ways. If the noun ends in s, simply add an apostrophe at the end of the word. If the noun does not end in s, add an apostrophe and s.

Examples:
Contraction: He **can't** button his sleeves.
Singular possessive: The **boy's** sleeves are too short.
Plural noun ending in s: The **ladies'** voices were pleasant.
Plural noun not ending in s: The **children's** song was long.

Directions: Use apostrophes to punctuate the sentences correctly. The first one has been done for you.

1. I can't understand that child's game.
2. The farmers' wagons were lined up in a row.
3. She didn't like the chairs' covers.
4. Our parents' beliefs are often our own.
5. Sandy's mother's aunt isn't going to visit.
6. Two ladies from work didn't show up.
7. The citizen's group wasn't very happy.
8. The colonists' demands weren't unreasonable.
9. The mothers' babies cried at the same time.
10. Our parent's generation enjoys music.

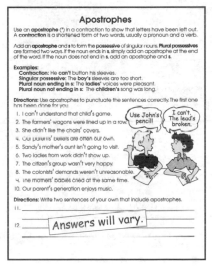

Use John's pencil!

I can't. The lead's broken.

Directions: Write two sentences of your own that include apostrophes.

11.
12.

Answers will vary.

Page 142

Singular Possessives

Directions: Write the singular possessive form of each word. Then, add a noun to show possession. The first one has been done for you.

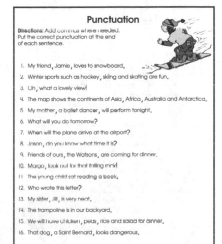

1. spider _spider's web_
2. clock _clock's_
3. car _car's_
4. book _book's_
5. Mom _Mom's_
6. boat _boat's_
7. table _table's_
8. baby _baby's_
9. woman _woman's_
10. writer _writer's_
11. mouse _mouse's_
12. fan _fan's_
13. lamp _lamp's_
14. dog _dog's_
15. boy _boy's_
16. house _house's_

(Nouns will vary.)

Page 143

Contractions

Examples:
he will = **he'll**
she is = **she's**
they are = **they're**
can not = **can't**

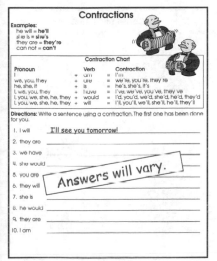

Contraction Chart

Pronoun		Verb		Contraction
I	+	am	=	I'm
we, you, they	+	are	=	we're, you're, they're
he, she, it	+	is	=	he's, she's, it's
I, we, you, they	+	have	=	I've, we've, you've, they've
I, you, we, she, he, they	+	would	=	I'd, you'd, we'd, she'd, he'd, they'd
I, you, we, she, he, they	+	will	=	I'll, you'll, we'll, she'll, he'll, they'll

Directions: Write a sentence using a contraction. The first one has been done for you.

1. I will _I'll see you tomorrow!_
2. they are
3. we have
4. she would
5. you are
6. they will
7. she is
8. he would
9. they are
10. I am

Answers will vary.

Page 144

Commas

A **comma** tells a reader to pause when reading a sentence. Use commas when combining two or more **complete** sentences with a joining word.

Examples: We raked the leaves, and we put them into bags.
Brian dressed quickly, but he still missed the school bus.

Do not use commas if you are not combining complete sentences.

Examples: We raked the leaves and put them into bags.
Brian dressed quickly but still missed the school bus.

If either part of the sentence does not have both a subject and a verb, do not use a comma.

Directions: Read each sentence below and decide whether or not it needs a comma. If it does, rewrite the sentence, placing the comma correctly. If it doesn't, write **O.K.** on the line.

1. The cat stretched lazily and walked out of the room.
_O.K._
2. I could use the money to buy a new shirt or I could go to the movies.
I could use the money to buy a new shirt, or I could go to the movies.
3. My sister likes pizza but she doesn't like spaghetti.
My sister likes pizza, but she doesn't like spaghetti.
4. Mom mixed the batter and poured it into the pan.
_O.K._
5. The teacher passed out the tests and she told us to write our names on them.
The teacher passed out the tests, and she told us to write our names on them.
6. The car squealed its tires and took off out of the parking lot.
_O.K._
7. The snow fell heavily and we knew the schools would be closed the next day.
The snow fell heavily, and we knew the schools would be closed the next day.
8. The batter hit the ball and it flew over the fence.
The batter hit the ball, and it flew over the fence.

Page 145

Punctuation

Directions: Add commas where needed. Put the correct punctuation at the end of each sentence.

1. My friend, Jamie, loves to snowboard.
2. Winter sports such as hockey, skiing and skating are fun.
3. Oh, what a lovely view!
4. The map shows the continents of Asia, Africa, Australia and Antarctica.
5. My mother, a ballet dancer, will perform tonight.
6. What will you do tomorrow?
7. When will the plane arrive at the airport?
8. Jason, do you know what time it is?
9. Friends of ours, the Watsons, are coming for dinner.
10. Margo, look out for that falling rock!
11. The young child sat reading a book.
12. Who wrote this letter?
13. My sister, Jill, is very neat.
14. The trampoline is in our backyard.
15. We will have chicken, peas, rice and salad for dinner.
16. That dog, a Saint Bernard, looks dangerous.

Summer Link Super Edition Grade 6

Page 146

Proofreading

Proofreading or "proofing" means to carefully look over what has been written, checking for spelling, grammar, punctuation, and other errors. At a newspaper, this is the job of a copyeditor. All good writers carefully proofread and correct their own work before turning it in to a copyeditor—or a teacher.
Here are three common proofreading marks:
Correct spelling ~~alrm~~ alarm
Replace with lower-case letter /
Replace with upper-case letter ≡

Directions: Carefully read the following paragraphs. Use proofreading marks to mark errors in the second paragraph. Correct all errors. The first sentence has been done for you.

A six-~~alrm~~ alarm fire at 2121 windsor Terrace on the

northeast side awoke apartment Residents at 3 A.M.

yesterday morning. ~~Eleven~~ Eleven people were in the ~~buliding~~ building.

No one was hurt in the ~~blaze~~ blaze, which caused $200,000

of property damage.

~~Property~~ Property manager Jim smith credits a perfectly Functioning smoke ~~alrm~~ alarm system for waking residents so they could get out safely. A ~~springler~~ sprinkler system ~~were~~ was also in ~~place~~ place. "There was ~~No~~ panick," Smith said proudly. "~~Everbne~~ Everyone was calm and Orderly."

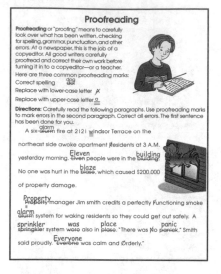

Page 147

Editing

Directions: Draw a line from the editing mark on the left to its meaning on the right.

com~~plain~~	Close up a word
The two boys came to class, The girls, though,	Insert an apostrophe
This is the best pie ever.	Insert a comma
thi~~s~~	Delete a word
copy editor	Transpose words
We went(zoo to the)	Transpose letters
There were two of us in the house.	Insert a space
Once upon a time, there were	Capitalize
leonardo da vinci	Move text down to line below
Thomas was the best.	Change letter to lower-case
The two girls came to class. The two boys never came back until the principal left.	Start a new paragraph
Now I will end the story	Move text up to line above
My mother, the best lady I know,	Insert a period
This is my mothers hat.	Insert a word

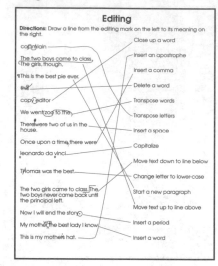

Page 148

Joining Sentences

Conjunctions are words that join sentences, words, or ideas. When two sentences are joined with **and**, they are more or less equal.
Example: Julio is coming, **and** he is bringing cookies.
When two sentences are joined with **but**, the second sentence contradicts the first one.
Example: Julio is coming, **but** he will be late.
When two sentences are joined with **or**, they name a choice.
Example: Julio might bring cookies, **or** he might bring a cake.
When two sentences are joined with **because**, the second one names the reason for the first one.
Example: I'll bring cookies, too, **because** Julio might forget his.
When two sentences are joined with **so**, the second one names a result of the first one.
Example: Julio is bringing cookies, **so** we will have a snack.

Directions: Complete each sentence. The first one has been done for you.
1. We could watch TV, or **we could play a game.**
2. I wanted to seize the opportunity, but_____
3. You had better not deceive me, because_____
4. My neighbor was on vacation, so_____
5. Veins take blood back to your heart, and_____
6. You can't always yield to your impulses, so_____
7. I know that is your belief, but_____
8. It could be reindeer on the roof, or_____
9. Brent was determined to achieve his goal, so_____
10. Brittany was proud of her height, because_____
11. We painted the ceiling, and_____

Answers will vary.

Page 149

Descriptive Sentences

Descriptive sentences give readers a vivid image and enable them to imagine a scene clearly.
Example:
Nondescriptive sentence: There were grapes in the bowl.
Descriptive sentence: The plump purple grapes in the bowl looked tantalizing.

Directions: Rewrite these sentences using descriptive language.
1. The dog walked in its pen.
2. The turkey was almost done.
3. I became upset when my computer wouldn't work.
4. Jared and Michelle went to the ice-cream parlor.
5. The telephone rang.
6. I wrote a letter.
7. The movie was excellent.
8. Dominique was upset that her friend was ill.

Sentences will vary.

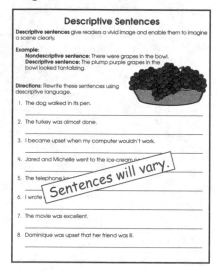

Page 150

Combining Sentences

When the subjects are the same, sentences can be combined by using appositives.
Examples:
Tony likes to play basketball. Tony is my neighbor.
Tony, **my neighbor**, likes to play basketball.

Ms. Herman was sick today. Ms. Herman is our math teacher.
Ms. Herman, **our math teacher**, was sick today.

Appositives are set off from the rest of the sentence with commas.

Directions: Use commas and appositives to combine the pairs of sentences.
1. Julie has play practice today. Julie is my sister.
   Julie, my sister, has play practice today.
2. Greg fixed my bicycle. Greg is my cousin.
   Greg, my cousin, fixed my bicycle.
3. Mr. Scott told us where to meet. Mr. Scott is our coach.
   Mr. Scott, our coach, told us where to meet.
4. Tiffany is moving to Detroit. Tiffany is my neighbor.
   Tiffany, my neighbor, is moving to Detroit.
5. Kyle has the flu. Kyle is my brother.
   Kyle, my brother, has the flu.
6. My favorite football team is playing tonight. Houston is my favorite team.
   My favorite football team, Houston, is playing tonight.
7. Bonnie Pryor will be at our school next week. Bonnie Pryor is a famous author.
   Bonnie Pryor, a famous author, will be at our school next week.
8. Our neighborhood is having a garage sale. Our neighborhood is the North End. **Our neighborhood, the North End, is having a garage sale.**

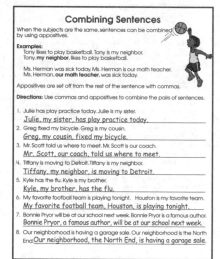

Page 151

Statements and Questions

A **statement** is a sentence that tells something. It ends with a period (.).
A **question** is a sentence that asks something. It ends with a question mark (?).
Examples:
Statement: Shari is walking to school today.
Question: Is Shari walking to school today?
In some questions, the subject comes between two parts of the verb. In the examples below, the subjects are underlined. The verbs and the rest of the predicates are bold.
Examples:
Is Steve **coming with us**?
Who **will be there**?
Which one **did** you **select**?
To find the predicate, turn a question into a statement.
Example: Is Steve coming with us? Steve is coming with us.

Directions: Write **S** for statement or **Q** for question. Put a period after the statements and a question mark after the questions.
S 1. Today is the day for our field trip.
Q 2. How are we going to get there?
S 3. The bus will take us.
Q 4. Is there room for everyone?
Q 5. Who forgot to bring a lunch?
S 6. I'll save you a seat.

Directions: Circle the subjects and underline all parts of the predicates.
7. Do (you) like field trips?
8. Did (you) bring your coat?
9. Will (it) be cold there?
10. Do (you) see my gloves anywhere?
11. Is (anyone) sitting with you?
12. Does the (bus driver) have a map?
13. Are (all the roads) this bumpy?

Page 152

Facts and Opinions

A **fact** is a statement based on truth. It can be proven. **Opinions** are the beliefs of an individual that may or may not be true.
Examples:
Fact: Alaska is a state.
Opinion: Alaska is the most magnificent state.

Directions: Write **F** if the statement is a fact. Write **O** if the statement is an opinion.
1. O The Grand Canyon is the most scenic site in the United States.
2. F Dinosaurs roamed Earth millions of years ago.
3. F Scientists have discovered how to clone sheep.
4. O All people should attend this fair.
5. O Purebreds are the best dogs to own because they are intelligent.
6. O Nobody likes being bald.
7. O Students should be required to get straight A's to participate in extracurricular activities.
8. F Reading is an important skill that is vital in many careers.
9. O Snakes do not make good pets.
10. F Many books have been written about animals.
11. F Thomas Edison invented the lightbulb.
12. O Most people like to read science fiction.
13. F Insects have three body parts.

Page 153

Facts and Opinions

A **fact** is information that can be proved.
Example: Hawaii is a state.
An **opinion** is a belief. It tells what someone thinks. It cannot be proved.
Example: Hawaii is the prettiest state.

Directions: Write **f** (fact) or **o** (opinion) on the line by each sentence. The first one has been done for you.
f 1. Hawaii is the only island state.
o 2. The best fishing is in Michigan.
o 3. It is easy to find a job in Wyoming.
f 4. Trenton is the capital of New Jersey.
f 5. Kentucky is nicknamed the Bluegrass State.
o 6. The friendliest people in the United States live in Georgia.
o 7. The cleanest beaches are in California.
o 8. Summers are most beautiful in Arizona.
f 9. Only one percent of North Dakota is forest or woodland.
f 10. New Mexico produces almost half of the nation's uranium.
f 11. The first shots of the Civil War were fired in South Carolina on April 12, 1861.
f 12. The varied geographical features of Washington include mountains, deserts, a rainforest, and a volcano.
f 13. In 1959, Alaska and Hawaii became the 49th and 50th states admitted to the Union.
f 14. Wyandotte Cave, one of the largest caves in the United States, is in Indiana.

Directions: Write one fact and one opinion about your own state.
Fact: _____
Opinion: _____

Answers will vary.

Page 154

Cause and Effect

Directions: Complete the chart by listing the cause and effect of each weather phenomenon.

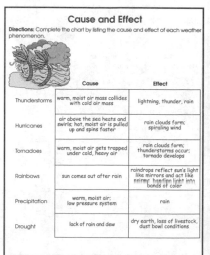

	Cause	Effect
Thunderstorms	warm, moist air mass collides with cold air mass	lightning, thunder, rain
Hurricanes	air above the sea heats and swirls; hot, moist air is pulled up and spins faster	rain clouds form; spiraling wind
Tornadoes	warm, moist air gets trapped under cold, heavy air	rain clouds form; thunderstorms occur; tornado develops
Rainbows	sun comes out after rain	raindrops reflect sun's light like mirrors and act like prisms, bending light into bands of color
Precipitation	warm, moist air; low pressure system	rain
Drought	lack of rain and dew	dry earth, loss of livestock, dust bowl conditions

Page 155

Venn Diagrams

A **Venn diagram** is used to chart information that shows similarities and differences between two things. The outer part of each circle shows the differences. The intersecting part of the circles shows the similarities.

Example.

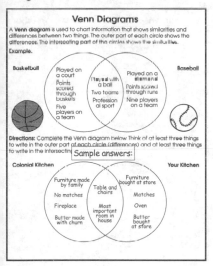

Basketball — Played on a court, Points scored through baskets, Five players on a team

Plays with a ball, Two teams, Professional sport

Baseball — Played on a diamond, Points scored through runs, Nine players on a team

Directions: Complete the Venn diagram below. Think of at least three things to write in the outer part of each circle (differences) and at least three things to write in the intersecting part.

Sample answers:

Colonial Kitchen — Furniture made by family, No matches, Fireplace, Butter made with churn

Table and chairs, Most important room in house

Your Kitchen — Furniture bought at store, Matches, Oven, Butter bought at store

Page 157

Following Directions

Directions: Read and follow the directions.

1. Draw a vertical line from the top mid-point of the square to the bottom mid-point of the square.
2. Draw a diagonal line from top left to bottom right of the square.
3. In each of the two triangles, draw a heart.
4. Draw a picture of a cat's face below the square.
5. Draw a horizontal line from the left mid-point to the right mid-point of the square.
6. Draw two intersecting lines in each of the two smaller squares so they are equally divided into four quadrants.
7. Draw a triangle-shaped roof on the square.
8. Draw a circle next to each heart.
9. Write your name in the roof section of your drawing.

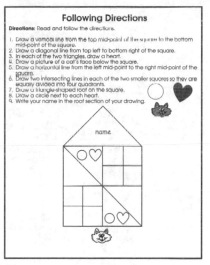

name

Page 158

Maps

Directions: Read the information about planning a map.

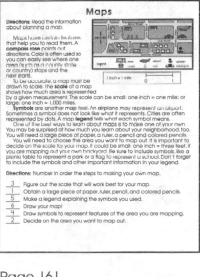

Maps have certain features that help you to read them. A **compass rose** points out directions. Color is often used so you can easily see where one area (such as a country, state or country) stops and the next starts.

To be accurate, a map must be drawn to scale. The **scale** of a map shows how much area is represented by a given measurement. The scale can be small: one inch = one mile; or large: one inch = 1,000 miles.

Symbols are another map tool. An airplane may represent an airport. Sometimes a symbol does not look like what it represents. Cities are often represented by dots. A map **legend** tells what each symbol means.

One of the best ways to learn about maps is to make one of your own. You may be surprised at how much you learn about your neighborhood, too. You will need a large piece of paper, a ruler, a pencil and colored pencils.

You will need to choose the area you want to map out. It is important to decide on the scale for your map. It could be small: one inch = three feet. If you are mapping out your own backyard. Be sure to include symbols, like a picnic table to represent a park or a flag to represent a school. Don't forget to include the symbols and other important information in your legend.

Directions: Number in order the steps to making your own map.

<u>3</u> Figure out the scale that will work best for your map.
<u>1</u> Obtain a large piece of paper, ruler, pencil, and colored pencils.
<u>5</u> Make a legend explaining the symbols you used.
<u>6</u> Draw your map!
<u>4</u> Draw symbols to represent features of the area you are mapping.
<u>2</u> Decide on the area you want to map out.

Page 159

Maps

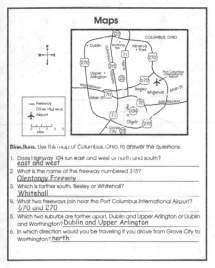

COLUMBUS, OHIO

Directions: Use this map of Columbus, Ohio, to answer the questions.

1. Does Highway 104 run east and west or north and south?
   <u>east and west</u>
2. What is the name of the freeway numbered 315?
   <u>Olentangy Freeway</u>
3. Which is farther south, Bexley or Whitehall?
   <u>Whitehall</u>
4. What two freeways join near the Port Columbus International Airport?
   <u>670 and 270</u>
5. Which two suburbs are farther apart, Dublin and Upper Arlington or Dublin and Worthington? <u>Dublin and Upper Arlington</u>
6. In which direction would you be traveling if you drove from Grove City to Worthington? <u>north</u>

Page 160

Creating a Map

Directions: In the space below, draw a map of your street or town. Be sure to include a compass rose, scale, symbols, and a map legend.

Maps will vary.

Page 161

It's Your Opinion

Your opinion is how you feel or think about something. Although other people may have the same opinion, their reasons could not be exactly the same because of their individuality.

When writing an opinion paragraph, it is important to first state your opinion. Then, in at least three sentences, support your opinion. Finally, end your paragraph by restating your opinion in different words.

Example:
I believe dogs are excellent pets. For thousands of years, dogs have guarded and protected their owners. Dogs are faithful and have been known to save the lives of those they love. Dogs offer unconditional love as well as company for the quiet times in our lives. For these reasons, I feel that dogs make wonderful pets.

Directions: Write an opinion paragraph on whether you would or would not like to have lived in Colonial America. Be sure to support your opinion with at least three reasons.

Answers will vary.

Writing Checklist
Reread your paragraph carefully.
☐ My paragraph makes sense.   ☐ I have a good opening and ending.
☐ There are no jumps in ideas.   ☐ I used correct spelling.
☐ I used correct punctuation.   ☐ My paragraph is well-organized.
                  ☐ My paragraph is interesting.

Page 162

Recalling Details: The Earth's Atmosphere

The most important reason that life can exist on Earth is its atmosphere—the air all around us. Without it, plant and animal life could not have developed. There would be no clouds, weather, or even sounds; only a deathlike stillness and an endlessly black sky. Without the protection of the atmosphere, the sun's rays would roast the Earth by day. At night, with no blanketing atmosphere, the stored heat would escape into space, dropping the temperature of the planet hundreds of degrees.

Held captive by Earth's gravity, the atmosphere surrounds the planet to a depth of hundreds of miles. However, all but 1 percent of the atmosphere is in a layer about 20 miles deep just above the surface of the Earth. It is made up of a mixture of gases and dusts. About 78 percent of it is a gas called nitrogen, which is very important as food for plants. Most of the remaining gas, 21 percent, is oxygen, which all people and animals depend on for life. The remaining 1 percent is made up of a blend of other gases—including carbon dioxide, argon, ozone and helium—and tiny dust particles. These particles come from ocean salt crystals, bits of rocks and sand, plant pollen, volcanic ash and even meteor dust.

You may not think of air as matter, as something that can be weighed. In fact, the Earth's air weighs billions and billions of tons. Near the surface of the planet, this "air pressure" is greatest. Right now, about 10 tons of air is pressing in on you. Yet, like the fish living near the floor of the ocean, you don't notice this tremendous weight because your body is built to withstand it.

Directions: Answer these questions about the Earth's atmosphere.

1. What is the atmosphere? <u>the air around us</u>
2. Of what is the atmosphere made? <u>a mixture of gases and dusts</u>
3. What is the most abundant gas in the atmosphere? <u>nitrogen</u>
4. Which of the atmosphere's gases is most important to humans and animals? <u>oxygen</u>
5. What is air pressure? <u>the weight of the air on Earth</u>

Page 163

Recalling Details: Clothing in Colonial Times

The clothing of the colonists varied from the north to the south, accounting for the differences not only in climate, but also in the religions and ancestries of the settlers. The clothes seen most often in the early New England colonies where the Puritans settled were very plain and simple. The materials—wool and linen—were warm and sturdy.

The Puritans had strict rules about clothing. There were no bright colors, jewelry, ruffles, or lace. A Puritan woman wore a long sleeved gray dress with a big white collar, cuffs, apron, and cap. A Puritan man wore long woolen stockings and baggy leather "breeches," which were knee-length trousers. Adults and children dressed in the same style of clothing.

In the middle colonies, the clothing ranged from the simple clothing of the Quakers to the colorful, loose-fitting outfits of the Dutch colonists. Dutch women wore more colorful outfits than Puritan women, with many petticoats and fur trim. The men had silver buckles on their shoes and wore big hats decked with curling feathers.

In the southern colonies, where there were no religious restrictions against fancy clothes, wealthy men wore brightly colored breeches and coats of velvet and satin sent from England. The women's gowns also were made of rich materials and were decorated with ruffles, ribbons, and lace. The poorer people wore clothes similar to the simple dress of the New England Puritans.

Directions: Answer these questions about clothing in colonial times.

1. Why did the clothing of the colonists vary from the north to the south?
   <u>differences in climate, religions and ancestries</u>
2. Why did the Puritans wear very plain clothing?
   <u>They had very strict rules and religious restrictions.</u>
3. What was the nationality of many settlers in the middle colonies?
   <u>Dutch</u>
4. From what country did wealthy southern colonists obtain their clothing?
   <u>England</u>

Page 164

Making Inferences: Cairo

- Cairo is the capital of Egypt.
- Cairo is the largest city of not only Egypt but all of Africa and the Middle East.
- The population of Cairo is almost 7 million people.
- Cairo is the cultural center for the Islamic religion.
- Cairo is a major industrial site for Egypt.
- Cairo is a port on the Nile River near the head of the Nile delta.
- Interesting sites include the Egyptian Museum, the Sphinx, the pyramids, and the City of the Dead.

Directions: Answer these questions about Cairo.

1. All the major cities discussed so far, including Cairo, have a seaport. Historically speaking, what is the importance of having access to the sea?

2. Cairo has a population of almost ... are three problems which could arise from ...
   1)
   2)
   3)

Answers will vary.

3. Would you ... visit Cairo? Why or why not?

Page 165

Making Inferences: Ottawa

- Ottawa is the capital of Canada and is located in Ontario.
- The federal government employs most people in the city. Manufacturing is another large employer.
- The Rideau Canal connects Ottawa to Lake Ontario.
- The population of Ottawa is over 300,000 people.
- Points of interest include the Peace Tower, Parliament Buildings, the Royal Canadian Mint and the Canadian Museum of Nature.

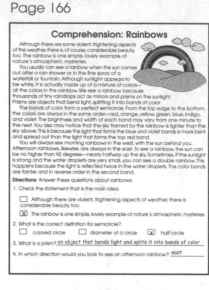

Directions: Answer these questions about Ottawa.

1. Who employs the most people in Ottawa, Canada? the federal government
2. What body of water connects Ottawa to Lake Ontario? Rideau Canal
3. In order from largest to smallest, list the six cities you have read about and their populations.

Cairo	7 million
London	6.5 million
Berlin	3.5 million
Sydney	3 million
Washington, D.C.	600,000
Ottawa	300,000

4. Canada is the United States' neighbor to the north. What problems could arise due to a shared border?
Answers will vary.

Page 166

Comprehension: Rainbows

Although there are some violent, frightening aspects of the weather, there is, of course, considerable beauty, too. The rainbow is one simple, lovely example of nature's atmospheric mysteries.

You usually can see a rainbow when the sun comes out after a rain shower or in the fine spray of a waterfall or fountain. Although sunlight appears to be white, it is actually made up of a mixture of colors—all the colors in the rainbow. We see a rainbow because thousands of tiny raindrops act as mirrors and prisms on the sunlight. Prisms are objects that bend light, splitting it into bands of color.

The bands of color form a perfect semicircle. From the top edge to the bottom, the colors are always in the same order—red, orange, yellow, green, blue, indigo, and violet. The brightness and width of each band may vary from one minute to the next. You also may notice that the sky framed by the rainbow is lighter than the sky above. This is because the light that forms the blue and violet bands is more bent and spread out than the light that forms the top red band.

You will always see morning rainbows in the west, with the sun behind you. Afternoon rainbows, likewise, are always in the east. To see a rainbow, the sun can be no higher than 42 degrees—nearly halfway up the sky. Sometimes, if the sunlight is strong and the water droplets are very small, you can see a double rainbow. This happens because the light is reflected twice in the water droplets. The color bands are fainter and in reverse order in the second band.

Directions: Answer these questions about rainbows.

1. Check the statement that is the main idea.
   - ☐ Although there are violent, frightening aspects of weather, there is considerable beauty, too.
   - ☒ The rainbow is one simple, lovely example of nature's atmospheric mysteries.
2. What is the correct definition for semicircle?
   ☐ colored circle ☐ diameter of a circle ☒ half circle
3. What is a prism? an object that bends light and splits it into bands of color
4. In which direction would you look to see an afternoon rainbow? east

Page 167

Comprehension: Causes/Effects of Weather

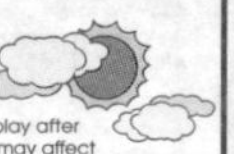

The behavior of the atmosphere, which we experience as weather and climate, affects our lives in many important ways. It is the reason no one lives on the South Pole. It controls when a farmer plants the food we will eat, which crops will be planted and also whether those crops will grow. The weather tells you what clothes to wear and how you will play after school. Weather is the sum of all the conditions of the air that may affect the Earth's surface and its living things. These conditions include the temperature, air pressure, wind and moisture. Climate refers to these conditions but generally applies to larger areas and longer periods of time, such as the annual climate of South America rather than today's weather in Oklahoma City.

Climate is influenced by many factors. It depends first and foremost on latitude. Areas nearest the equator are warm and wet, while the poles are cold and relatively dry. The poles also have extreme seasonal changes, while the areas at the middle latitudes have more moderate climates, neither as cold as the poles nor as hot as the equator. Other circumstances may alter this pattern, however. Land near the oceans, for instance, is generally warmer than inland areas.

Elevation also plays a role in climate. For example, despite the fact that Africa's highest mountain, Kilimanjaro, is just south of the equator, its summit is perpetually covered by snow. In general, high land is cooler and wetter than nearby low land.

Directions: Check the answers to these questions about the causes and effects of weather.

1. What is the correct definition for **atmosphere**?
   ☐ the clouds ☐ the sky ☒ where weather occurs
2. What is the correct definition for **foremost**?
   ☒ most important ☐ highest number ☐ in the front
3. What is the correct definition for **circumstances**?
   ☐ temperatures ☐ seasons ☒ conditions
4. What is the correct definition for **elevation**?
   ☒ height above Earth ☐ nearness to equator ☐ snow covering
5. What is the correct definition for **perpetually**?
   ☐ occasionally ☐ rarely ☒ always

Page 168

Poetry: Free Verse

Poems that do not rhyme and do not have a regular rhythm are called **free verse**. They often use adjectives, adverbs, similes, and metaphors to create word pictures.

My Old Cat

Curled on my bed at night,
Quietly happy to see me,
Soft, sleepy, relaxed,
A calm island in my life.

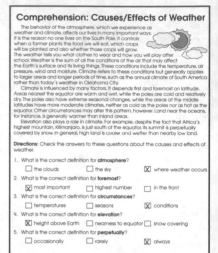

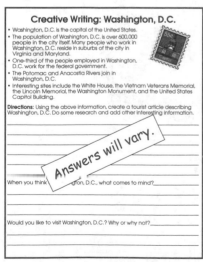

Directions: Write your own free verse. Use the guidelines for each poem.

1. Write a two-line free verse poem about a feeling. Compare it to some kind of food. For example, anger could be a tangle of spaghetti. Give your poem a title.
2. Think of how someone you know is like a color, happy like yellow, for example. Write a two-line free verse poem on this topic without naming the person. Don't forget a title.
3. Write a four-line free verse poem, like "My Old Cat," that creates a word picture of a day at school

Answers will vary.

Page 169

Poetry: Haiku

Haiku is a type of unrhymed Japanese poetry with three lines. The first line has five syllables. The second line has seven syllables. The third line has five syllables.

Example:

Katie

Katie is my dog.
She likes to bark and chase balls.
Katie is my friend.

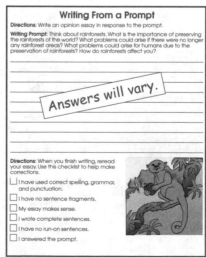

Directions: Write a haiku about a pet and another about a hobby you enjoy.

Be sure to write a title on the first line.

Pet

Hobby

Answers will vary.

Page 170

Persuasive Writing

Writing is usually more persuasive if written from the reader's point of view.

If you made cookies to sell at a school fair, which of these sentences would you write on your sign?
1. I spent a lot of time making these cookies.
2. These cookies taste delicious!

If you were writing to ask your school board to start a gymnastics program, which sentence would be more persuasive?
1. I really am interested in gymnastics.
2. Gymnastics would be good for our school because both boys and girls can participate, and it's a year-round sport we can do in any weather.

In both situations, the second sentence is more persuasive because it is written from the reader's point of view. People care how the cookies taste, not how long it took you to make them. The school board wants to provide activities for all the students, not just you.

Directions: Write **R** if the statement is written from the reader's point of view or **W** if it's written from the writer's point of view.

R 1. If you come swimming with me, you'll be able to cool off.
W 2. Come swimming with me. I don't want to go alone.
W 3. Please write me a letter. I really like to get mail.
R 4. Please write me a letter. I want to hear from you.

Directions: Follow these steps to write an "invitation" on another sheet of paper to persuade people to move to your town or city.

1. Think about reasons someone would want to live in your town. Make a list of all the good things there, like the schools, parks, annual parades, historic buildings, businesses where parents could work, scout groups, Little League, and so on. You might also describe your town's population, transportation, restaurants, celebrations, or even holiday decorations.
2. Now, select three or four items from your list. Write a sentence (or two) about each one from the reader's point of view. For example, instead of writing "Our Little League team won the championship again last year," you could tell the reader, "You could help our Little League team win the championship again this year."
3. Write a topic sentence to begin your invitation, and put your support sentences in order after it.
4. Read your invitation out loud to another person. Make any needed changes, and copy the invitation onto a clean sheet of paper.

Page 171

Creative Writing: Washington, D.C.

- Washington, D.C. is the capital of the United States.
- The population of Washington, D.C. is over 600,000 people in the city itself. Many people who work in Washington, D.C. reside in suburbs of the city in Virginia and Maryland.
- One-third of the people employed in Washington, D.C. work for the federal government.
- The Potomac and Anacostia Rivers join in Washington, D.C.
- Interesting sites include the White House, the Vietnam Veterans Memorial, the Lincoln Memorial, the Washington Monument, and the United States Capitol Building.

Directions: Using the above information, create a tourist article describing Washington, D.C. Do some research and add other interesting information.

Answers will vary.

When you think of Washington, D.C., what comes to mind?

Would you like to visit Washington, D.C.? Why or why not?

Page 172

Writing From a Prompt

Directions: Write an opinion essay in response to the prompt.

Writing Prompt: Think about rainforests. What is the importance of preserving the rainforests of the world? What problems could arise if there were no longer any rainforest areas? What problems could arise for humans due to the preservation of rainforests? How do rainforests affect you?

Answers will vary.

Directions: When you finish writing, reread your essay. Use this checklist to help make corrections.

- ☐ I have used correct spelling, grammar, and punctuation.
- ☐ I have no sentence fragments.
- ☐ My essay makes sense.
- ☐ I wrote complete sentences.
- ☐ I have no run-on sentences.
- ☐ I answered the prompt.

Page 173

Writing: Just the Facts

Some forms of writing, such as reports and essays, contain opinions that are supported by the writer. In other kinds of writing, however, it is important to stick to the facts. Newspaper reporters, for example, must use only facts when they write their stories.

Directions: Read the following newspaper story about a fire, and underline the sentences or parts of sentences that are opinions. Then rewrite the story in your own words, giving only the facts.

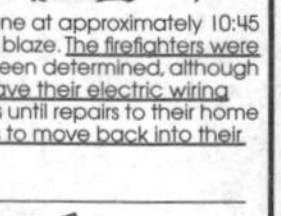

At around 10:30 p.m. last night, a fire broke out in a house at 413 Wilshire Boulevard. The house is in a very nice neighborhood, surrounded by beautiful trees. The family of four who lives in the house was alerted by smoke alarms, and they all exited the house safely, although they must have been very frightened. Firefighters arrived on the scene at approximately 10:45 p.m., and it took them over 3 hours to extinguish the blaze. The firefighters were very courageous. The cause of the fire has not yet been determined, although faulty electric wiring is suspected. People should have their electric wiring checked regularly. The family is staying with relatives until repairs to their home can be made, and they are probably very anxious to move back into their house.

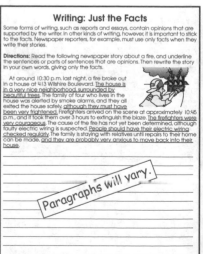

Paragraphs will vary.

Page 174

Friendly Letters

Directions: Study the format for writing a letter to a friend. Then answer the questions.

your return address

123 Waverly Road
Cincinnati, Ohio 45241
June 23, 1999

date

greeting

Dear Josh,

body

How is your summer going? I am enjoying mine so far. I have been swimming twice already this week, and it's only Wednesday! I am glad there is a pool near our house.

My parents said that you can stay overnight when your family comes for the 4th of July picnic. Do you want to? We can pitch a tent in the back yard and camp out. It will be a lot of fun!

Please write back to let me know if you can stay over on the 4th. I will see you then!

closing
signature

Your friend,
Michael

your return address

Michael Delaney
123 Waverly Road
Cincinnati, Ohio 45241

main address

Josh Sommers
2250 West First Ave.
Columbus, OH 43212

1. What words are in the greeting? _Dear Josh_

2. What words are in the closing? _Your friend_

3. On what street does the writer live? _Waverly Road_

Page 175

Friendly Letters

Directions: Write a friendly letter. Then address the envelope.

Letters should follow format given.

Page 176

Newswriting: Inverted Pyramid Style

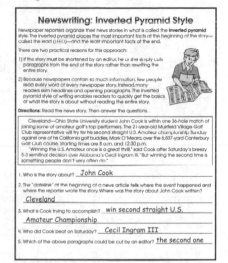

Newspaper reporters organize their news stories in what is called the **inverted pyramid** style. The inverted pyramid places the most important facts at the beginning of the story—called the lead (LEED)—and the least important facts at the end.

There are two practical reasons for this approach:

1) If the story must be shortened by an editor, he or she simply cuts paragraphs from the end of the story rather than rewriting the entire story.

2) Because newspapers contain so much information, few people read every word of every newspaper story. Instead, many readers skim headlines and opening paragraphs. The inverted pyramid style of writing enables readers to quickly get the basics of what the story is about without reading the entire story.

Directions: Read the news story. Then answer the questions.

Cleveland—Ohio State University student John Cook is within one 36-hole match of joining some of amateur golf's top performers. The 21-year-old Muirfield Village Golf Club representative will try for his second straight U.S. Amateur championship Sunday against one of his California golf buddies, Mark O'Meara, over the 6,837-yard Canterbury Golf Club course. Starting times are 8 a.m. and 12:30 p.m.

"Winning the U.S. Amateur once is a great thrill," said Cook after Saturday's breezy 5-3 semifinal decision over Alabama's Cecil Ingram III. "But winning the second time is something people don't very often do."

1. Who is the story about? _John Cook_

2. The "dateline" at the beginning of a news article tells where the event happened and where the reporter wrote the story. Where was the story about John Cook written?
   Cleveland

3. What is Cook trying to accomplish? _win second straight U.S._
   Amateur Championship

4. Who did Cook beat on Saturday? _Cecil Ingram III_

5. Which of the above paragraphs could be cut by an editor? _the second one_

Page 177

Writing: You're the Reporter

Directions: Now, write your own short newspaper story about an interesting event that occurred at your school or in your neighborhood. Find out who and what the story is about, where and when it happened, and why and how it happened. Take some notes, interview some of the people involved, and write your story. Give your story a title, and remember to stick to the facts! In the box, draw a picture (or "photo") to go with your story.

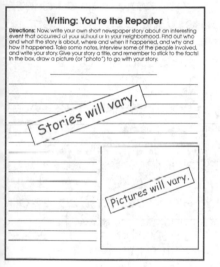

Stories will vary.

Pictures will vary.

Page 178

Personal Narratives

A **narrative** is a spoken or written account of an actual event. A **personal narrative** tells about your own experience. It can be written about any event in your life and may be serious or comical.

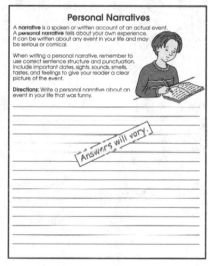

When writing a personal narrative, remember to use correct sentence structure and punctuation. Include important dates, sights, sounds, smells, tastes, and feelings to give your reader a clear picture of the event.

Directions: Write a personal narrative about an event in your life that was funny.

Answers will vary.

Page 179

Complete the Story

Directions: Read the beginning of this story. Then complete the story with your own ideas.

It was a beautiful summer day in June when my family and I set off on vacation. We were headed for Portsmouth, New Hampshire. There we planned to go on a whale-watching ship and perhaps spy a humpback whale or two. However, there were many miles between our home and Portsmouth.

We camped at many lovely parks along the way to New Hampshire. We stayed in the Adirondack Mountains for a few days and then visited the White Mountains of Vermont before crossing into New Hampshire.

My family enjoys tent camping. My dad says you can't really get a taste of the great outdoors in a pop-up camper or RV. I love sitting by the fire at night, gazing at the stars and listening to the animal noises.

The trip was going well, and everyone was enjoying our vacation. We made it to Portsmouth and were looking forward to the whale-watching adventure. We arrived at the dock a few minutes early. The ocean looked rough, but we had taken seasickness medication. We thought we were prepared for any kind of weather.

Stories will vary.

189

Summer Link Super Edition Grade 6

Curriculum Skills for Sixth Grade Reading Success

Parents and educators alike know that the School Specialty name ensures outstanding educational experience and content. *Summer Link Reading* was designed to help your child retain those skills learned during the past school year. With *Summer Link Reading,* your child will be ready to review and master new material with confidence when he or she returns to school in the fall.

Use this checklist—compiled from state curriculum standards—to help your child prepare for proficiency testing. Place a check mark in the box if the appropriate skill has been mastered. If your child needs more work with a particular skill, place an "R" in the box and come back to it for review.

Language Arts Skills

❑ Recognizes and correctly uses parts of speech: nouns, pronouns, verbs, adjectives, adverbs, articles, prepositions, and conjunctions.

❑ Understands and correctly uses mechanics conventions: capitalization, punctuation, subject and verb agreement, correct verb tense, and compound and complex sentences.

❑ Uses a variety of vocabulary strategies: synonyms, antonyms, homophones, homographs, multiple meanings, compound words, affixes, base words, phonics clues, context clues, and idioms.

❑ Understands and correctly uses a variety of writing purposes: business and friendly letters, journals, lists, instructions, poetry, narrative composition, outlining, paraphrasing, and webbing.

❑ Understands and correctly uses a variety of writing strategies: identifies persuasive, informal, and entertaining writing, uses literary devices like dialogue, suspense, figurative language, simile, and metaphor, and uses compare and contrast, cause and effect, and supporting details in writing.

❑ Can locate information in reference materials: dictionaries, thesaurus, encyclopedia, atlas, almanac, and the Internet.

Reading Skills

❑ Uses reading strategies to understand meaning: classification, themes, compare and contrast, cause and effect, context clues, and sequencing.

❑ Reads for different purposes: main idea, supporting details, following directions, predicting outcomes, making inferences, distinguishing fact/opinion, drawing conclusions.

❑ Recognizes story elements: character, setting, point of view, mood, plot, development, problem resolution, and character motivation.

❑ Distinguishes between fact and fiction and is familiar with different genres and forms of literature, such as: fantasy, fairy tale, folk tale, tall tale, fable, historical fiction, realistic fiction, science fiction, biography, autobiography, and poetry.

TEST PRACTICE

This page intentionally left blank.

Summer Link Test Practice
Table of Contents

Just for Parents

For All Students

Kinds of Questions

Subject Help

Practice Test and Final Test

About the Tests

What Are Standardized Achievement Tests?

Achievement tests measure what children know in particular subject areas such as reading, language arts, and mathematics. They do not measure your child's intelligence or ability to learn.

When tests are standardized, or *normed,* children's test results are compared with those of a specific group who have taken the test, usually at the same age or grade.

Standardized achievement tests measure what children around the country are learning. The test makers survey popular textbook series, as well as state curriculum frameworks and other professional sources, to determine what content is covered widely.

Because of variations in state frameworks and textbook series, as well as grade ranges on some test levels, the tests may cover some material that children have not yet learned. This is especially true if the test is offered early in the school year. However, test scores are compared to those of other children who take the test at the same time of year, so your child will not be at a disadvantage if his or her class has not covered specific material yet.

Different School Districts, Different Tests

There are many flexible options for districts when offering standardized tests. Many school districts choose not to give the full test battery, but select certain content and scoring options. For example, many schools may test only in the areas of reading and mathematics. Similarly, a state or district may use one test for certain grades and another test for other grades. These decisions are often based on the

amount of time and money a district wishes to spend on test administration. Some states choose to develop their own statewide assessment tests.

On pages 195–197 you will find information about these five widely used standardized achievement tests:

- California Achievement Test (CAT)
- Terra Nova/CTBS
- Iowa Test of Basic Skills (ITBS)
- Stanford Achievement Test (SAT9)
- Metropolitan Achievement Test (MAT)

However, this book contains strategies and practice questions for use with a variety of tests. Even if your state does not give one of the five tests listed above, your child will benefit from doing the practice questions in this book. If you're unsure about which test your child takes, contact your local school district to find out which tests are given.

Types of Test Questions

Traditionally, standardized achievement tests have used only multiple choice questions. Today, many tests may include constructed response (short answer) and extended response (essay) questions as well.

In addition, many tests include questions that tap students' higher-order thinking skills. Instead of simple recall questions, such as identifying a date in history, questions may require students to make comparisons and contrasts or analyze results, among other skills.

What the Tests Measure

These tests do not measure your child's level of intelligence, but they do show how well your child knows material that he or she has learned and that is

also covered on the tests. It's important to remember that some tests cover content that is not taught in your child's school or grade. In other instances, depending on when in the year the test is given, your child may not yet have covered the material.

If the test reports you receive show that your child needs improvement in one or more skill areas, you may want to seek help from your child's teacher and find out how you can work with your child to improve his or her skills.

California Achievement Test (CAT/5)

What Is the California Achievement Test?

The *California Achievement Test* is a standardized achievement test battery that is widely used with elementary through high school students.

Parts of the Test

The CAT includes tests in the following content areas:

Reading
- Word Analysis
- Vocabulary
- Comprehension

Spelling

Language Arts
- Language Mechanics
- Language Usage

Mathematics

Science

Social Studies

Your child may take some or all of these subtests if your district uses the *California Achievement Test*.

Terra Nova/CTBS (Comprehensive Tests of Basic Skills)

What Is the Terra Nova/CTBS?

The *Terra Nova/Comprehensive Tests of Basic Skills* is a standardized achievement test battery used in elementary through high school grades.

While many of the test questions on the *Terra Nova* are in the traditional multiple choice form, your child may take parts of the *Terra Nova* that include some open-ended questions (constructed-response items).

Parts of the Test

Your child may take some or all of the following subtests if your district uses the *Terra Nova/CTBS*:

Reading/Language Arts
Mathematics
Science
Social Studies

Supplementary tests include:
- Word Analysis
- Vocabulary
- Language Mechanics
- Spelling
- Mathematics Computation

Critical thinking skills may also be tested.

Iowa Test of Basic Skills (ITBS)

What Is the ITBS?

The *Iowa Test of Basic Skills* is a standardized achievement test battery used in elementary through high school grades.

Parts of the Test

Your child may take some or all of these subtests if your district uses the *ITBS*, also known as the *Iowa*:

Reading
- Vocabulary
- Reading Comprehension

Language Arts
- Spelling
- Capitalization
- Punctuation
- Usage and Expression

Mathematics
- Concepts/Estimate
- Problems/Data Interpretation

Social Studies

Science

Sources of Information

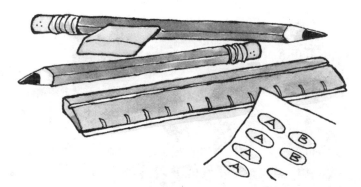

Stanford Achievement Test (SAT9)

What Is the Stanford Achievement Test?

The *Stanford Achievement Test, Ninth Edition (SAT9)* is a standardized achievement test battery used in elementary through high school grades.

Note that the *Stanford Achievement Test (SAT9)* is a different test from the *SAT* used by high school students for college admissions.

While many of the test questions on the *SAT9* are in traditional multiple choice form, your child may take parts of the *SAT9* that include some open-ended questions (constructed-response items).

Parts of the Test

Your child may take some or all of these subtests if your district uses the *Stanford Achievement Test:*

Reading
- Vocabulary
- Reading Comprehension

Mathematics
- Problem Solving
- Procedures

Language Arts

Spelling

Study Skills

Listening

Critical thinking skills may also be tested.

Metropolitan Achievement Test (MAT7 and MAT8)

What Is the Metropolitan Achievement Test?

The *Metropolitan Achievement Test* is a standardized achievement test battery used in elementary through high school grades.

Parts of the Test

Your child may take some or all of these subtests if your district uses the *Metropolitan Achievement Test:*

Reading
- Vocabulary
- Reading Comprehension

Mathematics
- Concepts and Problem Solving
- Computation

Language Arts
- Pre-writing
- Composing
- Editing

Science

Social Studies

Research Skills

Thinking Skills

Spelling

Statewide Assessments

Today the majority of states give statewide assessments. In some cases these tests are known as *high-stakes assessments*. This means that students must score at a certain level in order to be promoted. Some states use minimum competency or proficiency tests. Often these tests measure more basic skills than other types of statewide assessments.

Statewide assessments are generally linked to state curriculum frameworks. Frameworks provide a blueprint, or outline, to ensure that teachers are covering the same curriculum topics as other teachers in the same grade level in the state. In some states, standardized achievement tests (such as the five described in this book) are used in connection with statewide assessments.

When Statewide Assessments Are Given

Statewide assessments may not be given at every grade level. Generally, they are offered at one or more grades in elementary school, middle school, and high school. Many states test at grades 4, 8, and 10.

State-by-State Information

You can find information about statewide assessments and curriculum frameworks at your state Department of Education Web site. To find the address for your individual state, go to www.ed.gov, click on Topics A–Z, and then click on State Departments of Education. You will find a list of all the state departments of education, mailing addresses, and Web sites.

How to Help Your Child Prepare for Standardized Testing

Preparing All Year Round

Perhaps the most valuable way you can help your child prepare for standardized achievement tests is by providing enriching experiences. Keep in mind also that test results for younger children are not as reliable as for older students. If a child is hungry, tired, or upset, this may result in a poor test score. Here are some tips on how you can help your child do his or her best on standardized tests.

Read aloud with your child. Reading aloud helps develop vocabulary and fosters a positive attitude toward reading. Reading together is one of the most effective ways you can help your child succeed in school.

Share experiences. Baking cookies together, planting a garden, or making a map of your neighborhood are examples of activities that help build skills that are measured on the tests such as sequencing and following directions.

Become informed about your state's testing procedures. Ask about or watch for announcements of meetings that explain about standardized tests and statewide assessments in your school district. Talk to your child's teacher about your child's individual performance on these state tests during a parent-teacher conference.

Help your child know what to expect. Read and discuss with your child the test-taking tips in this book. Your child can prepare by working through a couple of strategies a day so that no practice session takes too long.

Help your child with his or her regular school assignments. Set up a quiet study area for homework. Supply this area with pencils, paper, markers, a calculator, a ruler, a dictionary, scissors, glue, and so on. Check your child's homework and offer to help if he or she gets stuck. But remember, it's your child's homework, not yours. If you help too much, your child will not benefit from the activity.

Keep in regular contact with your child's teacher. Attend parent-teacher conferences, school functions, PTA or PTO meetings, and school board meetings. This will help you get to know the educators in your district and the families of your child's classmates.

Learn to use computers as an educational resource. If you do not have a computer and Internet access at home, try your local library.

Remember—simply getting your child comfortable with testing procedures and helping him or her know what to expect can improve test scores!

Getting Ready for the Big Day

There are lots of things you can do on or immediately before test day to improve your child's chances of testing success. What's more, these strategies will help your child prepare him- or herself for school tests, too, and promote general study skills that can last a lifetime.

Provide a good breakfast on test day.

Instead of sugar cereal, which provides immediate but not long-term energy, have your child eat a breakfast with protein or complex carbohydrates, such as an egg, whole grain cereal or toast, or a banana-yogurt shake.

Promote a good night's sleep. A good night's sleep before the test is essential. Try not to overstress the importance of the test. This may cause your child to lose sleep because of anxiety. Doing some exercise after school and having a quiet evening routine will help your child sleep well the night before the test.

Assure your child that he or she is not expected to know all of the answers on the test. Explain that other children in higher grades may take the same test, and that the test may measure things your child has not yet learned in school. Help your child understand that you expect him or her to put forth a good effort—and that this is enough. Your child should not try to cram for these tests. Also avoid threats or bribes; these put undue pressure on children and may interfere with their best performance.

Keep the mood light and offer encouragement. To provide a break on test days, do something fun and special after school—take a walk around the neighborhood, play a game, read a favorite book, or prepare a special snack together. These activities keep your child's mood light—even if the testing sessions have been difficult—and show how much you appreciate your child's effort.

Taking Standardized Tests

No matter what grade you're in, this is information you can use to prepare for standardized tests. Here is what you'll find:

- Test-taking tips and strategies to use on test day and year round.
- Important terms to know for Language Arts, Reading, Math, Science, and Social Studies.
- A checklist of skills to complete to help you understand what you need to know in Language Arts, Reading Comprehension, Writing, and Math.
- General study/homework tips.

By opening this book, you've already taken your first step towards test success. The rest is easy—all you have to do is get started!

What You Need to Know

There are many things you can do to increase your test success. Here's a list of tips to keep in mind when you take standardized tests—and when you study for them, too.

Keep up with your school work. One way you can succeed in school and on tests is by studying and doing your homework regularly. Studies show that you remember only about one-fifth of what you memorize the night before a test. That's one good reason not to try to learn it all at once! Keeping up with your work throughout the year will help you remember the material better. You also won't be as tired or nervous as if you try to learn everything at once.

Feel your best. One of the ways you can do your best on tests and in school is to make sure your body is ready. To do this, get a good night's sleep each night and eat a healthy breakfast (not sugary cereal that will leave you tired by the middle of the morning). An egg or a milkshake with yogurt and fresh fruit will give you lasting energy. Also, wear comfortable clothes, maybe your lucky shirt or your favorite color on test day. It can't hurt, and it may even help you relax.

Be prepared. Do practice questions and learn about how standardized tests are organized. Books like this one will help you know what to expect when you take a standardized test.

When you are taking the test, follow the directions. It is important to listen carefully to the directions your teacher gives and to read the written instructions carefully. Words like *not, none, rarely, never,* and *always* are very important in test directions and questions. You may want to circle words like these.

Look at each page carefully before you start answering. In school you usually read a passage and then answer questions about it. But when you take a test, it's helpful to follow a different order.

If you are taking a Reading test, first read the directions. Then read the questions before you read the passage. This way, you will know exactly what kind of information to look for as you read. Next, read the passage carefully. Finally, answer the questions.

On math and science tests, look at the labels on graphs and charts. Think about what each graph or chart shows. Questions often will ask you to draw conclusions about the information.

Manage your time. *Time management* means using your time wisely on a test so that you can finish as much of it as possible and do your best. Look over the test or the parts that you are allowed to do at one time. Sometimes you may want to do the easier parts first. This way, if you run out of time before you finish, you will have completed a good chunk of the work.

For tests that have a time limit, notice what time it is when the test begins and figure out when you need to stop. Check a few times as you work through the test to be sure you are making good progress and not spending too much time on any particular section.

You don't have to keep up with everyone else. You may notice other students in the class finishing before you do. Don't worry about this. Everyone works at a different pace. Just keep going, trying not to spend too long on any one question.

Fill in answer sheets properly. Even if you know every answer on a test, you won't do well unless you enter the answers correctly on the answer sheet.

Fill in the entire bubble, but don't spend too much time making it perfect. Make your mark dark, but not so dark that it goes through the paper! And be sure you choose only one answer for each question, even if you are not sure. If you choose two answers, both will be marked as wrong.

It's usually not a good idea to change your answers. Usually your first choice is the right one. Unless you realize that you misread the question, the directions, or some facts in a passage, it's usually safer to stay with your first answer. If you are pretty sure it's wrong, of course, go ahead and change it. Make sure you completely erase the first choice and neatly fill in your new choice.

Use context clues to figure out tough questions. If you come across a word or idea you don't understand, use context clues—the words in the sentences nearby—to help you figure out its meaning.

Sometimes it's good to guess. Should you guess when you don't know an answer on a test? That depends. If your teacher has made the test, usually you will score better if you answer as many questions as possible, even if you don't really know the answers.

On standardized tests, here's what to do to score your best. For each question, most of these tests let you choose from four or five answer choices. If you decide that a couple of answers are clearly wrong but you're still not sure about the answer, go ahead and make your best guess. If you can't narrow down the choices at all, then you may be better off skipping the question. Tests like these take away extra points for wrong answers, so it's better to leave them blank. Be sure you skip over the answer space for these questions on the answer sheet, though, so you don't fill in the wrong spaces.

Sometimes you should skip a question and come back to it later. On many tests, you will score better if you answer more questions. This means that you should not spend too much time on any single question. Sometimes it gets tricky, though, keeping track of questions you skipped on your answer sheet.

If you want to skip a question because you don't know the answer, put a very light pencil mark next to the question in the test booklet. Try to choose an answer, even if you're not sure of it. Fill in the answer lightly on the answer sheet.

Check your work. On a standardized test, you can't go ahead or skip back to another section of the test. But you may go back and review your answers on the section you just worked on if you have extra time.

First, scan your answer sheet. Make sure that you answered every question you could. Also, if you are using a bubble-type answer sheet, make sure that you filled in only one bubble for each question. Erase any extra marks on the page.

Finally—avoid test anxiety! If you get nervous about tests, don't worry. *Test anxiety* happens to lots of good students. Being a little nervous actually sharpens your mind. But if you get very nervous about tests, take a few minutes to relax the night before or the day of the test. One good way to relax is to get some exercise, even if you just have time to stretch, shake out your fingers, and wiggle your toes. If you can't move around, it helps just to take a few slow, deep breaths and picture yourself doing a great job!

Terms to Know

Here's a list of terms that are good to know when taking standardized tests. Don't be worried if you see something new. You may not have learned it in school yet.

acute angle: an angle of less than 90°

adjective: a word that describes a noun (*yellow duckling*, *new bicycle*)

adverb: a word that describes a verb (*ran fast, laughing heartily*)

analogy: a comparison of the relationship between two or more otherwise unrelated things (*Carrot is to vegetable as banana is to fruit.*)

angle: the figure formed by two lines that start at the same point, usually shown in degrees

antonyms: words with opposite meanings (*big* and *small, young* and *old*)

area: the amount of space inside a flat shape, expressed in square units

article: a word such as *a*, *an*, or *the* that goes in front of a noun (*the chicken, an apple*)

cause/effect: the reason that something happens

character: a person in a story, book, movie, play, or TV show

compare/contrast: to tell what is alike and different about two or more things

compass rose: the symbol on a map that shows where North, South, East, and West are

conclusion: a logical decision you can make based on information from a reading selection or science experiment

congruent: equal in size or shape

context clues: language and details in a piece of writing that can help you figure out difficult words and ideas

denominator: in a fraction, the number under the line; shows how many equal parts a whole has been divided into ($\frac{1}{2}, \frac{6}{7}$)

direct object: in a sentence, the person or thing that receives the action of a verb (*Jane hit the ball hard.*)

equation: in math, a statement where one set of numbers or values is equal to another set (*6 + 6 = 12, 4 x 5 = 20*)

factor: a whole number that can be divided exactly into another whole number (*1, 2, 3, 4, and 6 are all factors of 12.*)

genre: a category of literature that contains writing with common features (*drama, fiction, nonfiction, poetry*)

hypothesis: in science, the possible answer to a question; most science experiments begin with a hypothesis

indirect object: in a sentence, the noun or pronoun that tells to or for whom the action of the verb is done (*Louise gave a flower to her sister.*)

infer: to make an educated guess about a piece of writing, based on information contained in the selection and what you already know

main idea: the most important idea or message in a writing selection

map legend: the part of a map showing symbols that represent natural or human-made objects

noun: a person, place, or thing (*president, underground, train*)

numerator: in a fraction, the number above the line; shows how many equal parts are to be taken from the denominator ($\frac{3}{4}, \frac{1}{5}$)

operation: in math, tells what must be done to numbers in an equation (such as add, subtract, multiply, or divide)

parallel: lines or rays that, if extended, could never intersect

percent: fraction of a whole that has been divided into 100 parts, usually expressed with % sign ($\frac{5}{100} = 5\%$)

perimeter: distance around an object or shape

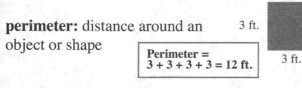

Perimeter = 3 + 3 + 3 + 3 = 12 ft.

3 ft.

3 ft. 3 ft.

3 ft.

perpendicular: lines or rays that intersect to form a 90° (right) angle

90°

predicate: in a sentence, the word or words that tell what the subject does, did, or has (*The fuzzy kitten had black spots on its belly.*)

predict: in science or reading, to use given information to decide what will happen

prefixes/suffixes: letters added to the beginning or end of a word to change its meaning (*reorganize, hopeless*)

preposition: a word that shows the relationship between a noun or pronoun and other words in a phrase or sentence (*We sat by the fire. She walked through the door.*)

probability: the likelihood that something will happen, often shown with numbers

pronoun: a word that is used in place of a noun (*She gave the present to them.*)

ratio: a comparison of two quantities, often shown as a fraction (*The ratio of boys to girls in the class is 2 to 1, or 2/1.*)

sequence: the order in which events happen or in which items can be placed in a pattern

subject: in a sentence, the word or words that tell who or what the sentence is about (*Uncle Robert baked the cake. Everyone at the party ate it.*)

summary: a restatement of important ideas from a selection in the writer's own words

symmetry: in math and science, two or more sides or faces of an object that are mirror images of one another

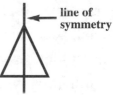

line of symmetry

synonyms: words with the same, or almost the same, meaning (*delicious* and *tasty, funny* and *comical*)

Venn diagram: two or more overlapping circles used to compare and contrast two or more things

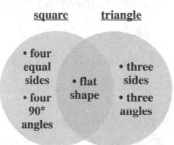

square   triangle

- four equal sides
- four 90° angles
- flat shape
- three sides
- three angles

verb: a word that describes an action or state of being (*He watched the fireworks.*)

writing prompt: on a test, a question or statement that you must respond to in writing

Multiple Choice Questions

You have probably seen multiple choice questions before. They are the most common type of question used on standardized tests. To answer a multiple choice question, you must choose one answer from a number of choices.

EXAMPLE	**Cheap has about the same meaning as _____.**

    Ⓐ generous   Ⓒ expensive

    Ⓑ stingy   Ⓓ charitable

Sometimes you will know the answer right away. But other times you won't. To answer multiple choice questions on a test, do the following:

- First, answer any easy questions whose answers you are *sure* you know.
- When you come to a harder question, circle the question number. You can come back to this question after you have finished all the easier ones.
- Eliminate any answers that you know are wrong. The last choice left is probably the correct one!
- Look for clue words like *same*, *opposite*, *not*, *probably*, *best*, *most likely*, and *main*. They can change the meaning of a question or help you eliminate answer choices.

Testing It Out
Now look at the example question more closely.

Think: I know that I'm looking for a synonym for *cheap*. I think that *cheap* means inexpensive or unwilling to spend money. Choice **A**, *generous*, means giving—that's the opposite of *cheap*.

I'm not sure what *stingy* means, so I'll come back to that one. Choice **C**, *expensive*, means "costs a lot." That's also the opposite of *cheap*, so that can't be the answer.

I'm not sure what *charitable* means, but I think it has something to do with charity, which is giving money away. If you give money away, you're not *cheap*, so that's probably not the answer.

Now back to **B**, *stingy* this is the only remaining choice, I'll try to use it in a sentence in place of *cheap*. "My brother is really *stingy* when it comes to buying birthday presents." Yes, that makes sense. So I'll choose **B**, *stingy*, as my synonym for *cheap*.

Fill-in-the-Blank Questions

On some tests, you will be given multiple choice questions where you must fill in something that's missing from a phrase, sentence, equation, or passage. These are called fill-in-the-blank questions.

> **EXAMPLE** **Aaron rides the roller coaster for the feeling of _____ through space.**
>
> Ⓐ strolling Ⓒ plummeting
>
> Ⓑ stirring Ⓓ plumbing

Directions: To answer fill-in-the-blank questions, do the following:

- Try to think of the answer even before you look at your choices. Even if the answer *is* one of the choices, check the other choices. There may be a better answer.
- Look for the articles *a* and *an* to help you. Since the word *a* must be followed by a consonant and *an* must be followed by words starting with vowel sounds, you can often use articles to eliminate choices.
- For harder questions, try to fit every answer choice into the blank. Which makes sense?
- If you get stuck, try filling in the blank on your own choice (not an answer provided). Then look for synonyms for your new word/words among the answer choices.

Testing It Out

Now look at the example question more closely.

Think: Roller coasters move very quickly; choice **A**, *strolling*, means walking not very fast. So choice **A** doesn't fit.

Choice **B** is *stirring*. I don't think that roller coasters have anything to do with stirring.

Choice **C** is *plummeting*. I think it has something to do with falling. "Aaron rides the roller coaster for the feeling of *falling* through space." That could be right.

Choice **D**, *plumbing*, is a noun that has to do with pipes in your house. That answer choice makes no sense.

So, I think *plummeting* makes the most sense. "Aaron rides the roller coaster for the feeling of *plummeting* through space." I'll choose **C**, *plummeting*, to fill in the blank.

True/False Questions

A true/false question asks you to read a statement and decide if it is right (true) or wrong (false).

EXAMPLE **Every year has 365 days.**

Ⓐ true

Ⓑ false

To answer true/false questions on a test, do the following:

- True/false sections contain more questions than other sections of a test. If there is a time limit on a test, you may need to go more quickly than usual. Do not spend too much time on any one question.
- First, answer all of the easy questions. Circle the numbers next to harder ones and come back to them later.
- If you have time left after completing all the questions, quickly double-check your answers.
- True/false questions with words like *always, never, none, only,* and *every* are usually false. This is because they limit a statement so much.
- True/false questions with words like *most, many,* and *generally* are often true. This is because they make statements more believable.

Testing It Out

Now look at the example question more closely.

Think: I know that 365 is the usual number of days in a year. Why would there be more or fewer days in a year? That's right, there's a leap year every four years. I can't remember how many days there are in a leap year, but it must be different than 365. So I'll answer **F** for false; every year does not have 365 days.

Matching Questions

Matching questions ask you to find words or phrases that are related in a certain way. The choices are often shown in columns.

Match items that mean the same, or almost the same, thing.

1	indigo	**A**	green	1	Ⓐ Ⓑ Ⓒ Ⓓ
2	scarlet	**B**	red	2	Ⓐ Ⓑ Ⓒ Ⓓ
3	ebony	**C**	black	3	Ⓐ Ⓑ Ⓒ Ⓓ
4	chartreuse	**D**	blue	4	Ⓐ Ⓑ Ⓒ Ⓓ

When answering matching questions on tests, follow these guidelines:

• Match the easiest choices first.
• For a difficult word, try using it in a sentence. Then repeat the sentence, substituting your answer choices. The answer that fits best in the sentence is probably the correct one.
• Some matching items contain phrases rather than single words. Begin with the column that has the most words. This column will usually give the most information.
• Work down one column at a time. It is confusing to switch back and forth.

Testing It Out
Now look at the example question more closely.

Think: Both columns contain colors, so I am looking for colors that are the same or closely related. I know that *indigo* comes after blue in the rainbow, so it must be either a kind of blue or purple. Since purple is not a choice, I'll match *indigo* to **D,** *blue*.

I'm pretty sure that *scarlet* is a kind of red, so the answer to number 2 is **B**.

I'm not sure what color *ebony* is, but I think it might be a kind of wood, and I've heard it used to describe keys on a piano. So it could be either black or white, but black makes more sense. I'll choose **C**.

The last item in the column is *chartreuse*, but I have no idea what that means. However, green is the only remaining choice and I'm fairly certain of my other answers. So I'll match 4, *chartreuse*, to **A,** *green*.

Analogy Questions

Analogies ask you to figure out the relationship between two things. Then you must complete another pair with the same relationship.

EXAMPLE   <u>**Contented**</u> **is to** <u>**uneasy**</u> **as** <u>**thoughtless**</u> **is to** _____.

   Ⓐ generous   Ⓒ rude

   Ⓑ considerate   Ⓓ mournful

Analogies usually have two pairs of items. In the question above, the two pairs are *contented/uneasy* and *thoughtless/* _____. To answer analogy questions on standardized tests, do the following:

- First, figure out how the first pair of items relate to each other. Try to form a sentence that explains how they are related.
- Next, use your sentence to figure out the missing word in the second pair of items.
- For more difficult analogies, try each answer choice in the sentence you formed.
- Decide if you are looking for a noun, verb, adjective, or other part of speech. If the first pair of words are nouns and the word you are looking to match is a noun, you're probably looking for a noun. So you can eliminate any choices that are not nouns.

Testing It Out

Now look at the example question more closely.

Think: How are *contented* and *uneasy* related? "*Contented* and *uneasy* are antonyms." So I am looking for the opposite of *thoughtless*.

A, *generous*, means giving. I guess this is very different from being *thoughtless*; perhaps it is even an antonym. This may be the answer.

I think that **B,** *mournful*, means sad. It's not really an antonym.

C, *rude*, is similar in meaning to *thoughtless*. It is not an antonym.

I know that **D,** *considerate*, means to be thoughtful. So *considerate* is definitely an antonym for *thoughtless*. So I'll choose **D,** *considerate*, as my answer.

Short Answer Questions

Some test questions don't give you answers to choose from. Instead, you must write short answers in your own words. They often ask you to respond to a passage or other information you have been given. These are called "short answer" or "open response" questions.

> **Gino knocked at Mark's back door. "Hey, Mark, want to check out the house they're building across the street? They just made stairs to the second floor, and I bet we could climb up to the roof if we wanted to!" he exclaimed.**
>
> **"Gee, I don't know," Mark said. "It sounds kind of dangerous. Why don't we go to the park instead?"**

1. Is Gino cautious or adventurous? How do you know? _____

2. In your own words, tell why Marcus doesn't want to go to the house across the street. _____

When you must write short answers to questions, follow these guidelines:

- Make sure to respond directly to the question that is asked, not details or statements that are given elsewhere in the body of the question.
- Your response should be short but complete. Don't waste time including unnecessary information, but be sure to answer the entire question, not just a part of it.
- Write in complete sentences unless the directions say you don't have to.
- Make sure to double-check your answers for spelling, punctuation, and grammar.

Testing It Out

Now look at the example question more closely.

Think: From the story, I can tell that Gino is adventurous. He wants to explore a house that isn't finished yet. Who knows what's inside?

1. Gino is adventurous. He wants to explore an empty, unfinished house even though it might be dangerous.

2. Marcus probably doesn't want to go into the house because there might be holes in the floor, tools lying around, or other things left unfinished. Also, going up to the roof is dangerous because it's high off the ground and who knows if they're even done building it yet!

Reading

Many standardized tests have sections called "Reading" or "Reading Comprehension." Reading questions test your ability to read for detail, find meaning in a sentence or passage, and use context clues to figure out words or ideas you don't understand.

Here is a list of topics covered on reading tests, along with tips and examples.

Word Meaning

Word meaning questions test your vocabulary and your ability to figure out unfamiliar words. When answering questions about word meaning, do the following:

- Look at words carefully to see if you can find prefixes, suffixes, or root words that give clues to their meaning.

- For clues to a more difficult word's meaning, look at the other words in the sentence or passage.

Literal and Inferential Comprehension

You will be asked to read short passages and think about their meanings in two ways:

Literal Comprehension: These questions ask about specific details in the story— they are generally "who," "what," "when," and "where" questions. You can find the answers by going back to the story and reading carefully.

Inferential Comprehension: These questions ask you to use the information in the story to draw conclusions or make predictions. They are generally "why" and "how" questions. These questions can be harder to answer because the specific information may not be found in the story. Start by eliminating unreasonable answer choices.

Main Idea

You will be asked to identify the main idea of some of the passages you read. The **main idea** is the most important idea about a topic or passage. Questions about the main idea might look like this:

What is the main idea of the passage?

What is the writer's purpose?

What would be a good title for this story?

Genre

You will probably be asked to identify the **genre** to which a passage belongs. **Genre** refers to different categories of writing in both fiction and nonfiction, such as science fiction, fantasy, adventure, persuasive writing, newspaper articles, and so on. You will probably also be asked to show whether a sentence expresses a **fact** or an **opinion**.

Language Arts

Standardized tests usually include questions about spelling, grammar, punctuation, and capitalization. These questions are often grouped together in sections called "Language Mechanics and Expression" or "Language Arts."

The following is a list of different topics included under Language Mechanics and Expression. Look at the tips and examples that go with each topic.

Grammar

Grammar is the set of rules that helps you write good, clear sentences. Follow these guidelines:

- Be sure that the verb in the sentence is in the correct tense.

> Yesterday I <u>swam</u> at the pool. (past tense)
>
> Today I <u>am swimming</u> at the pool. (present tense)
>
> Tomorrow I <u>will swim</u> at the pool. (future tense)

- Remember how to use different parts of speech such as nouns, verbs, adjectives, adverbs, and pronouns. Remember that an adjective describes a noun and an adverb describes a verb.

> The <u>shy</u> child hid behind the chair. (adjective)
>
> The child smiled <u>shyly</u>. (adverb)

Capitalization and Punctuation

You will probably be asked specific questions about capitals and punctuation marks, but you will also be required to use them when you write answers in your own words. Keep in mind:

- All sentences start with a capital letter, as do all proper nouns.

- Capitalize proper adjectives.

> Lucy was the only <u>C</u>hinese-<u>A</u>merican student in the competition.

- All sentences should end with a period, a question mark, or an exclamation point. Make sure you pick the one that best fits the meaning of the sentence.

- Use apostrophes to show possession.

> the <u>clown's</u> hat (singular possession)
>
> the <u>clowns'</u> hats (plural possession)

Language Arts

Spelling

You may be asked to pick out misspelled words or choose the correct spelling of a word that is already misspelled.

Watch your spelling with plural nouns. There are three basic ways to make a word plural:

- Add **s** (desks, lamps, pillows)
- Add **es** (foxes, beaches, marches)
- Change the **y** to **i** and add **es** (babies, ladies, diaries)

There are also common irregular plurals like *children*, *women*, *sheep*, and *fish*.

Sentence Structure

Keep in mind the parts of a complete sentence:

- The **simple subject** is the part of the sentence that is doing something.

> My friend's <u>dog</u> gnawed happily on his bone.

- The **complete subject** is the subject and all of the words which describe it.

> <u>My friend's dog</u> gnawed happily on his bone.

- The **simple predicate** is the part of the sentence that tells what the subject is doing.

> My friend's dog <u>gnawed</u> happily on his bone.

- The **complete predicate** is the predicate and all the words which describe it.

> My friend's dog <u>gnawed happily on his bone</u>.

Also keep in mind:

- A **sentence fragment** is a phrase that is missing either a subject or a predicate.

- You can often make two sentences more interesting by combining them. To do this, you can use conjunctions such as *and*, *but*, *so*, or *however*. You can also combine sentences with punctuation marks such as commas and semicolons. However, you must be careful not to change the meaning of the sentences you are combining.

> I like apples. I like pears. I don't like bananas.
>
> I like apples <u>and</u> pears, <u>but</u> I don't like bananas.

Writing

Many tests ask you to respond to a writing prompt. When responding to a writing prompt, follow these guidelines.

Read the Prompt

- Read the instructions carefully. Sometimes you will be given a choice of questions or topics to write about. You don't want to respond to more questions than you need to.

- Once you have located the prompt to answer, read it twice to be sure you understand it. Remember, there is no one right response to a writing prompt; there are only stronger and weaker arguments.

Prewrite

- Before you write your answer, jot down some details to include.

- You may find it helpful to use a chart, web, illustration, or outline to help you organize the information you want to include in your response.

A **web** is a way of organizing your thoughts. If you were writing about the advantages of having a dog as a pet, your web might look like this:

- Even if you aren't asked to, it is always a good idea to include facts and examples that support your answer. If the prompt asks you to respond to a reading passage, you can include specific examples from the passage to strengthen your argument.

Draft

- Begin your answer with a **topic sentence** that answers the prompt and gives the main idea.

- Write **supporting sentences** that give details and tell more about your main idea. All of these sentences should relate to the topic sentence.

- If you are allowed, skip lines as you write. That way you'll have space to correct your mistakes once you're done.

Proofread

- Make sure to proofread your draft for missing words, grammar, punctuation, capitalization, indentation, and spelling. Correct your mistakes.

Math: Trick Questions

Some test questions contain the word *not*. You must be careful to notice when the word *not* is used. These are a type of trick question; you are being tested to see if you have read and understood the material completely.

EXAMPLE   **Which of the following is not a fraction?**

Ⓐ $1\frac{2}{3}$

Ⓑ $4\frac{5}{9}$

Ⓒ $\frac{7}{16}$

Ⓓ 9.04

- When solving this type of problem, first figure out how the word *not* applies to the problem. In this case, you must find the number that is not a fraction.

- Next, you need to know what a fraction is and compare what you know to your answer choices.

You read the answer choices and decide that

$1\frac{2}{3}$ is a fraction.

$\frac{7}{16}$ is a fraction.

$4\frac{5}{9}$ is a fraction.

9.04 is a decimal.

- So the correct answer choice is **D**: 9.04 is not a fraction; it is a decimal.

When you are asked questions containing the word *not*:

❏ Read the problem carefully.

❏ Determine how the word is used in the problem.

❏ Solve the problem.

❏ Check your work.

Math: Paper and Pencil

On tests, it often helps to work a problem out using paper and pencil. This helps you to visualize the problem and double-check your answer. It is especially useful when you must solve an equation.

EXAMPLE **Mr. Thomas is planning the seating for a party he is having. There will be 167 guests altogether and 8 people can sit at one table. How many tables will Mr. Thomas need so everyone can have a seat?**

Ⓐ 23 tables

Ⓑ 20 tables

Ⓒ 21 tables

Ⓓ 18 tables

- Since it would be difficult to solve the problem mentally, you need to do the work for the problem using paper and pencil.
- Use paper and pencil to divide 167 by 8.

$$
\begin{array}{r}
20 \ \ R7 \\
8\overline{)167} \\
\underline{16} \ \ \ \\
7 \\
\underline{0} \\
7
\end{array}
$$

- There is a remainder of 7. Since Mr. Thomas needs enough tables to seat everyone, he must have 21 tables altogether. The correct answer is **C**.

When you use pencil and paper:

❏ Read the problem carefully.

❏ Write neatly so that you do not make errors.

❏ Solve the problem.

❏ Check your work.

Math: Estimation

Directions: Use estimation to help you narrow down answer choices on a multiple choice test.

| EXAMPLE | **A band gave 204 concerts in one year. One-fourth of these concerts were performed in the United States. How many concerts did the band perform in the United States?** |

Ⓐ 97 concerts   Ⓒ 59 concerts

Ⓑ 82 concerts   Ⓓ 51 concerts

- First, estimate the answer by rounding up or down. When rounding, you should round to the most precise place needed for the problem. In this case, you should round to the nearest ten, which happens to become the nearest hundred: 204 rounds to 200.
- You do not need to round $\frac{1}{4}$ because it multiplies and divides easily with 200. Now you can estimate the answer to the problem using these two numbers.
- You can cross off choices **A** and **B** since they do not have a five in the tens place.

$$\begin{array}{r} 50 \\ 4\overline{)200} \end{array}$$

- Find the exact answer by dividing:
$$\begin{array}{r} 51 \\ 4\overline{)204} \end{array}$$
- Now you can be sure that **D** is the correct answer.

When you estimate and answer:

❏ Read the problem carefully.

❏ Round the numbers you need to estimate the answer.

❏ Estimate the answer.

❏ Eliminate any answers not close to your estimate.

❏ Find the exact answer.

Math: Concepts

Standardized tests also test your understanding of important math concepts you will have learned in school. The following is a list of concepts that you may be tested on.

Number Concepts

- recognizing the standard and metric units of measure used for weighing and finding length and distance.

- recognizing place value (through the millions place and the thousandths place).

- telling time to the nearest minute.

- using a calendar.

- reading a thermometer.

- rounding up and down to the nearest whole number or five, ten, or hundred.

- prime numbers.

- mixed numbers and improper fractions.

- equivalent fractions.

- fraction/decimal equivalents.

Geometry

- identifying solid shapes such as prisms, spheres, cubes, cylinders, and cones.

- finding the area and perimeter of flat shapes.

- finding the line of symmetry in a flat shape.

- telling about the number of angles and sides of flat shapes.

- telling about the number of vertices, faces, and edges of a solid shape.

- recognizing parallel, perpendicular, and intersecting lines.

- recognizing congruent shapes.

- knowing the difference among acute, obtuse, and right angles.

Other Things to Keep in Mind

- If you come to a difficult problem, think of what you do know about the topic and eliminate answer choices that don't make sense.

- You may be given a problem that can't be solved because not enough information is provided. In that case, "not enough information" or "none of the above" will be an answer choice. Carefully consider each of the other answer choices before you decide that a problem is not solvable.

Math: Applications

You will often be asked to apply what you know about math to a new type of problem or set of information. Even if you aren't exactly sure how to solve a problem of this type, you can usually draw on what you already know to make the most logical choice.

When preparing for standardized tests, you may want to practice some of the following:

- how to use a number line with whole numbers and decimals.

- putting numbers in order from least to greatest and using greater than/less than symbols.

- recognizing complex number patterns and object patterns and extending them.

- writing an equation to solve a problem.

- solving time duration problems.

- reading bar graphs, tally charts, or pictographs.

- reading pie charts.

- reading simple line graphs.

- reading and making Venn diagrams.

- reading and plotting x-y coordinates.

Other Things to Keep in Mind

- When answering application questions, you may want to use scrap paper to work out some problems.

- If you come to a problem you aren't sure how to solve or a word or idea you don't recognize, try to eliminate answer choices by using what you do know. Then go back and check your answer choice in the context of the problem.

Introduction

The remainder of this book is made up of two tests. On page 225, you will find a Practice Test. On page 264, you will find a Final Test. These tests will give you a chance to put the tips you have learned to work. There is also a name and answer sheet preceding each test and an answer key at the end of the book.

Here are some things to remember as you take these tests:

- Be sure you understand all the directions before you begin each test.

- Ask an adult questions about the directions if you do not understand them.

- Work as quickly as you can during each test. There are no time limits on the Practice Test, but you should try to make good use of your time. There are suggested time limits on the Final Test to give you practice managing your time.

- You will notice little **GO** and **STOP** signs at the bottom of the test pages. When you see a **GO** sign, continue on to the next page if you feel ready. The **STOP** sign means you are at the end of a section. When you see a **STOP** sign, take a break.

- You can guess at an answer or skip difficult items and go back to them later.

- Use the tips you have learned whenever you can.

- It is OK to be a little nervous. You may even do better.

- When you complete all the lessons in this book, you will be on your way to test success!

- After you have completed your tests, check your answers with the answer key.

Practice Test Answer Sheet

Fill in **only one** letter for each item. If you change an answer, make sure to erase your first mark completely.

Unit 1: Reading, pages 225–239

A ABCD	**9** ABCD	**19** ABCD	**D** ABCD
B FGHJ	**10** FGHJ	**20** FGHJ	**28** ABCD
1 ABCD	**11** ABCD	**21** ABCD	**29** FGHJ
2 FGHJ	**12** FGHJ	**22** FGHJ	**30** ABCD
3 ABCD	**13** ABCD	**C** ABCD	**31** FGHJ
4 FGHJ	**14** FGHJ	**23** ABCD	**32** ABCD
5 ABCD	**15** ABCD	**24** FGHJ	**33** FGHJ
6 FGHJ	**16** FGHJ	**25** ABCD	
7 ABCD	**17** ABCD	**26** FGHJ	
8 FGHJ	**18** FGHJ	**27** ABCD	

Practice Test Answer Sheet

Unit 2: Language Arts, pages 240–250

A ABCD	**11** ABCD	**E** FGHJ	**34** FGHJ
1 ABCD	**12** FGHJ	**23** FGHJK	**35** ABCD
2 FGHJ	**13** ABCD	**24** ABCDE	**36** FGHJK
B ABCD	**14** FGHJ	**F** ABCD	**37** ABCD
3 ABCD	**15** ABCD	**25** ABCD	**38** FGHJ
4 FGHJ	**16** FGHJ	**26** FGHJ	**39** ABCD
5 ABCD	**17** ABCD	**27** ABCD	**40** FGHJ
6 FGHJ	**18** FGHJ	**28** FGHJ	**41** ABCDE
7 ABCD	**19** ABCD	**29** ABCD	**42** FGHJK
8 FGHJ	**D** ABCD	**30** FGHJ	**43** ABCDE
9 ABCD	**20** ABCD	**31** ABCD	**44** FGHJK
10 FGHJ	**21** FGHJ	**32** FGHJ	
C ABCD	**22** ABCD	**33** ABCD	

Practice Test Answer Sheet

Unit 3: Mathematics, pages 251–260

A ABCDE	**7** ABCD	**16** FGHJK	**24** ABCD
B FGHJK	**8** FGHJ	**17** ABCDE	**25** FGHJ
1 ABCDE	**9** ABCD	**18** FGHJK	**26** ABCD
2 FGHJK	**10** FGHJ	**19** ABCDE	**27** FGHJ
3 ABCDE	**11** ABCD	**20** FGHJK	**28** ABCD
4 FGHJK	**12** FGHJ	**21** ABCDE	**29** FGHJ
C ABCD	**13** ABCD	**D** ABCD	**30** ABCD
5 ABCD	**14** FGHJ	**22** ABCD	**31** FGHJ
6 FGHJ	**15** ABCD	**23** FGHJ	

Reading

Lesson 1 **Reading Nonfiction**

SAMPLE A

Walking briskly has been called the perfect exercise. If you keep up the pace and move your arms actively, you burn up calories and tone your muscles. In one respect, walking is even better than running—you aren't as likely to hurt your feet, knees, or lower back.

In this passage, the writer talks about "walking briskly." The word *briskly* probably means

A by yourself.

B with others.

C quickly.

D slowly.

SAMPLE B

Which sentence would best follow the last sentence in the passage?

F Best of all, walking is free.

G Another good sport is swimming.

H Back problems affect many people.

J Even so, people still run.

TIPS

Skim the story, then skim the questions. Answer the easiest questions first. Most answers can be checked in the story.

Look for key words in the question or the answer you think is right. Find these words in the story and you'll be able to check your answer.

Getting Around

In today's world, there are countless ways to travel, from space shuttles to plain old walking. In this part of the book, you'll read about two very different ways of getting around, one new and one very old.

GO

Name _____

Directions: Patricia wrote this report for a school project. She knew the topic well because she had just been on a school trip to England. Read the report, then do numbers 1–11.

Destination Europe

Airline travel is becoming so affordable and easy that many people are deciding to take vacations to far-away places, especially Europe. Flying to a foreign country is very different from flying from one American city to another, however, so it is important to prepare carefully.

Before taking an international flight, travelers must decide where they are going and when they want to go. Different countries are more enjoyable at certain times of the year. Then travelers must make a reservation and buy their tickets from a travel agent or airline. During busy times of the year, these steps must be taken several weeks or even months before the trip.

All international travelers need a passport, a legal document that lets them enter foreign countries and return to America. Passports look like thin, small books, with the traveler's home country written on the front. Inside is a picture of the person and important information about the traveler. In many respects, a passport is like a hall pass. Instead of letting you walk around school, it lets you travel in foreign countries.

Most airlines let each person bring only two suitcases, so travelers should choose carefully what to take with them. Of course, clothes and personal items are necessary. Since other countries use different kinds of money, most travelers buy some of the foreign money before leaving home. Flights from the United States to Europe last about nine hours, so it's a good idea to bring a book or a game to play to pass the time. Some planes fly overnight, so passengers can sleep part of the time.

On the day of the trip, travelers should arrive at the airport with their suitcases and tickets, along with their passports. The airline agent will exchange the ticket for a boarding pass and send the suitcases to a handler, who will put them on the plane. The agent will also check each passport to be sure everything is in order. Travelers then go to their gates and wait for the flights. Recently, some airlines have stopped giving paper tickets and started doing their ticketing electronically. This saves paper and time, and passengers like it because they can't lose their tickets.

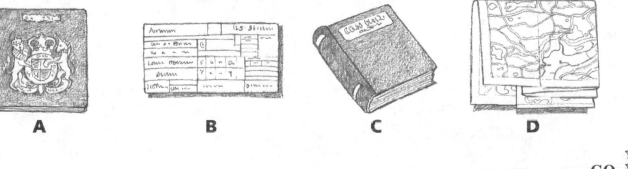

As people board the plane, they find the seats on their boarding passes and put their carry-on bags in a safe place. No plane can take off until the passengers are in their seats with their seat belts fastened. Airplane seats have high backs and armrests, like big armchairs. Some airline seats have plugs for headphones so passengers can listen to music. These headphones may also be used to enjoy a movie shown on a big screen. The newest planes even have a small video screen for each passenger.

The inside of an airplane looks a little like a big, fancy bus. The pilot and crew are in a little room at the front. The passengers sit in rows with a wide walkway down the middle. A small part of the plane is for the flight attendants, and there are also bathrooms.

Large planes have several flight attendants, who are there to make the flight safe and comfortable. When it is time to eat, flight attendants bring meals, which are served on small fold-down trays. These trays can also be used for other things, like playing cards. Some airline seats are next to the windows, giving passengers who sit in them a real bird's-eye view of the ground.

The most difficult thing about traveling to Europe is the time change. As the plane flies, it crosses time zones. Imagine that you leave New York at lunchtime and arrive in Paris, France, eight hours later. Your watch tells you it's time for dinner, but in Paris, it's 4:00 in the morning and most people in France are asleep. To remind you to change your watch, the pilot announces the local time before the flight ends.

Once the plane has landed, the suitcases are taken to an area of the airport called Customs. This is where special airport workers look at what travelers bring into the country. Then, after a passport check, the travelers are free to begin their visit.

As you can see, international air travel can be fun and exciting, as long as travelers plan ahead and know what to expect.

1   **Which picture shows what a passport looks like?**

A   **B**   **C**   **D**

GO

2 **Travelers need a passport to**

    F enter their own country after a trip.

    G leave their seats in the airplane.

    H get their baggage after arriving.

    J choose the dates they plan to travel.

3 **This passage is mostly about**

    A what happens in an airport.

    B taking a flight to another country.

    C flying in the United States.

    D the cost of international travel.

4 **From what you read, which of the following looks most like an airplane seat?**

     F   **G**   **H**   **J**

5 **The author compares a passport to a**

    A hall pass.

    B bus pass.

    C plane ticket.

    D parking ticket.

GO

6 The author of the passage would probably agree that international airline travel

F is too complicated.

G costs too much money.

H is usually frightening.

J can be fun and exciting.

7 Which of these statements about the passage best supports your answer choice for number 6?

A The passage is mostly about travel to distant places.

B The passage is mostly about living in a distant place.

C The passage is mostly about different ways to travel.

D The passage is mostly about airport terminals.

8 The author says that "no plane can take off until the passengers are in their seats with their seat belts fastened." The words *take off* probably mean

F come back.

G start the engine.

H stop moving.

J leave the ground.

9 Which idea helps you know that your answer to number 8 is right?

A Before the plane goes up in the air, passengers must be wearing their seat belts.

B Some planes have video screens for each passenger.

C Airline seats are a little like armchairs.

D Each airline seat has a seat belt, and some have headphones.

10 The author says that "As people board the plane, they find the seats on their boarding passes and put their carry-on bags in a safe place." The word *board* probably means

F walk around.

G get into.

H get out of.

J stand on.

11 If you wanted to learn more about the topic of the passage, which of these books would be most useful?

A *Train Guide to Europe*

B *International Travel Guide*

C *Flying Cheaply in the U.S.A.*

D *How to Get a Job With an Airline*

GO

Directions: Some of Patricia's friends wrote about travel experiences they had. These questions are about their writing.

12 **In which of these resources could Marty find information about travel agents in his town?**

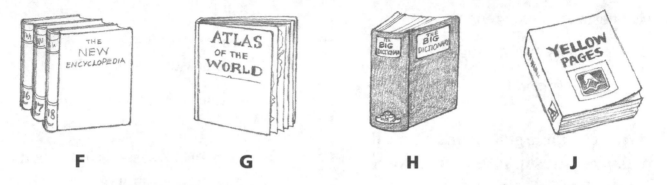

F   G   H   J

13 **Julia is reading an article about planes. Under which of these headings in the article should she look to find out what kinds of fuel different planes use?**

A Types of Engines

B Types of Wings

C Landing a Plane

D Steering a Plane

14 **Which of the sentences below best combines these two sentences into one?**

My brother has antique skis.
The antique skis are made of wood.

F Made of wood, my brother has antique skis.

G My brother has antique skis and the skis are made of wood.

H My brother has antique skis made of wood.

J Antique skis made of wood my brother has.

GO

Name _____

Directions: More than 70 years ago, an American athlete did something most everyone thought was impossible. This is the story of that great athlete and her accomplishment. Read the story, then do numbers 15–22.

First Lady of Swimming

Thousands of people cross the channel of water between France and England every day in planes, ferries, and even trains. An American athlete, Gertrude Caroline Ederle, however, used a different method. She was the first woman to swim across the English Channel.

Gertrude Ederle was born in New York City in 1906. She dedicated herself to the sport of swimming at an early age and enjoyed great success. Before long, she was on her way to becoming one of the most famous American swimmers of her time. When she was sixteen, Ederle broke seven records in one day at a swimming competition in New York. Two years later, in 1924, she represented the United States at the Olympic Games, winning a gold medal in the 400-meter freestyle relay.

After her Olympic victory, she looked for an even greater challenge. One of the most difficult swims is to cross the 21-mile English Channel. The seas in the channel can be rough, and the water is cold. In the past, the feat had only been accomplished by male swimmers. Most people believed that the swim was too difficult for a woman, but Ederle wanted to prove them wrong. She didn't make it on her first attempt, but in 1926 she tried again. Leaving from the coast of France, Ederle had to swim even longer than planned because of heavy seas. She went an extra fourteen miles and still managed to beat the world record by almost two hours. This accomplishment made her an instant heroine at the age of twenty.

After her triumph, Ederle traveled around the United States as a professional swimmer, delighting spectators of all ages. Unfortunately, a severe back injury kept her out of the pool for four years. It wasn't until 1939 that she swam in public again, in a swimming show at the New York World's Fair.

Later in life, Ederle worked as a swimming instructor for hearing-impaired children. She was also appointed to President Eisenhower's Youth Fitness Committee. Her dedication to the sport of swimming has made Gertrude Ederle a role model for athletes ever since. Because of her willingness to accept enormous challenges, she is a good example for anyone who wants to excel.

GO

15 According to the passage, why did Ederle decide to swim across the English Channel?

    A There weren't ferries across the Channel then.

    B She wanted to be the first woman to do it.

    C She wanted the attention it would bring her.

    D A friend had dared her to do it.

16 Which of these best describes why Ederle swam farther than 21 miles to cross the English Channel?

    F There were heavy seas that day.

    G She wanted to show off for the spectators.

    H Her start was slow, then she lost confidence.

    J She got lost because of the fog.

17 How did the public react after Ederle broke the world record for the swim across the English Channel?

    A They all wanted to do it, too.

    B They admired her courage and dedication.

    C They thought she hadn't really done it.

    D They wanted her to do it again.

18 Which of these is not one of Gertrude Ederle's accomplishments?

    F winning a gold medal in the Olympic Games

    G swimming in the coldest water in the world

    H breaking a world record for swimming the English Channel

    J being appointed to a presidential committee

GO

19 Which definition of the word *beat* is used in this sentence from the passage?

> She went an extra fourteen miles and still managed to beat the world record by almost two hours.

A to whip, like eggs

B to be faster than

C to hit, like a carpet

D the tempo of music

20 What does the author mean by the sentence reprinted in number 19?

F Setting world records isn't as important as swimming far.

G Miss Ederle failed to set a new record because she went too far.

H She was two hours late, and therefore didn't set the record.

J Miss Ederle set a new record even though she swam too far.

21 What is the main idea of the passage?

A Swimming can be a very profitable sport.

B Hard work and dedication can lead to great success.

C It's never too late to start learning something new.

D People who compete in the Olympics usually go far.

22 Here is a paragraph about another swimmer. Which sentence does not belong in the paragraph?

F Sentence 1

G Sentence 2

H Sentence 3

J Sentence 4

> [1]Sara Fernandez is a young athlete who has been swimming since she was six. [2]She also learned to ride a bike when she was young. [3] Sara has to use a wheelchair, but she has become a great swimmer. [4]Recently, she went to the state swimming championships and won two silver medals.

STOP

Lesson 2 Reading Fiction

SAMPLE C

The ski instructor helped Danny stand up. He gave Danny a little push, and the boy began sliding down the mountain. Just when Danny thought he would fall, the instructor caught him.

This is probably Danny's

A only vacation.

C first time skiing.

B last day of school.

D first time in the snow.

TIPS

If a question seems difficult, look at the answer choices, then read the question again.

As soon as you know which answer is right, mark it and go on to the next item. Check your answers only after you have tried all the items.

Directions: Here is a story about a family that is taking an exciting vacation, one that you might enjoy. Read the story and then do numbers 23–27.

Floating the River

"Aren't we there yet?" Shiloh asked. At last, she and her family were on their way to their annual tubing trip. Floating down Glenn River on an inner tube was one of Shiloh's favorite things. She was sure this year's trip would be the best ever. They would float five whole miles, all the way to Glenn Fork. They planned to stop along the way to eat their lunches, but only if the lunches stayed dry in their waterproof packs! There would also be time for swimming, another thing Shiloh loved to do.

With each passing mile, Shiloh smiled more and more as she thought of the fun they would have. When they finally reached Glenn Fork and parked the car, she jumped out, all ready to go.

GO

"Not so fast, Shiloh," said her mother. "Remember, we're just here to leave the car. We still have to drive up the river. After we float back here, we'll be able to drive the car upstream to the truck. Otherwise, we won't have any way to get home."

"Oh, yeah, false alarm," Shiloh said. She had forgotten the family's plan to leave one car at each end of the float.

Once the whole family was in the truck, they set out for Jenkins Bar, a sandy beach on a wide part of the river. It didn't take very long to get there on the road. But because of the river's many winding turns and slow current, it would take them about three hours to float back to Glenn Fork. "That's three wonderful hours of tubing," thought Shiloh, "and the fun is about to begin."

Shiloh's father helped her unload her backpack and shiny tube from the truck. Once everyone was ready, they left the truck and walked down to the river's bank. They all put their toes in the water, and Shiloh gasped as she felt how cold the water was. Since she was a little taller and stronger this time, she wasn't as afraid of the river's current. She remembered having to hold her mother's hand last year, the way her little sister was doing now. Shiloh took a deep breath and pushed herself out into the river. As she followed her family downstream, she thought to herself, "This will be the best tubing trip ever!"

23 **In the story, Shiloh decides that getting out of the car at Glenn Fork was a "false alarm." In this case, a _false alarm_ is a**

A warning   **C** misunderstanding

B funny story   **D** mistake

GO

24 **Why does Shiloh think that this year's trip will be the best ever?**

    F Her family has started down the river without her.

    G She is stronger and less afraid now.

    H They have decided to leave a car at each end of the trip.

    J She gets to carry her own tube and backpack.

25 **By the end of the passage, Shiloh's feelings have changed from**

    A (sadness) → (happiness)

    B (boredom) → (sadness)

    C (fear) → (impatience)

    D (impatience) → (excitement)

26 **This story is mostly about**

    F driving a car and a truck.

    G a one-day adventure.

    H a tiresome journey.

    J being older and stronger.

27 **The members of Shiloh's family seem to**

    A get along well.

    B worry about the weather.

    C compete with each other.

    D have long discussions.

STOP

Name _____

Lesson 3 Review

[1] My grandfather us visits almost every week. [2] He lives in a small town about an hour away.

Choose the best way to rewrite Sentence 1.

A Every week, my grandfather almost visits us.

B My grandfather visits us almost every week.

C My grandfather, who visits us almost every week.

D Almost every week, my grandfather visiting us.

Directions: Here is a daily journal written by a young boy visiting his cousins. There arc several mistakes that need correcting.

Monday, April 16

[1] Today I arrived in Glen Mill to stay with my cousins. [2] They live in a big house on a farm. [3] There are a lot of animals to care for and other things to do. [4] Farms usually have a main house, a barn, and lots of land. [5] Tomorrow I'll get to help with the calves. [6] We'll also make homemade jam. [7] It sounds like life on a farm is more busier than life in the city.

28 **Which is the best way to write Sentence 3?**

A There being a lot of animals to take care of and things to do.

B There is a lot of animals to take care of and things to do.

C Being a lot of animals to take care of and things to do.

D Best as it is

29 **Which sentence does not belong in the paragraph?**

F Sentence 1

G Sentence 4

H Sentence 5

J Sentence 7

GO

237   Summer Link Super Edition Grade 6

Journal

Wednesday, April 18

[1] Today was very busy. [2] Jane, Carl, and I went out around 8:00 to fill our buckets with blackberries. [3] It was hard work, and we didn't get back until it was time for lunch. [4] This afternoon, Aunt Mara showed us how to wash and sort the berries. [5] She did the cooking part, but she let us fill the jars and decorate the labels. [6] Now Aunt Mara is letting me take a jar of jam home for Mom she'll be surprised I made it. [7] I hope the rest of my stay here is as much fun as today was.

30 **Which sentence contains two complete thoughts and should be written as two sentences?**

   A Sentence 1

   B Sentence 3

   C Sentence 5

   D Sentence 6

31 **If students wanted to find out more information about life on a farm, it would be most helpful to look**

   F in an encyclopedia under "calves."

   G in a dictionary under "farming."

   H in an atlas under the heading "Glen Mill."

   J in a book about farm life.

GO

Directions: On this page, you will read about a girl named Rachel who lives on a very different kind of farm. Here are two paragraphs about where she lives.

32 **Choose the sentence that best fills the blank in the paragraph.**

> People laugh when I tell them what kind of farm we have. My family raises catfish! _____. We feed them pellets that look almost like the food you feed cats or dogs.

A Then the fish are sent to a store.

B The fish live in ponds on our farm.

C Before we raised cows and sheep.

D Even my little brother helps out.

33 **Rachel wrote about how her family's catfish farm works. Choose the sentence that best fills the blank in the paragraph.**

> A big tank truck filled with water comes to the farm. Inside the truck are thousands of baby catfish. The truck backs up to the edge of a pond. _____. My mother and I hold the other end in the pond. The truck driver opens up the tank, and the fish go from the tank into the pond.

F Then my father hooks one end of a big hose up to the truck.

G However, the driver is very busy.

H Each of us does a different thing.

J Afterward, the driver moves the truck to another pond.

STOP

Language Arts

Lesson 1   Vocabulary

Directions: For Sample A and numbers 1 and 2, read the sentences. Choose the word that correctly completes both sentences.

SAMPLE A

Is this your _____ of gum?
Gerry will _____ her bags.

   A stick

   B pack

   C move

   D piece

1 I threw the _____ at the target.
The bird _____ from the tree.

   A darts   **C** flies

   B balls   **D** jumps

2 Will you _____ the cheese for me?
A _____ covered the opening.

   F slice   **H** buy

   G lid   **J** grate

Directions: For Sample B and numbers 3 and 4, choose the word that means the **opposite** of the underlined word.

SAMPLE B

<u>bitter</u> taste

   A strange

   B sweet

   C dull

   D pleasant

3 <u>harvest</u> vegetables

   A eat   **C** pick

   B cook   **D** plant

4 sleepy <u>driver</u>

   F cyclist   **H** passenger

   G child   **J** officer

Use the meaning of a sentence to find the answer.

Think about the meaning of the answer choices.

GO

Directions: For numbers 5 and 6, read the sentences with the missing word and the question about that word. Choose the word that best answers the question.

5 This is the _____ part of the project. Which word means it was the first part of the project?

   A final   **C** reasonable

   B initial   **D** challenging

6 Louis had to _____ the floor. Which word means Louis had to clean the floor very well?

   F scrub   **H** deposit

   G rinse   **J** replace

Directions: For numbers 7 and 8, choose the word that means the same, or about the same, as the underlined word.

7 tiny **particle**

   A animal

   B package

   C piece

   D gift

8 <u>assist</u> him

   F bother

   G help

   H hinder

   J join

Directions: For numbers 9 and 10, read the paragraph. For each numbered blank, there is a list of words with the same number. Choose the word from each list that best completes the meaning of the paragraph.

   One of the most ___(9)___ books ever written almost went unpublished. Margaret Mitchell's novel *Gone with the Wind* was rejected by several editors. Eventually, it was published and received a Pulitzer Prize. Mitchell's epic about the Civil War became the best-selling book in American publishing history and was later turned into an ___(10)___ successful movie.

9 **A** humorous   **C** recent

     B famous   **D** difficult

10 **F** internally   **H** emotionally

     G equally   **J** originally

STOP

Lesson 2 Language Mechanics

Directions: For Sample C and numbers 11–14, look at the underlined part of the sentence. Choose the answer that shows the best capitalization and punctuation for that part.

SAMPLE C

The library will be closed this <u>week. It</u> will open again on Monday.

A week. it

B Week, it

C week it

D Correct as it is

---

11 <u>Mom: don't you</u> want me to go with you to the store?

A Mom. Don't you

B Mom? don't you

C Mom, don't you

D Correct as it is

12 While you were gone, Mr. Taylor <u>said "the party</u> starts at noon."

F said The party

G said, "The party

H said, "the party

J Correct as it is

13 Marisa has to go to the dentist <u>today But</u> she would rather stay home.

A today, but

B today. but

C today; but

D Correct as it is

14 On our trip to the beach, we found <u>rocks, shells, and starfish.</u>

F rocks shells and starfish.

G rocks, shells, and, starfish.

H rocks, shells and, starfish.

J Correct as it is

Compare the answer choices carefully.

Ask yourself: "Am I looking for a mistake or correct capitalization and punctuation?"

GO

Directions: For numbers 15 and 16, choose the answer that is written correctly and shows the correct capitalization and punctuation.

15
A How can Anthony stand to sleep for so long.

B Babies spend a lot of time sleeping

C When the alarm rings, try to wake up'?

D We like to sleep outside in the summer.

16
F Which boy didnt enter the photo contest?

G Angela can't see the winning photos from here.

H Mrs. Johnsons' class won first place in the contest.

J My cousin's always take photos on their vacation.

Directions: For numbers 17–19, read the letter and the underlined parts. Choose the answer that shows the best capitalization and punctuation for each part.

(17) November, 5 2001

(18) Dear Juan

I am sorry I missed your party last week. I had already been invited to my aunt's house by the Nueces River, we had a good time. Thanks for the invitation anyway.

(19) Your friend;

Nancy

17
A november 5, 2001

B November 5, 2001

C November 5 2001

D Correct as it is

18
F Dear Juan,
G dear Juan,

H Dear Juan:
J Correct as it is

19
A Your friend,
B Your Friend

C your friend
D Correct as it is

STOP

Lesson 3 Spelling

Directions: For Sample D and numbers 20–22, choose the word that is spelled correctly and best completes the sentence.

Directions: For Sample E and numbers 23 and 24, read each phrase. Find the underlined word that is not spelled correctly. If all the underlined words are spelled correctly, mark "All correct."

SAMPLE D The sports _____ is next week.

  A banquet

  B banqet

  C banguet

  D bancquet

SAMPLE E

  A not <u>allowed</u>

  B <u>youngest</u> child

  C funny <u>clown</u>

  D small <u>scratch</u>

  E All correct

20 Jenny _____ the math test.

  A paist   **C** passed

  B passded   **D** passted

21 Peter _____ his shirt before going to the party.

  F ironed   **H** iorned

  G ierned   **J** irnded

22 The hikers _____ the poison ivy.

  A uvoided   **C** avoided

  B evoided   **D** avoidid

23 **F** hotel <u>lobby</u>

   G famous <u>auther</u>

   H <u>steering</u> wheel

   J strange <u>journey</u>

   K All correct

24 **A** <u>wrinkled</u> shirt

   B <u>nursery</u> school

   C young <u>coach</u>

   D <u>useless</u> idea

   E All correct

Don't spend too much time looking at the words. Pretty soon, they all begin to look like they are spelled wrong.

STOP

Lesson 4 Writing

Directions: Read the paragraph about one student's mixed feelings about going to a new school.

    I have mixed feelings about going to a new school. I miss my friends from my old school, and I miss the city where we lived before. Still, this school is newer, and it even has a new gym. I'm making new friends here, and I can take classes I couldn't take at my old school.

Directions: Now think about something you have mixed feelings about. Write one or two sentences to answer each question below, and then use your answers to write a paragraph of your own.

What do you have mixed feelings about?

_____

What do you dislike about it? Why?

_____

_____

_____

What do you like about it? Why?

_____

_____

_____

Write your own paragraph on the lines below.

_____

_____

_____

_____

GO

Directions: Read the short story about one child's problem.

    Misha stood on the stage. His knees knocked. His heart pounded. His palms were drenched. His hands shook so hard that he could barely hold his violin. A hush fell over the audience. Hundreds of eyes bored holes through Misha. He couldn't move to leave, but he didn't want to stay.

    In the wings, he heard his friend whisper. "You can do it. Take a deep breath. Close your eyes. Pretend that you're standing in your den."

    Misha shut his eyes tight. In his mind, he saw the pictures on the wall in his den. He lifted the violin to his chin and played his solo perfectly from beginning to end.

Directions: Now think about a fiction story that you would like to write. Write one or two sentences to answer each question below, and then use your answers to write a paragraph of your own.

Think about your main character. Who is it? What is he or she like?

_____

_____

What is the setting of the story?

_____

_____

What kind of problem will the main character have? How will the character solve the problem?

_____

_____

Write your own short story on the lines below.

_____

_____

_____

STOP

Lesson 5 Review

Directions: For Sample F and number 25, read the sentences. Choose the word that correctly completes **both** sentences.

> **SAMPLE F** The dog caught the _____.
> Our school has a formal _____.
>
> **A** ball   **B** dance   **C** stick   **D** event

25 The _____ climbed the tree.
I can't _____ this heat.

A fox   **C** cat

B stand   **D** bear

Directions: For numbers 26 and 27, read the sentences with the missing word. Choose the word that best answers the question.

26 We hiked to a _____ campsite.
Which word means the campsite was far away?

F remote   **H** crowded

G pleasant   **J** level

27 Joe's _____ will be remembered.
Which word means what Joe said will be remembered?

A adjustment   **C** resource

B remark   **D** impatience

Directions: For number 28, choose the word that means the **opposite** of the underlined word.

28 <u>collect</u> money

F discover   **H** distribute

G spend   **J** save

Directions: For numbers 29 and 30, choose the word that means the same, or about the same, as the underlined word.

29 <u>depart</u> soon

A leave   **C** study

B win   **D** detect

30 <u>miniature</u> house

F huge   **H** expensive

G tiny   **J** unusual

GO

Directions: For numbers 31 and 32, choose the answer that is written correctly and shows the correct capitalization and punctuation.

31 **A** Chip shouted "I found the book here under my bed!"

B "Are books always so long" he asked.

C Madeleine said, "Please bring me my book, Daddy."

D Our teacher always says, "don't leave your books at home.

32 **F** "Roller coasters scare me, but they're fun, he whispered.

G Nouria shouted "it's the biggest roller coaster in the country!"

H My mom said, you're too young to go on the roller coaster.

J "Let's go on the roller coaster," Jeremy suggested.

Directions: For numbers 33–36, read the paragraph and the underlined parts. Choose the answer that shows the best capitalization and punctuation for each part.

(33)   We are reading an article called <u>Food For Thought</u>.
(34)   It is about what we should and <u>shouldnt</u> eat as snacks.
(35)   Some of the ideas in the article are very <u>good like</u> choosing an apple instead of chips. The article
(36)   made me <u>think; but</u> it also made me hungry.

33 **A** "Food for Thought."

B "food for thought."

C food for thought.

D Correct as it is

35 **A** good. Like

B good Like

C good, like

D Correct as it is

34 **F** shouldn't

G should'nt

H shouldnt'

J Correct as it is

36 **F** think, But

G think, but

H think but

J Correct as it is

GO

Directions: For numbers 37–40, choose the word that is spelled correctly and best completes the sentence.

37 We'll be _____ after this run.

A thirsdy

B thirsty

C thursty

D thirstie

38 We were in a harmless _____ yesterday.

F accident

G acident

H accidint

J accadent

39 Make sure to _____ the cans from the bottles.

A seperate   C separat

B sepparate   D separate

40 Please _____ me when you get home.

F tellephone   H telefone

G telaphone   J telephone

Directions: For numbers 41–44, read each phrase. Find the underlined word that is **not** spelled correctly. If all the underlined words are spelled correctly, mark "All correct."

41 A crowded stadium

  B memorize words

  C substitute teacher

  D ancient ruins

  E All correct

42 F hard to swallow

  G happy occasion

  H locate the station

  J usuelly right

  K All correct

43 A important meeting

  B diffrent route

  C among the best

  D autumn leaves

  E All correct

44 F three quarts   **J** two teaspoons

  G one acre   **K** All correct

  H ten minites

GO

Directions: Read the paragraph that tells about a challenging experience that one student had.

I've never been as scared as I was the first time I tried to go inline skating. My legs felt like jelly. The skates kept slipping out from under me. I'd thought I'd just soar through the air in jumps and spins, but I found out that skating isn't as easy as it looks. Since then, I've been practicing, and I'm getting better. With even more practice, I know that I'll continue to improve.

Directions: Now, think about a challenging experience you have had. Write one or two sentences to answer each question below, and then use your answers to write a paragraph of your own.

What is a challenging experience you have faced?

_____

_____

_____

_____

Why was the experience challenging? How did you feel when you first tried it?

_____

_____

_____

_____

Write your own paragraph on the lines below.

_____

_____

_____

_____

_____

STOP

Mathematics

Lesson 1   Computation

SAMPLE A			
	413	**A**	320
	+ 133	**B**	446
		C	546
		D	556
		E	None of these

SAMPLE B			
55 − 19 =	**F**	34
	G	44
	H	46
	J	74
	K	None of these

 **TIPS**

Skim the problems and do the easiest ones first. Check your answer by the opposite operation.

1

7291	**A**	7005
+ 296	**B**	6587
	C	7585
	D	7587
	E	None of these

3

3106	**A**	3109
× 3	**B**	9418
	C	9318
	D	9609
	E	None of these

2

4008	**F**	2027
− 2021	**G**	1987
	H	2987
	J	6029
	K	None of these

4

$\frac{1}{3} + \frac{1}{3} =$	**F**	0
	G	$\frac{1}{6}$
	H	$\frac{11}{13}$
	J	$\frac{1}{8}$
	K	None of these

STOP

Lesson 2 Mathematics Skills

SAMPLE C

What is the area of the shaded figure?

A 5 square units

B $5\frac{1}{2}$ square units

C 6 square units

D $6\frac{1}{2}$ square units

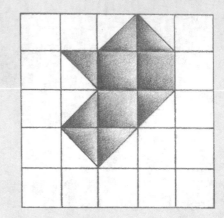

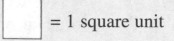 = 1 square unit

Think about what you are supposed to do before you start working.

Eliminate answers you know are wrong.

Before you mark your answer, compare it with the question. Does your answer make sense?

Name _____

Our Hockey Team

5 Carla has 6 hockey cards. Ed and Carla together have 16 hockey cards. Judith and Ed together have 25 hockey cards. How many hockey cards does Judith have?

A 6

B 9

C 15

D 20

6 The table shows the number of goals Luke, Jacques, Pierre, and Roland have scored during the hockey season. If the trend continues, which player is most likely to score a goal in the next game?

Players	Luke	Jacques	Pierre	Roland
Number of Goals	✓✓✓✓✓ ✓	✓✓✓✓✓ ✓✓✓✓✓ ✓✓✓✓	✓✓✓✓✓ ✓✓✓	✓✓✓

F Luke

G Jacques

H Pierre

J Roland

7 The number of people watching a hockey game is 900 when rounded to the nearest hundred and 850 when rounded to the nearest ten. Which of these could be the number of people watching the game?

A 847

B 849

C 856

D 852

GO

8 After the hockey game, each of these players bought a can of soda from a machine that takes both coins and bills.

Soda
70¢

– Luke used only dimes.

– Jacques used only quarters.

– Pierre used only half-dollars.

– Roland used a dollar bill.

Which two players got the same amount of change?

F Luke and Jacques

G Jacques and Pierre

H Pierre and Roland

J Roland and Luke

9 The Card Shop receives a shipment of trading cards each month. There are 8 hockey cards in a pack, 12 packs in a box, and 16 boxes in a shipping crate. Which is the total number of hockey cards in the shipping crate?

A 1536

B 672

C 1436

D 662

8 cards
in a pack

12 packs
in a box

16 boxes
in a crate

GO

Hair Color

Directions: The tally chart shows the hair color of some 5th-grade students. Study the chart. Then do numbers 10–12.

10 **Which of these questions could you answer using the information on the tally chart?**

F How often do the students get their hair cut?

G How many students dye their hair?

H Which students have long hair?

J How many more brown-haired students are there than blond-haired students?

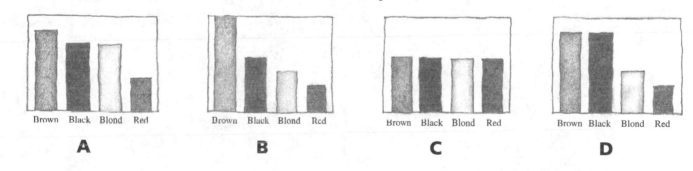

11 **Which graph below shows the data on the tally chart?**

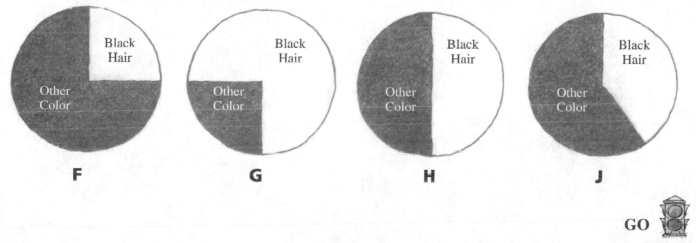

12 **Which circle shows the fraction of the students on the tally chart that have black hair?**

13 Lori's class used hobby sticks to make skeletons of solid figures. Study the picture of the prism and its skeleton.

How many hobby sticks would be needed to make a skeleton of a rectangular pyramid?

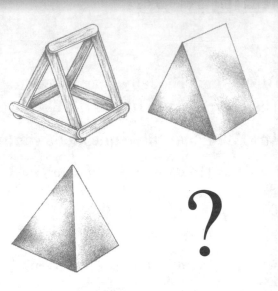

A 9

B 8

C 7

D 4

14 How many pairs of congruent figures are on the grid?

F 4

G 5

H 6

J 7

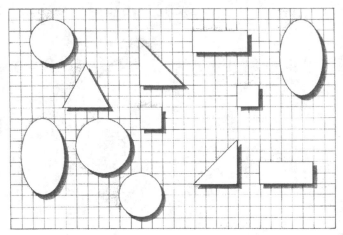

15 If 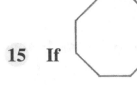 = 1, then which of these pictures represents $1\frac{3}{8}$?

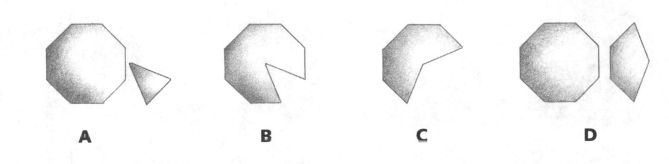

| A | B | C | D |

16   1.14
       + 4.53

F   5.57

G   5.66

H   5.76

J   5.77

K   None of these

17 $20\frac{7}{8}$
       $- 5\frac{3}{8}$

A $25\frac{1}{2}$

B $15\frac{1}{2}$

C $14\frac{1}{2}$

D $15\frac{2}{7}$

E   None of these

18   3000
       $\times$ 42

F   126,000

G   120,420

H   300,420

J   300,042

K   None of these

19 $31\overline{)1085}$

A   34

B   34 R1

C   35

D   35 R1

E   None of these

20 $\frac{5}{6} - \frac{2}{3} =$

F $\frac{1}{3}$

G $1\frac{1}{9}$

H $\frac{1}{6}$

J   1

K   None of these

21 $490 \div 7 =$

A   70

B   90

C   420

D   560

E   None of these

STOP

Lesson 3 Review

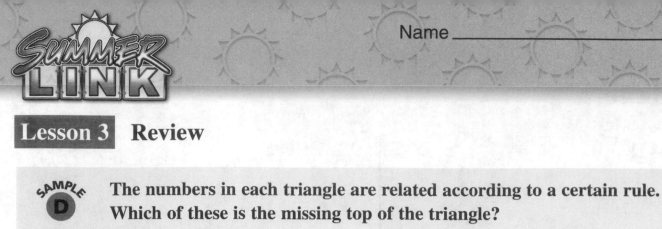

SAMPLE
D

The numbers in each triangle are related according to a certain rule. Which of these is the missing top of the triangle?

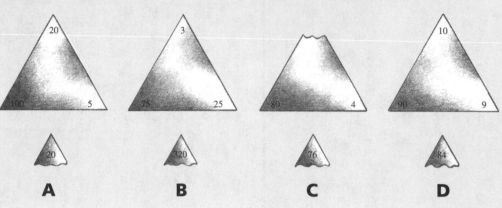

| A | B | C | D |

Directions: For numbers 22–25, you do not need to find exact answers. Use estimation to choose the best answer.

22 Jay took a test that had a true/false section, a matching section, and a multiple choice section. Look at the score card below. Which of these is the best estimate of his point total on the multiple choice section?

A 20 points

B 30 points

C 40 points

D 50 points

True/False	1-10
1 Wrong	
Matching	1-15
2 Wrong	
Multiple	
Choice	1-25
5 Wrong	
2 pts. per question.	

23 5700 ÷ 7

The answer to this problem is about

F 8000

G 800

H 80

J 8

24 Which of these is the best estimate of 57.4 + 79.7?

A less than 100

B between 100 and 150

C between 150 and 200

D greater than 200

25 Sharon earned $125.50 baby-sitting on weekend nights. She had $46.89 left after she bought some new clothes. Which of these is the best estimate of the cost of her clothes?

F $20.00

G $40.00

H $60.00

J $80.00

GO

Our Favorite Subjects

Directions: The 5th graders at Memorial School voted for their favorite subject in school. They made a graph to show how they voted.

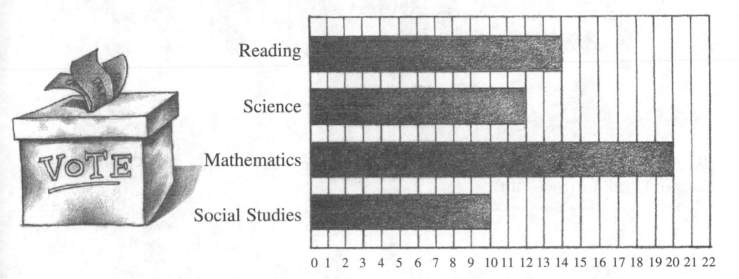

26 How many more students voted for mathematics than voted for science?

A 2   **C** 6

B 4   **D** 8

27 Which of these could not happen if 8 more 5th graders added their votes to the graph?

F Social studies could have the most votes.

G Science and math could have the same number of votes.

H Science could have more votes than reading.

J Social studies could have more votes than science.

28 Which of these statements about the vote is true?

A More than three-quarters of the 5th graders voted for mathematics.

B Exactly one-quarter of the 5th graders voted for reading.

C More than one-quarter of the 5th graders voted for social studies.

D Exactly one-quarter of the 5th graders voted for science.

GO

29 Which shape is exactly two-thirds shaded?

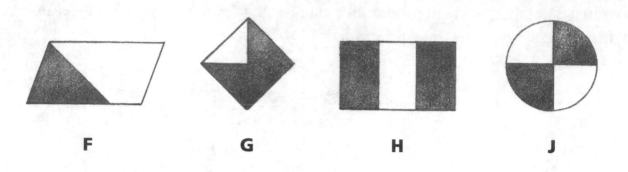

F G H J

30 Xavier cut an eight-sided piece of paper along a line of symmetry. Which of these could not be the result?

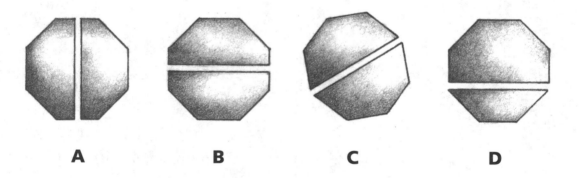

A B C D

31 Which of these points shows about where 3×87 would be put on the number line?

F Point A

G Point B

H Point C

J Point D

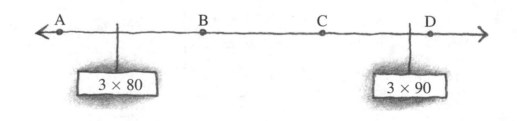

STOP

Final Test Answer Sheet

Fill in **only one** letter for each item. If you change an answer, make sure to erase your first mark completely.

Unit 1: Reading, pages 264–269

A ABCD	7 ABCD	14 FGHJ	21 FGHJ
1 ABCD	8 FGHJ	15 ABCD	22 ABCD
2 FGHJ	9 ABCD	16 FGHJ	23 ABCD
3 ABCD	10 FGHJ	17 ABCD	24 ABCD
4 FGHJ	11 ABCD	18 FGHJ	25 ABCD
5 ABCD	12 FGHJ	19 FGHJ	
6 FGHJ	13 ABCD	20 FGHJ	

Name _____

Final Test Answer Sheet

Unit 2: Language Arts, pages 270–278

A ABCD	10 FGHJ	21 ABCD	32 FGHJ
1 ABCD	11 ABCD	22 FGHJ	33 ABCD
B ABCD	12 FGHJ	23 ABCD	34 FGHJ
2 FGHJ	13 ABCD	24 FGHJ	35 ABCD
3 ABCD	14 FGHJ	25 ABCD	36 FGHJ
4 FGHJ	15 ABCD	26 FGHJ	37 ABCD
5 ABCD	16 FGHJK	27 ABCD	38 FGHJ
6 FGHJ	17 ABCDE	28 FGHJ	39 ABCD
7 ABCD	18 FGHJK	29 ABCD	
8 FGHJ	19 ABCDE	30 FGHJ	
9 ABCD	20 FGHJ	31 ABCD	

Name _____

Final Test Answer Sheet

Unit 3: Mathematics, pages 279–287

A ABCD	10 FGHJ	22 FGHJ	34 FGHJ
B FGHJK	11 ABCD	23 ABCD	35 ABCD
1 ABCDE	12 FGHJ	24 FGHJ	36 FGHJ
2 FGHJK	13 ABCD	25 ABCD	37 ABCD
3 ABCDE	14 FGHJ	26 FGHJ	38 FGHJ
4 FGHJK	15 ABCD	27 ABCD	39 ABCD
5 ABCDE	16 FGHJ	28 FGHJ	40 FGHJ
6 FGHJK	17 ABCD	29 ABCD	41 ABCD
C ABCD	18 FGHJ	30 FGHJ	42 FGHJ
7 ABCD	19 ABCD	31 ABCD	43 ABCD
8 FGHJ	20 FGHJ	32 FGHJ	
9 ABCD	21 ABCD	33 ABCD	

Reading

Directions: Read the paragraph, then answer the question.

SAMPLE A
John practiced playing piano every day after school. Sometimes it wasn't easy, especially on days when the other kids were playing sports. He enjoyed sports, especially basketball, but he loved piano even more.

On a rainy Saturday, John would probably

A play basketball.

B watch basketball on television.

C play piano.

D play another musical instrument.

Directions: When Kiki and her family were shipwrecked on an island, they began a new life. Read the story about Kiki's home, then do numbers 1–9.

Survivors

As far as Kiki was concerned, the island had always been her home, and she loved it. She had been just about a year old when the ship she and her family had been on was caught in a great storm. She didn't remember their home in England, where she had been born, or boarding the sailing ship for Australia. Kiki certainly didn't remember how her family and a few dozen others had arrived on the island in lifeboats, or even how they had built houses and made new lives. Kiki's first memory was sitting in the warm lagoon with her mother's arms around her. Her brother and sister were splashing in the waves, and her father was in a small boat spearing fish.

The Martin family and the others who had survived the shipwreck had worked hard to make the island livable. Now, ten years after the disaster, the island was a wonderful place to grow up. Everyone had a comfortable home with furniture made out of wood, palm leaves, and vines. Their food came from the sea, from jungle plants, or from small gardens the survivors had planted. They were able to accomplish so much because chests of seeds, tools, and food had washed up on the beach in the weeks following the wreck. These chests gave the survivors a chance to build a new life on the island.

GO

Kiki and the other children went to school just like other children, with the grownups taking turns teaching the children. They learned to write on large leaves using burnt sticks and to read from books that had been in several of the chests. They also learned arithmetic, science, history, and geography. But most of all, they learned about their island. Part of every school day was spent exploring the island and discovering more and more about its plants, animals, and geography.

It was on one of these outings to explore the island that Kiki and her friends saw the great ships. They had climbed to the highest peak on the island to learn about the sea birds that nested on the cliffs below. When the children reached the top of the peak, they spent a few minutes looking at the ocean all around them. Kiki spotted the four ships first, with their huge sails billowing in the wind. She shouted to her teacher, and soon everyone saw them. The ships were clearly headed toward the island.

By the time Kiki and her friends climbed down the mountain, the ships had reached the island, and the captain and crew were surprised to find other English settlers there. They had known about the shipwreck, of course, but had no idea there were survivors. The ships were heading to Australia, and the survivors were welcomed to join the crew on board.

That, however, was the problem. Almost all the survivors didn't want to leave the island, especially the children like Kiki who had spent most of their lives there or the dozen who had been born there. For them, the island was their world, and they couldn't imagine leaving it.

GO

Name _____

1 **This story is mostly about**

A a family leaving England for Australia.

B survivors being rescued years later.

C how people lived after a shipwreck.

D children discovering sailing ships.

2 **Which of these best describes Kiki's feelings at the end of the story?**

F She was frightened by the great ships.

G She loved the island and didn't want to leave.

H She wanted to finish the journey to Australia.

J She was grateful for being rescued.

3 **Which ideas from the story support your answer to number 2?**

A The children couldn't imagine leaving the island.

B Kiki saw the great ships from a mountain top.

C The survivors were welcomed to board the ship.

D They had survived a terrible storm.

4 **Which of these actions led to Kiki's spotting the ships?**

F splashing in the lagoon

G spearing fish in the lagoon

H climbing the mountain

J looking for wood and palm leaves

5 **The survivors were able to make the island a good place to live because they**

A were skilled at building things from wood.

B found the chests with seeds, tools, and food.

C decided not to continue to Australia.

D believed that they would be rescued some day.

6 **Imagine that the children were given a chance to vote on whether to leave the island or stay. Which of these would probably happen?**

F Most would vote to stay.

G Most would vote to go.

H It would be a tie vote.

J They would not want to vote.

GO

7 In the year after the shipwreck, the feelings of the survivors probably changed from

A fear to anger.

B boredom to tolerance.

C joy to confusion.

D sadness to acceptance.

8 The story states that, "It was on one of these outings to explore the island" that the ships were seen. Used in this way, the word outings probably means

F a brief voyage.

G a walking trip.

H an open field.

J an empty cave.

9 Here is a time line of what happens in the passage.

Families board ship	Storm wrecks ship	Chests are found	?	New ships appear

Which of these events should go in the empty box?

A Kiki grows up

B Settlers reach America

C Kiki is born

D Settlers leave England

GO

Directions: Read the passage. Then answer the questions.

There are many differences between frogs and toads. Frogs have narrow bodies and ridges down their backs. They have large, round ear membranes and small teeth in their upper jaws. Their long hind legs **enable** them to take long leaps. They have smooth, moist, soft skin. Most frogs are water-dwellers. They lay clumps of eggs in their watery habitat.

In contrast, toads have chubby bodies and ridges on their heads. Toads make their homes on land and their skin is thick, dry, and bumpy. A toad's short legs **limit** it to short leaps only. Their ear membranes are smaller than frogs'. They have no teeth. Although toads are land-dwellers, they deposit their eggs in water as frogs do. However, they lay eggs in strings rather than clumps.

10 **What would be a good title for this passage?**

   F "Laying Eggs in Water"

   G "Frogs and Toads: What's the Difference?"

   H "Amphibians"

   J "Similarities Between Frogs and Toads"

11 **In this passage, the word *limit* means**

   A to restrict or hold back.

   B boundary.

   C the greatest number or amount allowed.

   D restriction.

12 **Which word is an antonym for *enable*?**

   F prevent

   G assist

   H inedible

   J teach

13 **Which of the following is not a fact?**

   A Toads have chubbier bodies than frogs.

   B Frogs have longer hind legs than toads.

   C Toads have smaller ear membranes than frogs.

   D Frogs are more attractive than toads.

GO

Directions: Choose the best answer for each of the following. Mark the letter of your choice for each next to the correct number on your answer sheet.

14 Raise is to uplift as bring down is to _____.

F depress   H pull

G undo   J rely

16 Email is to write as telephone is to _____.

F speak   H ring

G listen   J download

15 Millimeter is to meter as gram is to _____.

A liter

B kilometer

C kilogram

D milligram

17 Biographer is to life story as reporter is to _____.

A science fiction

B personal narrative

C newspaper

D newspaper article

Directions: Match words with the same meanings.

18 silence   F bcratc

19 belittle   G amusement

20 questionable   H quiet

21 entertainment   J unreliable

Directions: Match words with the opposite meanings.

22 create   A darken

23 illuminate   B repulse

24 impress   C destroy

25 deny   D admit

STOP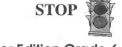

Language Arts

Directions: For Sample A and number 1, read the sentences. Choose the word that correctly completes **both** sentences.

Directions: For Sample B and numbers 2 and 3, choose the word that means the **opposite** of the underlined word.

SAMPLE A We can _____ at the park.
I'll see you at the track _____.

    A play   **C** relax

    B competition **D** meet

SAMPLE B <u>spoiled</u> fruit.

    A fresh

    B rotten

    C moldy

    D dirty

1 This _____ of books is heavy.
The book is about an unsolved _____.

    A box   **C** case

    B crime   **D** bag

2 <u>smile</u> at her

    F frown   **H** whisper

    G yell   **J** wink

3 <u>expected</u> result

    A anticipated   **C** disappointing

    B surprising   **D** pleasing

Directions: For numbers 4 and 5, read the paragraph. For each numbered blank, there is a list of words with the same number. Choose the word from each list that best completes the meaning of the paragraph.

For many years, jigsaw puzzles have entertained both children and adults. In recent years, puzzles have become even more ___(4)___ and enjoyable. Now there are three-dimensional puzzles that look exactly like the things they ___(5)___. For example, you can find 3-D puzzles that represent castles, famous buildings, and even a camera. Amazingly, the camera can even take pictures.

4 **F** boring   **H** simple

    G inexpensive   **J** challenging

5 **A** imitate   **C** improve

    B replace   **D** assemble

GO

Directions: For numbers 6 and 7, choose the answer that is written correctly and shows the correct capitalization and punctuation.

6 **F** You know that I don't like carrots Aunt Latifa.

    G Have you ever made carrot salad, Inez?

    H Dad! do I have to finish my carrots?

    J Molly can you remember to water the carrots tomorrow?

7 **A** Rain is good for plants and, it provides water for people.

    B When it rains, the sky gets dark; and the temperature drops.

    C The sound of rain is usually quiet, but, during a storm it can be loud.

    D The rain fell steadily, and the fields began to flood.

Directions: For numbers 8–11, look at the underlined part of the paragraph. Choose the answer that shows the best capitalization and punctuation for that part.

(8)   Leo wrote an article called "<u>lizards</u>" for the school paper.
(9) He <u>didn't</u> expect anyone to get excited about it, but they did.
(10) His teacher <u>was. Pleased</u> that Leo had done such a good job.
(11) "This was the best story you ever <u>wrote she</u> said.

8 **F** lizards

    G "Lizards"

    H lizards.

    J Correct as it is

9 **A** didnt

    B didnt'

    C did'nt

    D Correct as it is

10 **F** was? Pleased

    G was pleased.

    H was pleased

    J Correct as it is

11 **A** wrote," she

    B wrote she,"

    C wrote." She

    D Correct as it is

GO

Name _____

Directions: For numbers 12–15, choose the word that is spelled correctly and best completes the sentence.

12 I'll be there in a _____.

  F minit

  G minite

  H minnute

  J minute

13 Marsha will meet us _____.

  A afterward

  B afterword

  C afterwerd

  D aftirward

14 What a _____ mistake we made!

  F terible   **H** terrible

  G terribull   **J** terrable

15 My birthday is on the _____.

  A twelth   **C** twelfeth

  B twelveth   **D** twelfth

Directions: For numbers 16–19, read each phrase. Find the underlined word that is *not* spelled correctly. If all the underlined words are spelled correctly, mark "All correct."

16 F <u>division</u> problem

  G be <u>pateint</u>

  H <u>brightly</u> colored

  J was <u>frightened</u>

  K All correct

17 A small <u>apartment</u>

  B <u>heavier</u> package

  C <u>special</u> place

  D next <u>century</u>

  E All correct

18 F <u>cuccumber</u> seeds

  G <u>pursue</u> her dream

  H <u>reference</u> section

  J political <u>campaign</u>

  K All correct

19 A <u>ceiling</u> fan   **D** <u>eighth</u> in line

  B <u>chief</u> of police   **E** All correct

  C <u>niether</u> of them

GO

Directions: For numbers 20–25, mark the letter of the punctuation mark that is needed to complete each sentence correctly.

20 "Mark and Alex where are you going?" asked Mrs. Anderson.

    ;   ,   .   none

    F   **G**   **H**   **J**

21 Please add these items to our shopping list bread, milk, orange juice, lettuce, apples, and eggs.

    :   ,   !   none

    A   **B**   **C**   **D**

22 We listened to the Presidents inaugural address in class today.

    ,   .   '   none

    F   **G**   **H**   **J**

23 "What an incredible sight this is" exclaimed one of the tourists.

    ?   !   ,   none

    A   **B**   **C**   **D**

24 Maria plays the French horn and cello; Lisa plays piano, flute, and piccolo.

    ,   :   .   none

    F   **G**   **H**   **J**

25 "Unless you combine and mix the ingredients thoroughly, warned Mom, "the batter will be lumpy."

    "   '   ,   none

    A   **B**   **C**   **D**

GO

Directions: For numbers 26–29, mark the letter of the sentence that is written correctly and shows the correct punctuation and capitalization.

26 **F** Pittsburgh, Pennsylvania the "Steel City," has over 700 bridges.

G The allegheny and the monongahela, two rivers bordering downtown Pittsburgh, join to form the ohio river.

H In 1758, General John Forbes built a fort near the fork of the two rivers and named it Fort Pitt in honor of the prime minister of Great Britain.

J Soon after, british settlers began to build a community outside the fort which Forbes named Pittsburgh.

27 **A** Did you know that the Grand Coulee dam, on the Columbia River, is the largest concrete dam in the world?

B Mrs James our social studies teacher showed us photos of the dam and all the other neat places she visited on her trip to Washington.

C I didn't realize that mount Ranier was actually a volcano like mount st Helens!

D I'd really like to visit the space needle and ride the monorail in Seattle Washington.

28 **F** The travel brochures for Arizona and New Mexico are on Dads desk?

G Lets look up some of these places online before we decide.

H Don't you think it would be fantastic to visit the grand canyon, the painted desert, and the petrified forest?

J Well, Mom and Dad want to see New Mexico's Carlsbad Caverns.

29 **A** "Mrs. Wilson and I," Began Mr. Wilson, our neighbor, have visited all 50 states."

B "Which state did you like the most, Mr. Wilson," asked Adam?

C "That's really a hard question to answer," he said, "because every state has so many interesting things to see and do."

D "We're going to Maine in august, said Adam, so maybe you can show us some of your videos."

GO

Directions: For numbers 30–35, mark the letter of the word or words that correctly complete each sentence.

30 Mai's brother walks _____ than she does.

   F rapider

   G more rapidly

   H rapidlier

   J more rapid

31 My brother and I taught _____ to swim.

   A himself

   B myself

   C themselves

   D ourselves

32 Tom misses school _____.

   F real infrequently

   G really infrequent

   H really infrequently

   J real infrequent

33 _____ are very good friends.

   A He, she, and I

   B He, she, and me

   C Him, her, and I

   D He, she, and me

34 Which one of _____ shirts do you prefer?

   F them

   G these

   H this

   J that

35 We have to replace the sidewalk _____ the weather turns too cold.

   A while

   B until

   C before

   D after

GO

Directions: For numbers 36–39, mark the letter of the sentence that is correctly written.

36 **F** She don't have nothing to do.

G You can't tell nobody nothing about this.

H He doesn't have anything more to say.

J Nobody wants none of that salad.

37 **A** Ann and I was walking in the woods yesterday.

B I am picking berries when I noticed the poison ivy.

C Now my arms and legs are covered with blisters.

D These pills and this cream is supposed to stop the itching.

38 **F** I felt worst today than I did yesterday.

G I hope I feel more better soon.

H The doctor says it could get worser tomorrow.

J I have never felt so sick before.

39 **A** Kwanzaa is an African-American holiday based on an African festival.

B The festival beginning on December 26 and lasting seven days.

C Comes from the Swahili phrases *matunda ya kwanza* meaning *first fruits*.

D In 1966 in the United States by M. Ron Karenga, a professor.

STOP

Directions: Read the paragraph below about what one student does to help at home. Then think of one thing you do to help at home. Write a paragraph that explains how to do it. Use words such as *first, next, then, finally,* and *last*.

     I help out at home by doing the wash. First, I separate clothes to be washed in cold water and in hot water. Next, I put the clothes into the water. Then I add detergent. When the clothes are clean, I put them into the dryer. Finally, I hang them up or fold them. This chore is a big contribution to my family, and I get to put away my own clothes exactly the way I like them!

_____

_____

_____

_____

_____

_____

_____

_____

_____

_____

_____

_____

_____

_____

_____

_____

_____

GO

Directions: Read the paragraph below that compares two kinds of vacations. Then think of two other things to compare and contrast, such as different sports, musicians, or books. Use your ideas to write a paragraph. As you write, use words such as *same, like, different, unlike, but,* and *however*.

A beach vacation and a ski vacation are alike in some ways and different in others. On both kinds of vacations, people can relax and spend time with friends and family. However, some people prefer the beach, because, unlike the ski slopes, the beach is usually warm. Other people find skiing much more exciting than sitting in a beach chair and splashing in the waves. Whether it is a beach vacation or a ski vacation, it all comes down to what you like to do more.

_____

_____

_____

_____

_____

_____

_____

_____

_____

_____

_____

_____

_____

_____

_____

_____

_____

STOP

Mathematics

SAMPLE A

469
+ 225

- **A** 244
- **B** 684
- **C** 694
- **D** 695
- **E** None of these

SAMPLE B

87.8
− 72.4

- **F** 5.4
- **G** 14.5
- **H** 16.2
- **J** 15.4
- **K** None of these

1

23
× 32

- **A** 736
- **B** 636
- **C** 55
- **D** 115
- **E** None of these

4 $5\frac{7}{8} - 2\frac{3}{8} =$

- **F** $2\frac{1}{2}$
- **G** $3\frac{3}{4}$
- **H** $3\frac{3}{8}$
- **J** $3\frac{1}{2}$
- **K** None of these

2 $6.00 − $0.35

- **F** $6.35
- **G** $5.65
- **H** $5.75
- **J** $5.35
- **K** None of these

5 $510 \times 38 =$

- **A** 19,380
- **B** 548
- **C** 51,038
- **D** 18,390
- **E** None of these

3 $18\overline{)90}$

- **A** 5
- **B** 4
- **C** 4 R2
- **D** 5 R4
- **E** None of these

6

89.7
+ 25.6

- **F** 114.3
- **G** 64.3
- **H** 105.3
- **J** 104.3
- **K** None of these

GO

SAMPLE C Points M and N represent certain numbers on the number line. Which of these problems would give an answer of about 10?

A N + M

B N − M

C N × M

D N ÷ M

7. **Parallelogram QRST slid to a new position on the grid as shown. Which moves describe the slide?**

A 1 right, 4 down

B 1 right, 5 down

C 2 right, 4 down

D 1 right, 3 down

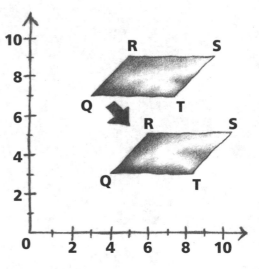

8. **Study this pattern. If the pattern continues, how many stars will be in the fourth position?**

F 14

G 16

H 18

J 20

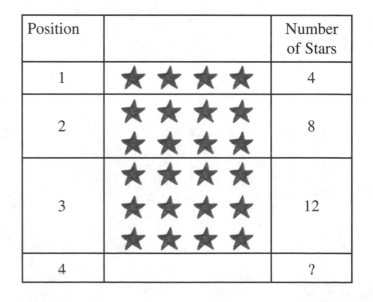

Position		Number of Stars
1	★ ★ ★ ★	4
2	★ ★ ★ ★ ★ ★ ★ ★	8
3	★ ★ ★ ★ ★ ★ ★ ★ ★ ★ ★ ★	12
4		?

GO

The Hundreds Hunt

Directions: Mr. Pontario's students are making number charts and labeling the squares from 1 to 100. Use Harry's number chart to do numbers 9 and 10.

9 Liza is making a number chart. If she shades only the multiples of 4, her chart will have

  A about three-fourths as many shaded numbers as Harry's.

  B about two-thirds as many shaded numbers as Harry's.

  C about one-half as many shaded numbers as Harry's.

  D about twice as many shaded numbers as Harry's.

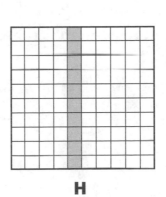

10 Tenisha just made a number chart on which she shaded all the multiples of 5. Which pattern shows the shading on her number chart?

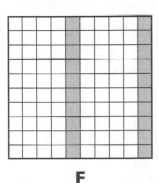
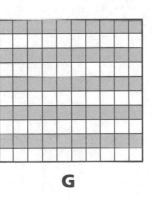

F   **G**   **H**   **J**

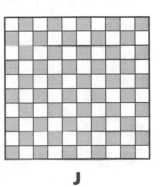

GO

11 Which of these number sentences could be used to find the cost of 6 dozen pens?

   A $\$4.59 + 6 =$

   B $\$4.59 - 6 =$

   C $\$4.59 \times 6 =$

   D $\$4.59 \div 6 =$

12 Mrs. Lynch showed a container of jelly beans to her class. She said she would give it to the student who guessed the correct number of jelly beans inside it. The first four students guessed 352, 267, 195, and 454, respectively. What was the average of these four guesses?

   F   300

   G   317

   H   320

   J   323

13 If all these chips were put into a bag, what is the probability that you would pick a chip with a letter that comes before M in the alphabet?

   A $\frac{3}{5}$

   B $\frac{3}{8}$

   C $\frac{5}{3}$

   D $\frac{5}{8}$

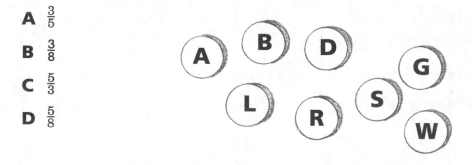

Bake Sale

Directions: The 5th grade is having a bake sale for the rest of the school and the outside community. Numbers 14–17 are about the bake sale.

14 There are 120 students in the fifth grade. Only 87 of these students contributed baked goods. How many students did not contribute baked goods?

F 87

G 207

H 43

J 33

15 The oatmeal cookies are small, so there are 3 cookies in each plastic bag. There are 45 bags of these cookies. How many oatmeal cookies are there in all?

A 48

B 120

C 135

D 15

16 The local bakery donated 112 blueberry muffins. There are 16 blueberries in each muffin. How many blueberries did the bakery use in all?

F 784   **H** 1782

G 128   **J** 1792

17 Thelma and Arnold collected the money. Thelma sat 71.52 inches from the exit door, and Arnold sat 63.31 inches farther from the exit door than Thelma sat. How far from the door did Arnold sit?

A 134.83 in.

B 135.83 in.

C 8.21 in.

D 9.21 in.

GO

Directions: Find the correct answer to solve each problem.

18 **What number does CXVII represent?**

F 62   **H** 117

G 67   **J** 542

19 **What is the name of this figure?**

A sphere

B rectangular prism

C triangular prism

D cylinder

20 **What is 456,517 rounded to the nearest thousand?**

F 460,000

G 457,000

H 454,000

J 456,000

21 **Which of the following is a right triangle?**

A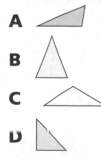

B

C

D

22 **What letter represents point 4, 2?**

F A

G C

H B

J D

23 **What is the square root of 16?**

A 256   **C** 4

B 8   **D** 1

24 **Which figure shows intersecting lines, but not perpendicular lines?**

F S

G _____

H X

J

25 **What number has an 8 in the millions place and a 2 in the ten-thousands place?**

A 8,912,703

B 8,721,034

C 8,241,037

D 2,781,654

GO

26 **What figure has vertical and horizontal symmetry?**

F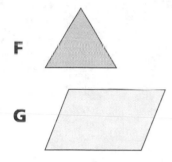

H

G

J

27 **Which animal is longer than 156 inches and shorter than 216 inches?**

A   African elephant

B   Hippopotamus

C   White rhinoceros

D   Giraffe

Animal	Length (in feet)	Weight (in pounds)
African Elephant	24	14,432
White Rhinoceros	14	7,937
Hippopotamus	13	5,512
Giraffe	19	2,257

28 **What is the perimeter of this figure?**

F   101 inches

G   98 inches

H   76 inches

J   38 inches

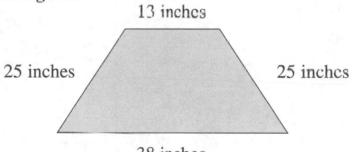

13 inches

25 inches   25 inches

38 inches

29 **Which is the best estimate for the height of a room?**

A   3 inches

B   3 feet

C   3 yards

D   3 miles

GO

Directions: Find the correct answer to solve each problem.

30 23,300 – 17,984 =

   F 5,316

   G 5,326

   H 6,626

   J 41,284

31 0.36 ☐ $\frac{3}{5}$

   A >

   B =

   C <

   D Not enough information

32 78.576 + 412.82 =

   F 1,198.58

   G 491.396

   H 490.396

   J 119.848

33 1984 – 894.5 =

   A 986.5

   B 1,089.5

   C 1,189

   D 2,879

34 24,000 ÷ 60 =

   F 4,000

   G 400

   H 40

   J None of these

35 765 + 456 + 835 + 490 =

   A 2,056

   B 2,456

   C 2,546

   D None of these

36 Find the average for this set of numbers: 47, 83, 15, 22, 67.

   F 58.5   **H** 43.5

   G 47   **J** None of these

37 $\frac{1}{3} + 2\frac{1}{3} + \frac{4}{9}$ =

   A $3\frac{1}{9}$

   B 3

   C $2\frac{2}{3}$

   D None of these

GO

Directions: Find the correct answer to solve each problem.

38 Five friends each had 36 prize tokens from the arcade. Two other friends each had 25 prize tokens. The 7 friends decided to combine their tokens and then divide them equally. How many tokens will each friend get?

F 8 tokens   **H** 32 tokens

G 25 tokens   **J** 33 tokens

39 James earned $15.85 each week for his chores. If James saves all of his money for 8 weeks, how much money will he have?

A $12.68

B $120.00

C $125.40

D $126.80

40 Luca finished his homework at 8:37 p.m. If he started his homework 92 minutes earlier, at what time did Luca begin his homework?

F 7:05 p.m.

G 7:09 p.m.

H 7:35 p.m.

J 11:09 p.m.

41 Martin made a bowl of punch using 14 gallons of juice. How many quarts of punch did Martin make?

A 112 quarts   **C** 28 quarts

B 56 quarts   **D** None of the above

42 Jaime read for 30 minutes on Monday, 47 minutes on Tuesday, 64 minutes on Wednesday, and 81 minutes on Thursday. Which statement describes Jaime's pattern for reading?

F Add 15 minutes each day

G Subtract 17 minutes each day

H Add 12 minutes each day

J Add 17 minutes each day

43 An aquarium has a collection of 148 fish. It is going to expand its collection to 500 fish. If 8 new fish are added each week, how long will it take to get to 500 fish?

A 15 weeks

B 19 weeks

C 43 weeks

D 44 weeks

STOP

Grade 5 Answer Key

Page 225
A. C
B. F

Page 227
1. A

Page 228
2. F
3. B
4. H
5. A

Page 229
6. J
7. A
8. J
9. A
10. G
11. B

Page 230
12. J
13. A
14. H

Page 232
15. B
16. F
17. B
18. H

Page 233
19. B
20. J
21. B
22. G

Page 234
C. C

Page 235
23. D

Page 236
24. G
25. D
26. G
27. A

Page 237
D. B
28. D
29. G

Grade 5 Answer Key

Page 238
30. D
31. J

Page 239
32. B
33. F

Page 240
A. B
1. A
2. J
B. B
3. D
4. H

Page 241
5. B
6. F
7. C
8. G
9. B
10. G

Page 242
C. D
11. C
12. G
13. A
14. J

Page 243
15. D
16. G
17. B
18. F
19. A

Page 244
D. A
20. C
21. F
22. C
E. E
23. G
24. E

Grade 5 Answer Key

Page 247
- **F.** A
- **25.** D
- **26.** F
- **27.** B
- **28.** H
- **29.** A
- **30.** G

Page 248
- **31.** C
- **32.** J
- **33.** A
- **34.** F
- **35.** C
- **36.** G

Page 249
- **37.** B
- **38.** F
- **39.** D
- **40.** J
- **41.** E
- **42.** J
- **43.** B
- **44.** H

Page 251
- **A.** C
- **B.** K
- **1.** D
- **2.** G
- **3.** C
- **4.** K

Page 252
- **C.** D

Page 253
- **5.** C
- **6.** G
- **7.** D

Page 254
- **8.** H
- **9.** A

Page 255
- **10.** J
- **11.** B
- **12.** F

Grade 5 Answer Key

Page 256
13. B
14. G
15. D

Page 257
16. K
17. B
18. F
19. C
20. H
21. A

Page 258
D. A
22. C
23. G
24. B
25. J

Page 259
26. D
27. F
28. B

Page 260
29. H
30. D
31. H

Page 264
A. C

Page 266
1. C
2. G
3. A
4. H
5. B
6. F

Page 267
7. D
8. G
9. A

Page 268
10. G
11. A
12. F
13. D

Grade 5 Answer Key

Page 269

14. F
15. C
16. F
17. D
18. H
19. F
20. J
21. G
22. C
23. A
24. B
25. D

Page 270

A. D
1. C
B. A
2. F
3. B
4. J
5. A

Page 271

6. G
7. D
8. G
9. D
10. H
11. A

Page 272

12. J
13. A
14. H
15. D
16. G
17. E
18. F
19. C

Page 273

20. G
21. A
22. F
23. B
24. J
25. A

Grade 5 Answer Key

Page 274
26. H
27. A
28. J
29. C

Page 275
30. G
31. D
32. H
33. A
34. G
35. C

Page 276
36. H
37. C
38. J
39. A

Page 279
A. C
B. J
1. A
2. G
3. A
4. J
5. A
6. K

Page 280
C. B
7. A
8. G

Page 281
9. D
10. F

Page 282
11. C
12. G
13. D

Page 283
14. J
15. C
16. J
17. A

Page 284
18. H
19. C
20. G
21. D
22. G
23. C
24. H
25. B

Grade 5 Answer Key

Page 285
   26. G
   27. C
   28. F
   29. C

Page 286
   30. F
   31. C
   32. G
   33. B
   34. G
   35. C
   36. J
   37. A

Page 287
   38. H
   39. D
   40. F
   41. B
   42. J
   43. D

Grade 5 Answer Key

Page 245

Answers will vary, but should identify something specific that students have mixed feelings about, such as their neighborhood.

Answers will vary, but should include a specific example of something students do not like about their topic. Sample answer: I don't like all the traffic that travels through our neighborhood.

Answers will vary, but should include a specific example of something students like about their topic. Sample answer: I like the way our neighbors all get together outside on summer nights.

Paragraphs will vary, but should reflect the content of students' answers for the previous questions and include a topic sentence followed by detail sentences in logical order. See sample paragraph in writing prompt.

Grade 5 Answer Key

Page 246

Answers will vary, but should include a fictional character that could support a story. Students' reasoning should clearly identify some of the character's traits. Sample answer: I would write about Ling, a girl who always wants to win, but doesn't want to be a team player. She will be the main character because she has an important lesson to learn, and finding out how she learns this lesson will be interesting for the reader.

Answers will vary, but should include one or more settings. Sample answer: The story will take place now on playing fields at Ling's school and other schools nearby.

Answers will vary, but should include a clear problem and solution. More sophisticated answers might include a character's inner personal conflict, as well as the conflict happening externally within the story. Sample answer: José has a friend who needs to be a star in practice to make the team. This is his friend's dream. José decides to back away and stop taking all the attention to let his friend shine during the practice.

Stories will vary, but should reflect the content of students' answers for the previous questions and a clear sequence of events. See sample paragraph in writing prompt.

Grade 5 Answer Key

Page 250

Answers will vary, but should state a specific challenging experience, rather than a vague idea. Sample answer: I have learned to dive off the high board.

Answers will vary, but should clearly explain why the experience was challenging. Sample answer: This experience was challenging because the board was very high, and I had always been afraid of heights.

Paragraphs will vary, but should reflect the content of students' answers for the previous questions. See sample paragraph in writing prompt.

Grade 5 Answer Key

Page 277

Paragraphs will vary, but should tell how to do only one activity. Paragraphs should show knowledge of an informative how-to paragraph, including time-order words. The order of the steps should be logical. Topics might include: how to take care of the lawn or how to clean the kitchen thoroughly. See sample paragraph in writing prompt.

Page 278

Paragraphs will vary, but should compare and contrast at least two items clearly. Key words such as *same, like, different, unlike, but,* and *however* should be included. See sample paragraph in writing prompt.

Test Practice Worksheet

Test Practice Worksheet

Test Practice Worksheet

Test Practice Worksheet

Test Practice Worksheet

Test Practice Worksheet

Test Practice Worksheet

Test Practice Worksheet

Test Practice Worksheet

Test Practice Worksheet

Test Practice Worksheet

Test Practice Worksheet

Test Practice Worksheet

Test Practice Worksheet

Test Practice Worksheet

Test Practice Worksheet

Test Practice Worksheet

Test Practice Worksheet

Test Practice Worksheet

Test Practice Worksheet

Test Practice Worksheet

Test Practice Worksheet